Of Literature and Knowledge

Explorations in narrative thought
experiments, evolution, and game theory

Peter Swirski

 Routledge
Taylor & Francis Group

LONDON AND NEW YORK

First published 2007
by Routledge
2 Park Square, Milton Park, Abingdon, Oxon OX14 4RN

Simultaneously published in the USA and Canada
by Routledge
270 Madison Avenue, New York, NY 10016

Routledge is an imprint of the Taylor & Francis Group, an informa business

© 2007 Peter Swirski

Typeset in Baskerville by Taylor & Francis Books
Printed and bound in Great Britain by Antony Rowe Ltd, Chippenham, Wiltshire

British Library Cataloguing in Publication Data
A catalogue record for this book is available from the British Library

Library of Congress Cataloging in Publication Data
A catalog record for this book has been requested

ISBN10: 0-415-42059-8 (hbk)
ISBN10: 0-415-42060-1 (pbk)
ISBN10: 0-203-96586-8 (ebk)

ISBN13: 978-0-415-42059-4 (hbk)
ISBN13: 978-0-415-42060-0 (pbk)
ISBN13: 978-0-203-96586-3 (ebk)

This book is dedicated to William John Kyle and Edward O. Wilson, scientists and humanists

Contents

List of figures

Acknowlededgment

The author gratefully acknowledges the support from the Hong Kong's Research Grants Council in the form of a Competitive Earmarked Research Grant.

Introduction

I wrote a novel because I had a yen to do it. I believe this is sufficient reason to set out to tell a story. Man is a storytelling animal by nature.

Umberto Eco, *The Name of the Rose* (Postscript)

Stories, stories everywhere. From cradle to grave we tell stories with hardly a pause from work, play, and sleep. We read bedtime stories to children, concoct stories about our fishing exploits, and confide "you'll never believe this" stories to friends, and hairdressers. We shed tears over *Love Story*, titillate with the *Story of O.*, devour inside stories, and flock to see the sequels to *The Neverending Story*. We rehash triumphs at work as quest sagas, failures in romance as Aeschylean tragedies, and holiday hunts for that no-frills Athens hotel near Omonia Square as mini-odysseys. Late for work, we feed stories to the boss from the hallowed repertoire of traffic snarls, ailing relatives, and automobile malfunctions. Late at night we even dream stories, sometimes in beta-wave equivalent of Panasonic and Technicolor.

Beside ubiquity, our propensity for storytelling has other characteristics. First of all, it is universal. Every culture we know has developed its preferred range and type of stories.[1] Matter of fact, oftentimes we learn much of these chronologically or geographically distant societies through the stories they preserved in their versions of *Thousand and One Nights* or the *Eddas*. Second, the impulse to tell, invent, make up, construct, create, write, recite – in short, narrate – stories is inseparable from being *Homo sapiens sapiens*. We string words into sentences, sentences into plots, and from then we're off on life's journey to add our own stories to the stock of those that came before.

Finally, many of our stories are recognizable from culture to culture. To be sure, details of setting or character differ. One community's elves become another people's peris. One people's tall tales and tricksters are another's picaresques and picaros. But the underlying intercultural form is common because the human experience is common. Over the years a persuasive case has been mounted, in fact, for a variety of such translit-erary – or more exactly transcultural – universals. Michelle Sugiyama's recent "Narrative Theory and Function: Why Evolution Matters" made it even for such basic elements of storytelling as characters, goal-oriented action, and resolution.

Other literary evidence for human universals comes from multicultural analyses of folk and fairy tales.[2] Not that any of this would surprise Russian and Central European formalists, who already a century ago stressed liter-ature's transnational and transcultural invariance. The first to document narratological regularities in the "deep structures" of many enduring story types, Propp, Shklovskii, and Eikhenbaum were also the first to systemati-cally investigate the evolutionary dimension in literature and folklore. Yet, for all their acumen, the Russian scholars did not comment much on another aspect of our stories: their made-up character.

To be sure, many recurrent stories are grounded in real-life experience. Not to look too far, the assassination of JFK or the machinations of Nixon's Watergate "plumbers" were the subject of endless tellings and retellings in books, films, reports, editorials *et al*. We have even evolved sophisticated forms of telling stories with factual veracity and scholarly aplomb, so much so that they have come to be called histories and accepted as true. This is no less true in literature where the genre of (auto)biography rides coattails on the veracity and legitimacy of history. Reconstruction of real lives and events for a better understanding of the human condition, the edification of posterity, or both, was the averred goal of writers as sundry as Plutarch, Franklin, and Churchill.

But stories grounded in real life and fashioned with a view to their accu-racy are not the only kind we like to write and consume. For all its vaunted historical aplomb and slice-of-life immediacy, nonfiction has always had to contend for cultural supremacy with literary make-believe. No doubt to the chagrin of historians, the earliest societies for which records survive even mixed them freely into a mythopoetic stew. Today, a visit to a local book-store or cineplex is all it takes to become convinced that people love fictions with a passion that belies their unreal character.

We love to make-believe about a ruddy elf with a Yeltsin nose and a posse of reindeer living at the North Pole – the same North Pole that Robert Peary flew over in 1908 and saw nothing but frozen wasteland. We devour stories about an ace detective domiciled at 221b Baker Street, even though London town's municipal records show that Mrs. Hudson's address was not even residential property in the days of "A Study in Scarlet." Generation after generation we return to the story of Donkey Hote (*pace* some of my "mondegreening" students) doing his knight-errant bit after leaving La Mancha.[3] Ditto for Ahab's vendetta on an albino whale, for postmen ringing twice for love-triangled couples, and for humanoid robots with positron brains behaviorally restricted by three asinine "laws" of robotics. Ditto for countless other fictions, none of which existed, and some that could not even exist.

What is it in literary fictions, these stories of make-believe, that makes readers while away hours, days, and in the case of literature professors even lives on them? The standard answer is that literature instructs and entertains. This is true and it would take a philistine to deny that stories attract by skilful execution, artistic flair, complex design, and a penchant for coloring a colorless day. Fictions take us to faraway places, exercise the imagination, offer a chance for self- and group-identification, and entertain us with humor, horror, hyperbole, and whatever other technique is in their arsenal.

Good fiction is, in other words, very much like good nonfiction – except that the latter is *ex definitio* about real events in the real world. Not that nonfictions are all, or even necessarily, true. Claudius Ptolemy's geocentric nonfiction certainly wasn't, and the Warren Report had all the makings of a great nonfiction without convincing anyone it was true. But, unlike made-up stories designed to generate the reflexive attitude of make-believe, in nonfiction the default design on the part of the author is the genesis of belief.[4]

There is little point in debating whether fiction – make-believe and made up as it is – can affect us in a real, nonfictional way. We all know it can, even without Marianne Moore's sage "Poetry" of imaginary gardens with real toads in them. We even dismiss a certain type of stories as tear-jerkers calculated to exploit our capacity to shed real tears over unreal people. A cathartic reaction to a piece of fiction implies, naturally, a proximate causal link between its contents and the reader's mental disposition. Tautologically almost, some kind of information transfer must be taking place.

Even so, this is quite a-ways from showing that narrative fiction is, and therefore should be approached as, an effective information bearer and an effective information processor. Emotional affect is not the same, after all, as intellectual gain. It is possible to be profoundly affected in a non-cerebral fashion, for example when the limbic system autonomically alters one's disposition during a sudden onset of a "fight or flight" stimulus. Is it truly and demonstrably information, rather than any other type of affectation, that is the currency of this literary exchange?

The question leads straight to the larger question of people's enduring interest in producing and consuming fiction. Why do we value stories *prima facie* grounded in fantasy or, less charitably, falsehood? Why do we emote with nonexistent characters overcoming unreal obstacles? Logically and ontologically we ought not to take fiction seriously, yet the opposite is often the case. Time and again narrative fantasies dramatically prove their power to encroach on our real-life existence. The case of Heinrich Schliemann, who, with a copy of Homer's *Iliad* in hand, went to Asia Minor to unearth the historical Troy, is perhaps extreme. Still, it vividly demonstrates the abiding power of fiction to inform and cognitively enrich our lives.

If fictions are fairy tales for adults with no cognitive bite, then something else has to explain Abraham Lincoln's quip about Harriet Beecher Stowe's little fiction that started the Civil War. The same something else presumably lies behind the blacklisting of *Animal Farm* and *1984* by Big Brother censors in various parts of the globe. But if our ontological fantasies have real cognitive bite, where does the bite come from? That, as you may have surmised, is the mother of all questions for the book in your hands.

> *Whatever knowledge is attainable, must be attained by scientific method, and what science cannot discover, mankind cannot know.*
>
> Bertrand Russell, "Science and Ethics"

The basic premise behind *Of Literature and Knowledge* is that the capacity of literary fictions for generating nonfictional knowledge owes to their capacity for doing what philosophy and science do – generating thought experiments. Not that *all* knowledge in literature can be traced to thought experiments. Historical novels transmit knowledge of history much in the same manner that historians transmit it. Moreover, in *thought* experiments there is no question of equipment setup and instrumental manipulation, the goal of which is the production of data by means of which a hypothesis can be (dis)confirmed. Armchair inquiries may therefore look nothing like the paradigmatic goings-on among researchers in scientific institutes.

In literature they may even take the form of folktales, such as the one about Indian King Sharim and his vizier, Sissa Ben Dahir, the inventor of chess. Pleased with the game, the monarch is said to have offered a reward of sixty-four pieces of gold (one for each square) to the vizier. The offer was countered by Ben Dahir's request for a grain of wheat for the first square, two for the second, four for the third, and so on. Deceived by its apparent modesty, the king acceded to the proposal, unaware that all the grain in the world then and now could not cover the amount. In this canonical account, the story of the invention of chess models a mathematical function, namely a differential equation of exponential growth ($y' = 2y$).

The same function animates other thought experiments, for example folding a sheet of paper fifty times over. The counterfactual abstracts away the struggle of dealing with tiny paper folds and focuses only on the thickness of the resulting wad. For most people it will not be very thick at all: a couple of feet or a couple of meters, but not – as in the correct answer – so thick as to reach beyond the sun. To make the thought experiment even more robust, one might manipulate the key variables – the number of folds or the thickness of the paper. In the story of the king and vizier, one could vary the number of squares on the chessboard (which would no longer be a chessboard) or the number of coins. Either way, the onset of numerical explosion will exhibit the dramatic difference between exponential and polynomial equations.

As an artform, literature has traditionally been studied less for its modeling than for its aesthetic value. In the words of one philosopher of art, "the attempt to orient research towards the literary specificity of texts and utterances has amounted to focusing on what may be loosely identified as their aesthetic qualities."[5] Doing so, it is assumed, we study literature *qua* literature. Even before New Criticism, this may have been a not unreasonable program for an energetic but amorphous area of academic activity hot in pursuit of field-specific methodology (and, through it, disciplinary identity). But over the course of history the focus on aesthetics – and whatever else went into the crucible in accordance with the winds of interpretive fashion – precipitated a neglect of literature as an instrument of inquiry.

That we learn from stories is a truism. Moreover, it is a truism held for so long and by so many that, like falling apples or the vector of time, it has wormed its way into our collective subconscious. As a consequence it has come to be regarded as pretheoretical and thus in no need of inquiry. A paucity of research into *how* we learn from literary fictions has, in turn, impoverished our understanding of *what* we may learn from them. Next to the epistemology of science – better known as the theory of confirmation – the epistemology of letters is, after all, a fledgling enterprise. As a result, the informational transfer between real life and narrative make-believe, and the cognitive mechanisms behind such a transfer, remain under-investigated and not fully understood.

Today's aestheticians and metacritics are less inclined to aesthetic autonomy when explaining the processes behind the composition and reception of literary works. Equally, for many (though obviously not all) writers and readers the cognitive dimension of literature is as vital as the literary. It may be, to paraphrase Richard Feynman, that booklovers need a sound theoretical underpinning to how they learn from stories as much as birds need ornithology. But scholars of literature, humanists, and even general readers alarmed by the political hegemony of scientism at the expense of *belles lettres* might be keen to find out how literature relates to science in cognitive terms. They might be no less keen to find out what a puissant intellectual tool it is in its own right.

Historians, sociologists, ethnographers, cultural anthropologists, and, not least, storytellers and story scholars have always recognized the cognitive power of fiction. But epistemically one needs to square this fact with the perception that truth and nonfiction are one thing, whereas fiction is, well . . . just fiction. It is for no other reason that "telling stories" is a colloquial synonym for lying, or that you can sweep away a child's fear for the heroine in distress with an ontological bracket: "It's just a story." There is something inherently puzzling about milking real knowledge from unreal cows, and this something is the principal explanatory challenge for any account of literature as an instrument of inquiry.

I suggest that by placing literary fictions on the level of thought experiments, a well-established and increasingly well-understood instrument of learning, we may come closer to disentangling the riddle. Stories are adaptive tools to help us navigate more efficiently – or more colorfully, imaginatively, and memorably, which deep down still comes down to more efficiently – our time on earth. Philosophic and scientific counterfactuals, that is, propositions that map consequences of events that by definition did not occur, generate knowledge as part of their field-specific hunts for knowledge. My contention is that a significant chunk of narrative fiction generates knowledge in a similar manner and, at least in part, for similar reasons.[6]

Given that philosophers and scientists engage in research, does it follow that literary fictions can be a research tool, too? The litterateurs, for one, have no doubt. *Hypotheses fingo*, proclaimed Poe, setting out in his cosmological poem *Eureka* to construct a "train of ratiocination as rigorously logical as that which establishes any demonstration in Euclid."[7] Italo Calvino echoed Poe's confidence by identifying his own *t zero* as an attempt "to make narrative out of a mere process of deductive reasoning." In a Harvard lecture Bernard Malamud defended a proposition that an outline for a novel "is the equivalent of a scientific hypothesis." In "The State of the Novel" Walker Percy insisted that literature is cognitive because it "discovers and knows and tells, tells the reader how things are, how we are, in a way that the reader can confirm with as much certitude as a scientist taking a pointer-reading."

Taking my cue from the writers, I hold that the answer to the question "Can literature be an effective instrument of inquiry?" is affirmative. I believe, in other words, that literature is a form of knowledge or, what amounts to the same thing, that it can generate knowledge while coursing through the minds of its creators and/or consumers. I also believe that, like so many other things that human beings do naturally, universally, and transculturally, our aptitude for imagining other worlds is rooted in evolutionary adaptation. Notwithstanding sporadic attempts to put creation "science" on equal footing with evolution in some part of the United States, the way to knowledge through fiction is via the neo-Darwinian paradigm.

Knowledge of the world and the experience of life can of course take many forms. While for some writers the production of literary knowledge involves abstract ideas, testable hypotheses, and perhaps even cumulative data, for many others it manifestly does not. In their hands literature is an enterprise and experience that is inalienably personal, emotive, and subjective. In these respects it diverges from both theoretical science and philosophy to the extent that their goals and practices are interpersonal, empirical, and objective. And that's exactly the way it should be, for whatever unified inquiry means, it does *not* mean confusing tigers with zebras, even though both wear disciplinary stripes.

Thought experiments are devices of the imagination used to investigate the nature of things.
Stanford Encyclopedia of Philosophy

"There is reason to believe," concludes William Poundstone in *Labyrinths of Reason*, "that the ability to conceive of possible worlds is a fundamental part of human intelligence."[8] His synopsis of more than a century of research on the subject echoes what Ernst Mach, dean of scientists and philosophers of science, wrote in *Knowledge and Error* during the golden age of mechanics:

> The planner, the builder of castles in the air, the novelist, the author of social and technological utopias is experimenting with thoughts; so too is the hardheaded merchant, the serious inventor and the enquirer. All of them imagine conditions, and connect with them their expectations and surmise of certain consequences: they gain a thought experience.[9]

More than any others, three studies have of late revitalized work on how counterfactual thinking leads to a gain in thought experience. Setting in motion a thriving research program, they continue to inform most debates on the nature and scope of this remarkable method of discovery. In order of appearance, the three are James R. Brown's *The Laboratory of the Mind* (1991), Tamara Horowitz and Gerald J. Massey's collection *Thought Experiments in Science and Philosophy* (1991) and Roy A. Sorensen's *Thought*

Experiments (1992). Reflecting the common ground between them, Sorensen lays his cards on the table in terms of "gradualistic metaphilosophy."[10] This ungainly term hides a simple, although by no means straightforward, thesis. Thought experiments in philosophy, argues the author, are continuous with experiments in science, differing from them not in kind but only in degree. This assumption lies, in fact, behind most analytic work in philosophy. In *The Cambridge Dictionary of Philosophy*, for example, John Heil finds little unanimity in the ranks except, among others, "a conviction that philosophy is in some sense continuous with science."[11]

In this sense, you could say that my own book starts where *Thought Experiments* left off. This is because I extend the above precept to literary epistemology in general, and to literary fictions in particular. In line with Sorensen's gradualistic metaphilosophy, *Of Literature and Knowledge* may be taken, therefore, as a book-length argument for gradualistic metacognition. Its centerpiece is that, when considered in cognitive terms, literary narratives lie on a continuum with philosophical thought experiments, differing from them not in kind but only in degree.

Lest there be any misunderstanding, I immediately reiterate that not all literary knowledge owes something to thought experiments. Nor is knowledge all there is to literary fictions or, a wiseass might remark, they would never be as fun to read as they are. But the many narratives that do rely on thought experiments justify the attempts to put literary knowledge on a level with that found in the social sciences. Needles to say, my central thesis, much as any of the subsidiary ones, is open to critique and falsification. It would be presumptuous to imagine that the chapters that follow are the last word on the matter.

On the other hand, should conclusive refutations be found wanting, it is hard to overestimate the implications for literary cognition. With no categorical difference between thought experiments in literature and philosophy – and with *Gedankenexperimente* in philosophy different only in degree from science – thought experiments in literature may also be removed from their cousins in the sciences only by a matter of degree. If corroborated, such a continuity would furnish a clear link between the disciplinary varieties of the same cognitive tool used by scientists, philosophers, as well as scholars and writers of fiction.

And corroboration is no longer a far-fetched notion. The 1990s ushered in a rich analytical harvest, more than ever before inclined to recognize the storytelling component in our mental and thought-experimental calisthenics. Terms such as "literary," "narrative," or "process-narrative" are increasingly yoked to analyses of thought experiments by a growing number of historians, philosophers, and sociologists of science.[12] This narrative turn reflects, in turn, the growing awareness of the extent to which human minds categorize and memorize experience in storytelling terms. We think and remember best not in bits and bytes but in plots and stories (more on this in Chapter 4).

Given the surge of interest in the narrative dimension of thought experiments, it is rather odd that few philosophers, not to mention literature specialists, have actually studied literary narratives from this angle.[13] It is odder still when you consider that approaching knowledge in fiction through thought experiments holds a great deal of promise for tackling the mechanisms of narrative comprehension. But then again, maybe it isn't. In the philosophical hierarchy, disciplines like aesthetics, narrative theory, and discourse analysis are frequently just a cut above cultural studies.

Be that as it may, the need to probe the cognitive connection between stories and thought experiments is quite urgent. Only by applying the analytic apparatus of philosophy and science to *literary* thought experiments can we find out, after all, how apposite these narrative analogies and metaphors really are. There is, of course, nothing in the above research program to endorse a reduction of *belles lettres* to a handmaiden of analytic philosophy or the social sciences. Thought experiments provide a constructive way of investigating how knowledge in literature works. But that's not all there is to telling and reading stories.

At the risk of repeating myself, for all the cognitive analogies with philosophy and science, literature is quite a different bird from both. First and foremost it is distinct by virtue of its gift for emotional renditions of subjective human experience. Any epistemological model – including my own – that identifies a common "knowledge factor" between literature, philosophy, and science will thus never amount to the whole story about any of them. The identity of these different approaches to discovering the world will, in other words, never be exhausted by what they have in common.

The focus on cognition in storytelling is not, therefore, meant to take anything away from fiction as an emotional chronicler of human experience. That would be madness akin to that which overpowers Lear, making him override his love for and profound emotional dependence on Cordelia in the name of a "higher" principle. In the spirit of Edward Wilson's arguments for the deep unity of all knowledge, my goal is simply to harness literary research to a more *consilient* program of inquiry. And with few philosophers lining up to pick up the gauntlet, the study of narratives as thought experiments is tantalizingly open to scholars of literature.

What has changed? Perhaps it is the gradual the encroachment of science upon issues that were once the sole preserve of the humanities.

John Barrow, *Between Inner Space and Outer Space*

To examine literature as a variety of thought experiment means to examine the ways in which it cognitively works in the manner comparable to established research disciplines. Approaching narrative fictions as the same *kind* of tool – though vastly different in *degree* – as the *Gedankenexperimente* of philosophy and science, this book is underwritten by three related epistemological claims. The first is that literary works can be powerful instruments of knowledge. The second that a significant portion of this knowledge can be fruitfully assessed in interdisciplinary – and thus interpersonal and objective – terms. The third is that these interdisciplinary terms are framed by field-specific tools of inquiry whose cross-section is the cognitive Swiss army knife: thought experiment.

All three assumptions bring us face to face with the thorny question of the relation between literary and scientific modes of inquiry. The problem is indisputably complex, so much so that many humanists have fallen prey to the impression that there is little chance of untangling its multifarious positions and oppositions. Yet on closer inspection the relation between literature and the sciences loses its aura of messy intractability. Many of its apparent dichotomies turn out to be illusory, particularly those advanced by cognitive anti-realists, constructivists, conventionalists, solipsists, and other relativists.[14]

The recent years ushered in a number of censures from outside the humanities directed at its lax intellectual standards. Laying siege to deconstruction and other facets of postmodernism in the name of rationality and reason, intellectuals from Alan Sokal to John Searle must be applauded for their readiness to engage in such crossover peer review. But their focus on only one, albeit vociferous, bloc amounts to throwing out the baby with the bathwater. The methodological poverty of *some* parts of the humanities validates neither the neglect of its non-constructivist elements nor the dismissal of literary research *in toto*. Rarely acknowledged in the exposés of humanists' quarrels with science are the alternatives prospected *within* literary scholarship which resolutely chip away at the façade of interpretive relativism and intellectual anarchy.

When Charles Percy Snow delivered the "Two Cultures" lecture in 1959, he may not have imagined that the rift between the scientific and literary cultures would linger past Y2K. Though his eyes were on the future, Snow's title harked back to an 1845 novel by Disraeli, whose *Sybil: The Two Nations* was a cry of indignation over social conditions that rent Britain into a nation of haves and have-nots. Picking up the gauntlet, Snow targeted the socio-political dangers lurking in the separation of literature and science which, to his mind, lay at the root of such social conditions. Science, he lamented, with all the means at its disposal, foundered on the lack of humanistic and political vision. Literature, with its aesthetics *du jour*, was adrift in the industrial and informational age.

With hindsight of almost fifty years, Snow's campaign seems a gallant – if failed – effort to correct the imbalance with which we valorize the type of knowledge harvested in the sciences and the arts. Nowhere is this more apparent than in the way we train future generations of citizens and decision-makers. Humanities and liberal arts are garroted by funding shortages, while science faculties bloom, nurtured by donations and endowments from return-on-the-dollar-savvy school boards and governments. Between a genetics lab and a department of critical theory, the funding alternative is frequently a no-brainer. Next to the research colossi of modern science, literary studies must appear a cottage industry. Under the banner of postmodern "theory," its intellectual harvest is often no more relevant than Thomist scholasticism, giving additional ammunition to near-sighted humanities-bashers.

Today in the high-tech reality of breeder reactors, Energia boosters, bio-computing, quantum tunneling, or antigen monocloning, the educated public's exposure to science has, indeed, increased manifold. It goes without saying that we need a better understanding of science and of the reasons why it works so well. The stakes of the post-industrial society do not leave much room for this type of ignorance. Not, at least, if we hope to survive. The question worth asking, of course, is how much of such journalistically hyped-up exposure has transmuted into the grasp of the nature of things.

But we need a better understanding of literature no less. Literature is not a crutch but an intellectual and emotional laboratory as we time-travel to the future one day at a time. It contains the narrative and cognitive machinery for examining issues that challenged thinkers of yesterday, and will continue to challenge thinkers of tomorrow. Because – good old-fashioned artificial intelligence notwithstanding – we are not just information processors but storytelling homeostats who experience the world much in the same fashion, and for much the same reasons, as in the days of *Gilgamesh*.

Briefly, then, the plan of action. The book is divided into five chapters, each of which illuminates a different aspect of the relation between narrative fiction and knowledge. Chapter 1, "Literature and knowledge," carries out an anatomy of the contemporary critical scene with a view to mapping the different schools of thought on cognition in literature. Differentiating their sundry positions goes a long way towards fashioning a middle ground between postmodern excesses, on the one hand, and detractors who misjudge the discipline by focusing on these excesses, on the other. Absence of evidence is not evidence of absence, and critiques that turn a blind eye on advanced work in select areas of literary studies ought not to be taken as gospel.

Chapter 2, "Literature and modeling," is organized around a comparative analysis of modeling and cognitive representation. The opening sections discuss the modeling capacity of literature and mathematics, aiming to highlight the not always obvious analogies (perhaps even homologies) between these two methods of inquiry. The remainder of the chapter develops a comprehensive typology of literary models, in both narrative practice and narratological theory. Based on their degree of anti-mimeticism, it maps out the sundry ways in which literary thought experiments depart from conventionally realistic representation, illustrating the principles and pitfalls of narrative modeling.

The central part of the book comprises Chapters 4 and 5. Both address themselves to the central investigative task, namely the analysis of the nature of thought experiments and of their role in literary investigations. Chapter 3, "Literature and evolution," conducts a double task of sorting out the key dilemma of thought experiments – where does the knowledge come from? – and determining the evolutionary adaptations of story-telling. The two are closely related. The rebuttals of those who disparage armchair inquiry in philosophy and science apply with equal persuasiveness to narrative mind experiments. At the same time, arguments about cognitive and adaptive compensations of fiction-making boost hypothetical reasoning *sensu lato*.

Chapter 4, "Literature and thought experiments," opens with a defense from critiques that have dogged their use. It then delves into the philosophical theories on how we learn from *Gedankenexperimente* and into the psychological theories on how we learn from narrative fictions. Describing things that never were, and in some cases that never could be, literature mines for knowledge using the same range of mechanisms that allow cognitive gain in other domains. The explanatory challenge here concerns the mechanisms that drive the learning process during armchair inquiry. A survey of five models of mental "mining": recollection, rearrangement, transformation, homuncular, and cleansing, as well as their narrative equivalents, prompts a range of solutions to how real-world knowledge can be extracted from (literary) thought alone.

Reflected in the ascendance of theory and formalism, literary studies seeks analytical frameworks to support its disciplinary and interdisciplinary research ambitions. Chapter 5, "Literature and game theory," develops one such framework by adapting a modern branch of analysis known as the theory of games.[15] Even though the subject is not new and has even gained some notoriety in the critical circles, the present reintroduction is designed to dispel the misconceptions perpetuated by its current use. Matrix analyses of *Memoirs Found in a Bathtub* by the late Stanislaw Lem, one of the century's most acclaimed and science-expert writers, capture both the literary-analytic potential of game theory and the cognitive complexity of this novel.[16]

Throughout, my selection of literary case studies and illustrations cuts across established divisions into, for example, American and European, canonical and popular, or realistic and fantastic. On top of securing a viable study sample, this reflects my belief that the narrative use of counterfactuals is not confined to any specific author, genre, period, country, or level of literary acclaim. We can learn from all varieties of fiction, and a good way of determining how is to examine how thought experiments perform in a narrative setting – and, conversely, what insights we gain by looking at literature in this way. With this cross-disciplinary premise in mind, *Of Literature and Knowledge* is written in a language that aims to be transparent to knowledge-hunters of all stripes.

Whether it succeeds in this conceit, and whether the sum of its insights exceeds the sum of inevitable errors, I leave up to the reader.

1 Literature and knowledge

The most I have attempted to do here is to show how much fraud and pretense are sometimes used to deceive the unwary, and how much so-called learning is empty of significance.

Johann Burkhard Mencken, *The Charlatanry of the Learned*

The list of things to do with literature is long. It begins with reading for pleasure or, in a more refined lexicon, aesthetic gratification. Others read to keep up with the Winfreys, foraging for books noted for being noted. Some turn to fiction to escape the mundane, *in extremis* shading into Bovarism. Others read to kill time during flights. Some look for the inside dope, getting their civics from McBain, westlore from McMurtry, spyware from Le Carré, and tips for romance from Jackie Collins. Others approach literature as an extension of ideology and, indexed by their politics, applaud or combat its progressivist or bourgeois trends. Professionals in the business preview, review, and e-view books to advance the world of publishing. Some of us mine fiction for the advancement of learning.

No motivation is intrinsically more equal than others. All are legitimate in their contexts. Nor is any one reason to read likely to come uncontaminated by the others. Pleasure, for instance, features high on all readers' menu, including academics for whom pleasure frequently coincides with pushing the frontiers of knowledge. Still, like politicians or courtroom attorneys, literary theorists today appear only to agree to disagree on what the disciplinary pairing of literature and knowledge signifies. The full range of responses to cognition in literature and to cognition in general runs, in fact, the gamut from utter condemnation to more or less dedicated affirmation.

Broadly speaking, literary epistemology comes in two flavors. The first is dismissive of the traditional approaches to truth, objectivity, and cognition. The dismissive camp falls into two main factions. The revisionists struggle to revise the traditional canons of inquiry, trying to make them over into something better. The abolitionists don't even try because they deem it impossible – they sweep them aside wholesale. On the other hand, the permissive camp embraces truth, objectivity, and cognition, albeit in the name of quite diverse stakes. They fall into three factions: negative, dualist, and affirmative, with the latter splitting again three ways according to how literature mines for knowledge: illustrative, hypothetical, and systematic.

The notion of literature as only one of several avenues to a single type of propositional knowledge is, of course, hardly the winning ticket in lit-crit today. More typical are sentiments that see such a notion as not even admissible, if at all desirable. The world of these academic refuseniks is, however, a bleak and sterile place. Disarmed by their own epistemic fiat, scholars cannot assert anything since they deny the idea of objective rationality. If they arrive at an insight whose truth they wish to defend – for example that truth and rationality are passé – they can't do so because truth and rationality are constructed to be constructed.

Needless to say, they cannot even defend the truth of epistemic relativism. Cultural and epistemic constructivists ask us, after all, to believe that our beliefs cannot be evaluated in terms of truth or falsehood, or even that they could be both true and false at the same time. "The question," insists one of its luminaries "is no longer: is it true? but what is its use?"[1] But not to worry. In the end, either relativism (or any one of its postmodern hydra-heads) is true, or not. If it's true, then as per its own adumbrations it cannot be said to be true. And if it's not true, then it's not true – so it's not true. *Quod erat demonstrandum.*

Even by postmodernist standards, shooting yourself in the foot is hardly an auspicious way to convert others to the soundness of your vision, quite apart from being left without a leg to stand on. Aware of this awkward fact, some scholars prefer to embrace less totalizing (not to say militant) tactics. They do not dismiss old-time epistemological principles and epistemic practices outright. Instead, they campaign on behalf of swapping them for Age-of-Aquarius-type notions such as "rightness" or "fitting." But no matter how lofty the goals of new epistemologists, getting rid of truth and knowledge is never that simple.

For one, both the revisionists and the abolitionists situate themselves in opposition to a hoary and hardly ever practiced, even if historically influential, model of inquiry, namely logical positivism. Their straw man, however, is no longer available for an all-out tilting practice. Decades in development, modern pragmatic models of inquiry smoothly (gradualistically) segue from the natural to the social sciences to the humanities. These consilient bridges, spanning in some cases remarkably diverse fields of inquiry, are sensitive as much to core methodological similarities as to their field-specific differences.[2]

Second, the revisionists are inconsistent at best and self-refuting at worst, referring to truth and falsehood even as these notions are supposed to be retired. If anything, this suggests a fundamental incoherence of pursuing inquiry without the notion of truth. In practice the New Age counterthrust is unsustainable and rapidly degenerates into relativism. "Our hypotheses, descriptions, depictions cannot be checked against the inaccessible [*sic*] 'external world,'" profess the authors of the influential *Reconceptions in Philosophy*, heedless of the argumentative ice cracking under their feet. The epistemic bullet, bitten gamely by the revisionists, is predictable: "pluralism results."[3]

The authors, Nelson Goodman and Catherine Z. Elgin, are neither the most recent nor the most egregious proponents of epistemological revisionism. Andrew Ross's *Strange Weather: Culture, Science and Technology in the Age of Limits* (1991) is more strident in its formulations of alternative epistemology. In our own millennium, another guru of New Age science, Arkady Plotnitsky, also dreams of nonclassical thought, postclassical theory and anti-epistemology, judging by his book titles. But in Goodman (who called himself an irrealist), the revisionists can boast not only a philosopher of impeccable credentials, but one whose arguments are both more measured and more cogent than most.[4]

Readers sympathetic to either of Goodman and Elgin's proposals will find little to cheer below. This is because, to put it bluntly, in my view literature is a rich springwell of knowledge about the accessible external world. Moreover, checked against the external world in terms of its truth value, this knowledge is indispensable to the understanding of humanity's actual yesterdays and possible tomorrows. To this end I defend two principles. First, the cognitive approach is not only legitimate, but indispensable *vis-à-vis* a number of literary fictions – though by no means all of them. Second, consilient interdisciplinary methodology is not only legitimate, but indispensable in any mature form of literary *research*.

This is far from contending that cognitive studies is the only game in town, even though, insofar as one can generalize on its status in literary criticism, it is a gravely neglected one. Goals of storytellers and story-scholars vary and are duly reflected in a variety of methods mining fiction for aesthetic, cathartic, or mimetic gold. Interpreting fictions in terms of their contribution to knowledge is only one strategy among several that may fruitfully mediate between art, us, and the world. But to the extent such efforts contribute to knowledge, they must conform to core principles and practices of rational inquiry. Conversely, to the extent such efforts are in opposition to interdisciplinary knowledge and method, they are not a form of research but merely an ideological formation.

You are metaphysicians. You can prove anything by metaphysics; and having done so, every metaphysician can prove every other metaphysician wrong – to his own satisfaction. You are anarchists in the realm of thought.

Jack London, *Iron Heel*

Programmatically leery of truth, objectivity, and cognition – and truth, objectivity, and cognition in fiction in particular – the dismissive camp splits into two strains of thought. Indexed by their take on (literary) knowledge, both revisionists and abolitionists bear the imprint of cultural constructivism or relativism. Both owe it, in turn, to critical "theory" with its obligatory elevation of ideology to the order of an epistemological precept. With an almost anarchistic aplomb, the abolitionist faction seeks, for example, to dispense with the classical principles of research and confirmation altogether. By their own admission, their goal is not to further knowledge but "to reveal a *politics* of truth, logic and reason."5

On this radical remake, instead of contributing to an interdisciplinary body of knowledge, research becomes part of an all-inclusive, semantically unstable, and semiotically self-erasing activity. All signs of this activity, including science, medicine, and even technology, are said to be no more than culturally contingent conventions played out against the backdrop of power politics. This is roughly the position defended with varying degrees of subtlety by logocentrism, textualism, deconstruction, and other post-modern schools of philosophy and criticism.

Somewhat more moderately, the revisionists seek to transform the reigning paradigm of inquiry by replacing it with one decidedly less analytic and scientific in character. Though not always apparent at first glance, the difference between the weaker and stronger strains of postmodernism is frequently more in emphasis than substance. This is so even though, unlike the abolitionists, the revisionists do not automatically, categorically, and globally reject epistemic values. Instead, knowledge and its concurrent goals of truth and rational justification are deemed replaceable with other notions, such as understanding or fitting.

Goodman and Elgin's above-cited revisionist manifesto, *Reconceptions in Philosophy*, contains some of the most explicit theses to that effect. These theses are in turn embedded in a sweeping methodological redescription which aims to establish the humanities as a non-denotative form of reference *vis-à-vis* other arts and sciences. Valiant as it is, the project leaves itself open to a number of caveats from the get-go. Some are fundamental enough to shake the very argumentative ground on which the revisionist program is to stand.

To begin with, the pivotal concept – understanding – by virtue of which the authors would undo centuries of science is beset with problems. Far too inclusive and indeterminate to be of consequence, it is identified only as "the cognitive faculty in an inclusive sense."[6] The entire epistemological edifice rests, thus, on a distinctly vague (not to say ill-defined) notion. As the core of the proposed reconceptions, the notion of understanding needs much conceptual and methodological fleshing out before it could foster a measure of understanding in keeping with its constructors' design. This is to say nothing about becoming a serious contender to the core principles and methods of inquiry as practiced over centuries, if not millennia.

Compounding the problem, this fundamental term is employed in an almost indiscriminate fashion. At various junctures it is used to denote a process, an accomplishment, and a skill. Cut it any way you like, the new epistemology is a matter of understanding understanding with understanding, a nebulous metaphor at the best of times. A conspicuous absence of any defense of this key notion is matched by the absence of any defense of the theses supposed to ensue from it. Such vagueness and appeal to suggestion rather than rational suasion cannot but cast a pall over the entire scheme. Aware of racing a lame duck, the revisionists preemptively concede that their confidently titled *Reconceptions* only manages to "sketch, in the scantiest way, some first steps in the proposed reconception."[7]

In one form or another revisionist schemes have been advanced even before Goodman and Elgin, to say nothing of the decades since. Thus, in defense of feminist epistemology, Elizabeth Grosz declares that her mentor, Luce Irigaray, "remains indifferent to such traditional values as 'truth' and 'falsity'." She adds: "This does not mean that her work could be described as 'irrational,' 'illogical,' or 'false.' On the contrary, her work is quite logical, rational and true in terms of quite *different criteria*."[8] Clearly, while the form is different, the content has not changed an iota. This is all the more remarkable in the face of a thousand and one critiques of epistemological revisionism, of which Richard Rudner's "On Seeing What We Shall See" is not only one of the earliest but one of the aptest.

Given this against-all-odds commitment to revising the canons of rational inquiry, it seems not inappropriate to pause over the motives in trying to replace knowledge with understanding. In the case of Goodman and Elgin the rationale is not to be found until their closing statements, and it is an anti-climax. Apparently the reason for doing away with *epistēme* as we know it is to "construct something that works cognitively, that fits together and handles new cases, that may implement further inquiry and invention."[9] One can hardly be faulted for concluding that two prominent scholars were caught trying to reinvent the wheel, calling it a circular-motion vehicular device. Grand as their goals are, the scientific enterprise under attack has always excelled in doing no less.

The theoretical conundra surrounding the mainstay of the scientific method – induction – are well known, and we will return to them in Chapter 3. The most persistent ones are encapsulated in a procession of classic paradoxes, from Hempel's contrapositive ravens to Goodman's own category-smashing paradox involving grue-bleen (green before *T*, blue thereafter) emeralds. Showing the incompleteness of the best models of confirmation theory, they drive home the message that some scientific principles and procedures are employed on no better grounds than the faith in their efficacy. There are other, no less famous riddles of induction, such as the Gettier paradoxes. Via trains of coincidence as far-out as those in Dickens's *A Tale of Two Cities*, they illustrate why a justified belief in the true state of affairs may not be enough as a basis for knowledge.

Cast in the form of thought experiments, all these paradoxes trip the classic trinity of criteria of knowledge (belief, justification, and truth). All are designed to prove – and do so with remarkable precision – that our theoretical accounts of how and why science works are incomplete. But scientists do not need the imprimatur of philosophers to get busy. Although its logical and methodological foundations may not be unassailable, the science of Galen, Galileo, and Gell-Mann works cognitively, fits together, handles new cases, and implements further inquiry with spectacular results. And as such it reduces the revisionist program to a flash in the philosophical pan.

Seen in this light, the revisionist variety of the dismissive stance has little to offer in the way of improving on, let alone challenging, the classical model of inquiry. The burden of proof remains squarely with the authors of such putative reconstructions. This is all the more so since, speaking of knowledge and truth in the arts, scholars do not speak in any special way distinct from the sciences. As E. D. Hirsh painstakingly documented in *The Aims of Interpretation*, then in "Value and Knowledge in the Humanities," despite the vaunted dissimilarities between humanistic and scientific inquiry, the cognitive elements in both are exactly the same in character.

What is the nature of the reading process, after all? We try to formulate true hypotheses about the hypothetical storyworld and formulate more or less precise descriptions of how it feels to experience it. By that token literary scholarship is a unique blend of literary science engaged in a search for objective knowledge, and – for lack of a better term – art criticism engaged in a search for discernments of taste. In principle, scholarship can suppress the latter part. Motivated by research considerations, research can deliberately focus on the objective, interpersonal, and interdisciplinary aspects of literature. Trying to unravel the puzzle of the cognitive power of storytelling, *Of Literature and Knowledge* exemplifies this approach.

But it seems hardly possible to entirely forswear the objective part. No one in practice ever does – never mind the theory. Even the wildest relativists purport to render an objective account of *their* version of events, whether on the level of the work or on the meta-level of epistemological reflections adduced by it. The point is simple. Emphasis on the emotive and experientially subjective aspects of fiction does not establish any of the relativist theses. Emotions and *qualia* are, and forever will be, central to the experience of literature in a manner they are not to philosophy and science. But that in no way precludes studying the non-subjective elements of literary fictions with a view to non-subjective knowledge.

> *It is by no means sufficient to raise a pair of relativist hands and give benediction for everything. The denial of reason, decisive, impersonal, is doing an ill service indeed to culture itself.*
>
> Karel Čapek, in *Man Against Destruction*

Leaving revisionism aside, in literary-critical circles the turn against the classical theory of knowledge is frequently more categorical. Fueled by the precepts of postmodernism, radical postulates of displacement of rationality and truth are often coupled with a negation of even the possibility of systematic knowledge in literature. Abolition of epistemology as we know it is said to secure a privileged portal to a different kind of academic enterprise. Politicized to the core, it is oriented not at the external world (posited to be unknowable) but at the otherwise unattainable, subjective, and esoteric (to the point of ineffability) facets of what Habermas called *Sonderwissen*.

Sketching alternatives to the regnant theory of knowledge – in itself a move with a better-than-average chance of striking out through self-contradiction – is but one part of this ambitious epistemological program. Equally importantly, the abolitionists seek to cast doubt on the type of inquiry pursued in other disciplines. This is thought to be achievable by means of postulating a radical fragmentation of knowledge by some form of irony, general negativity, or skeptical *arrhepsia*. The assault on literary studies as a domain of interdisciplinary research, tasked with conforming to the basic principles of rationality and consilience, is thus often a preamble to even more radical theses.

These radical theses range from more or less sophisticated relativism to outright epistemic anarchy. They champion the abolition of scientific *epistēme* by the deconstructing pantextuality of institutional, socio-political, economic, racial, sexual, and gender discourses. The socio-cultural contingency of the latter is said to preclude once and for all a recourse to classical logic and the application of even the most fundamental *modi operandi* of science. In a politically motivated move – the consequences of which are said to be politically liberating – science and its epistemological foundations are dismissed as oppressive, hegemonic, and pre-postmodern. Professors of this ideology range from famous to obscure. Richard Rorty is wholly typical when he professes – one presumes truthfully – "I don't have much use for notions like 'objective truth.'" Anne Carson disparages – one presumes non-deceptively – the "delusion that there are such things as facts, and they do not deceive us." Presumably not irrationally, Donald E. Polkinghorne observes: "Our observations cannot be trusted to represent the real, nor can our rationality be assumed to mirror the order of the real." And Pierre Machery – who clearly didn't exist before I thought him into being by subjecting him to this rational investigation – warns: "rigorous knowledge must beware all forms of empiricism, for the objects of any rational investigation have no prior existence but are thought into being."[10]

To be fair, postmodernism has raised the level of consciousness about the constructive elements in some aspects of our lives, including how categories of knowledge may be used in power relationships. It's been a burr in the saddle of scientism, the political ideology that, masquerading as progressive and rational, usurps all resources and attributes all solutions to the false idol of increasingly militarized and regimented science. The light it has brought to bear on the day-to-day conduct of science has usefully stressed its less rational or idealistic motivations. In some cases it's not even incompatible with traditional inquiry. Meanings are indeed not fixed by a transcendent linguistic entity but subject to social forces, historical processes, and ideological agendas. Constructivist history may differ in emphasis from standard historical research, without being a different species of it.

But that's about as good as it gets. Most of the time, most practitioners of postmodernism are neither coherent nor moderate. Illustrating his own point – though not the way he intended – Jameson states, for example, that postmodernity is "at one with the demonstration of the necessary incoherence and impossibility of all thinking." More incoherent thinking is in evidence in Eagleton, who rejects all knowledge – and the methods that culled this knowledge – culled over the last half-millennium. In his capsule definition: "Postmodernity is a style of thought, which is suspicious of classical notions of truth, reason, identify and objectivity." Only in this dismissive climate could Sandra Harding get away with claiming that it's "illuminating and honest" to see Newton's laws of motion as a "rape manual."[11]

Karl Popper is only one of many thinkers who condemned the irrationality and intellectual sloppiness issued in the name of the abolitionist program as the most serious menace hovering over our society.[12] Another philosopher of science, Mario Bunge, exemplifies the views of the forty contributors to the 1996 annals of the New York Academy of Sciences – tellingly entitled *The Flight from Science and Reason*. "Walk a few steps away from the faculties of science, engineering, medicine, or law, towards the faculty of arts. Here you meet another world, one where falsities and lies are tolerated, nay manufactured and taught. Here the unwary student may take courses in all manner of nonsense and falsity. Here some professors are hired, promoted, or given power for teaching that reason is worthless, empirical evidence unnecessary, objective truth nonexistent."[13]

Symptomatically, abolitionist denials of objectivity and rational validation are made with no regard for their consequences. The subversion of the so-called outmoded forms of knowledge always fails, for instance, to subvert the insights of the subverters. No reasons are ever offered for the sacredness of their epistemic Ararat in the raging seas of constructivism, because none exist. Claims are tacitly made in terms of epistemic rationality, even as these very claims posit an erosion and erasure of epistemic norms, together with all forms of justification of rational belief. We are asked to believe that beliefs cannot be evaluated in terms of truth or falsehood, or even that they could be both true and false at the same time.

Dissected in Harvey Siegel's *Relativism Refuted* under the mantle of UVNR (undermines the very notion of rightness) and NSBF (necessarily some beliefs are false), such abolitionist theses are incoherent and self-refuting. Dismissals of knowledge in general, and literary knowledge in particular, could never achieve what they set out to do. The presence of *some* constructivist elements in scientific theories does not make epistemological abolitionism, with its totalizing relativism and incoherence, a viable alternative. Literary and cultural scholars would also be well advised to take note of the contemporary philosophy and history of science. Capping their own velvet revolution, epistemologists are divesting the theory of confirmation of the last vestiges of its unreasonably exclusive positivist legacy.[14]

Unfortunately, a decline in the epistemic standards in the humanities is not exactly a novel phenomenon, albeit one that has gained in notoriety of late. John M. Ellis's *Literature Lost: Social Agendas and the Corruption of the Humanities* (1999) is only one of a torrent of studies to draw attention to the remarkable *volte-face* by academic liberals. Erstwhile champions of truth and rationality in the name of Enlightenment and social reform, today's humanists have forsworn them for the dubious recompense of pomo neoscholasticism – politically correct jargon notwithstanding. Scenting blood, a number of science-mindful literary scholars, philosophers, and scientists have joined the fray, charting the doctrine's self-destructive trajectory. Within this chorus of critiques none has, of course, bred more diatribe than Alan Sokal and his notorious experiment.

When I was in England I experimented with marijuana a time or two. And I didn't like it, and I didn't inhale.

Bill Clinton, 1992 presidential campaign MTV interview

It is perhaps fitting that an outsider, and a scientist to boot, should highlight the fact that what passes for postmodern scholarship is a crafty rearrangement of the deckchairs on theW *Titanic*. A *cause celèbre* whose coverage spilled into the public media, Sokal's hoax will forever be remembered in the annals of cultural studies as the one to rank – and rankle – with the best of Poe's. The experimenter, a physicist at NYU, penned a test article in the gobbledygook jargon emblematic of postmodernism. Christening it "Transgressing the Boundaries: Toward a Transformative Hermeneutics of Quantum Gravity" – in other words, pure gibberish – he submitted it to a leading journal of cultural studies, *Social Text*, only to see it published in the Spring/Summer 1996 issue.

The central tenet of this parody was the denunciation of the Enlightenment "dogma" that there exists an external world, whose attributes are for the most part independent of human inquiry. With no arguments to back his wild assertions, the author brazenly claimed that the physical *reality* – not theories of it – is a social and linguistic construct. Evidently the editors of *Social Text* were comfortable accepting this and other, equally outrageous and opaque, absurdities in the essay. In a post-mortem of the whole affair, published as "A Physicist Experiments with Cultural Studies," Sokal jeered: "Anyone who believes that the laws of physics are mere social conventions is invited to try transgressing those conventions from the windows of my apartment. (I live on the twenty-first floor)."[15]

Sokal's point is that, even as they advance ever more radical theories, their proponents conspicuously fail to abide by them in their academic practice, to say nothing of their daily lives. In one form or another, the same hypocrisy has been taken to task countless times before and since. Dr. Johnson put Berkley's idealism in its place by kicking a real stone. Psychologist Barbara S. Held shrugs: "no therapist I know of treats it [reality] as such [a nonreal linguistic construction], despite his or her antirealist epistemological declarations."[16] Indeed, postmodern principles all are refuted in practice. What's the point of arguing, and what is the argument about in the first place, if discourse is all ideology, the world unknowable, facts nonexistent, meanings unstable, and reality socially constructed?

Predictably enough, the overriding riposte from literary and cultural studies was no different than the reaction to the no less devastating critique delivered by a biologist and a mathematician on the pages of *Higher Superstition: Academic Left and Its Quarrels with Science* (1994). That earlier blood-letting was met, on the one hand, by platitudes about the alleged rigors of literary "theory," and on the other by imputations of the scientists' lack of training to judge the work in the humanities. The riposte to Sokal's muckraking exposé and its sequel, *Fashionable Nonsense: Postmodern Intellectuals' Abuse of Science*,[17] was no different. The only change was an additional charge of a breach of professional ethics.

According to the protesters, the physicist broke a code of academic conduct by cooking up his parody in "bad faith." The implications are startling, insofar as they appear to exonerate the shoddy research practices in the humanities. Editors whose competence does not extend to the esoterica of science need not, it would appear, solicit expert opinion to evaluate submissions. Rather, they may publish incomprehensible gobbledygook when it conforms with their political agenda. No word about the duty to banish pseudo-intellectual chaff from disciplines that, as a great number of humanists and scientists have labored to point out, to this day misconstrue such core notions as "theory" and "research."[18]

Except for sporadic outcries of having been misunderstood or having never said anything so radical, there has been no change in business as usual. No recantation from the authors of the targeted errors – Aronowitz, Baudrillard, Deleuze, de Man, Derrida, Guattari, Lacan, Lyotard, Latour *et al.* – that remain for all to see in the by-now bestselling critiques. No engagement with the critics on the level of specific argument and evidence. No systematic dialogue informed by expert scientific knowledge and deference to canons of rational inquiry. It's one thing, after all, to claim that there are incompatible *truth claims*, and another to confuse this sensible point with wild proclamations about incompatible *truths* and hence constructed realities. Everyone is entitled to their own opinion, but not to their own facts.

Joseph Carroll's *Evolution and Literary Theory*, a veritable compendium of the sundry howlers perpetrated in the name of postmodern metacriticism, makes this point clear. Capping this epic-sized anatomy of how *not* to conduct literary theory, his forecast for the undisciplined discipline engaged in anti-cognitive behavior makes for an apt, if acerbic, summary:

> [A] very large proportion of the work in critical theory that has been done in the last twenty years will prove to be not merely obsolete but essentially void. It cannot be regarded as an earlier phase of a developing discipline, with all the honor due to antecedents and ancestors. It is essentially a wrong turn, a dead end, a misconceived enterprise, a repository of delusions and wasted efforts.[19]

Given that the holes in the postmodern doctrine are big enough for an elephant to waltz through, one is sympathetic to Anne Applebaum's irritation at the inordinate amount of cultural space it hogs. But it is hard to agree when she shrugs off deconstruction and constructivism as rubbish patent enough not to need another book. The point is not that postmodern "theory" is by and large epistemological rubbish. If that was all, the debate would have ended decades prior with the first conclusive refutation, of which there are myriad.[20] The point is that such rubbish, resistant to internally and externally administered rubbish-cide, continues to choke rational voices in scholarship.

If cognitive openness and rational critique are to become more than empty slogans, literary studies must rally behind critics who, in a paradigmatic display of cross-disciplinary solidarity, take time away from science to instruct humanists on how to get their research right. Dispelling argumentative sleights of hand and faulty logic is often more than half the victory in getting the intellectual zeppelin off the ground. But where does it leave humanists who feel that, sniping at the extremists, Gross/Levitt and Sokal/Bricmont fail to acknowledge the rational and constructive voices *within* literary studies?

When Carl Sagan applied himself to refuting the kooky but trendy astro-mysticism of Velikovsky, first at the forum of the American Association for the Advancement of Science and subsequently in *Scientists Confront Velikovsky* and his own *Broca's Brain*, he enjoined his fellows not to begrudge such efforts. As vital as doing science, maintained Sagan, is exposing intellectual fraud, which, simplistic and trendy, creates fertile ground for all sorts of irrational beliefs. One must thus applaud the debunkers for debunking the slipshod intellectual habits of the abolitionist brigade. This includes its pretension to interdisciplinarity in which selective aprioritizing of scientific authority (while leaving out the actual methodology) is the order of the day.

But this is no grounds for imputing – even if only by omission – that no sophisticated work is conducted in other domains of the humanities. Absence of evidence is not evidence of absence, and the critiques of postmodern excesses are hardly the last word on literary studies. There are literary scholars who for years have advocated the interdisciplinary methods and procedures that have proven their worth across campus. Frederick Crews is only one among many to impel humanists to "cultivate the scientist's alertness against doctored evidence, circular reasoning, and wilful indifference to counterexamples."[21] These words appeared more than a decade and a half ago in a tellingly titled *After Poststructuralism*, one of a number of studies overlooked by the quality-control taskforce.

To them, I said, the truth would be literally nothing but the shadows of the images.
Plato, *The Republic*

Dismissals of rationality and science have little chance of improving on the inherited model of inquiry. Let us move, then, to the permissive end of our cognitive menu. Here one can distinguish three types of views on literature and knowledge: negative, dualist, and affirmative. In contrast to the abolitionists and revisionists, all take classical epistemology to be firmly in place. All allow for appraisal of literature in terms of its contribution to knowledge. To the question "Is knowledge, including literary knowledge, in the classical sense possible, and is truth the best criterion for its evaluation?," all reply with a resolute "Yes." This is also where most similarities among them end.

For a succinct but forceful articulation of the negative position we can turn to Plato's condemnation of poetic mimesis in *The Republic*. Fiction, twice corrupt by dint of describing objects already an ontological level below the ideal forms, is a source of perilous, because appealingly mimetic, illusion. As such, argues the Hellene, it is useless and frequently deceptive in the search for knowledge. Even though his goal is the pursuit of truth through rational inquiry, Plato feels that literature will only get in the philosopher's way. Hence, as he puts it, "from of old a quarrel between philosophy and poetry."[22]

In Plato's eyes fiction is a villain, all the more dangerous for assuming an alluring shape. It breeds irrationality by luring writers and readers away from the philosophically untainted apprehension of ideal forms. This is quite a stretch from the book in your hands, in which literature and philosophy are more like running mates on the same cognitive ticket than zero-sum competitors for knowledge and supremacy. Still, although well publicized, mostly by association with Plato, the negative stance does not command the spotlight in academic circles. It's just as well, for it would spell the end of literature and literary studies.

By and large it is some form of dualism – the second item on the permissive side of the ledger – that passes for the dominant ideology in the humanities. In a simple paraphrase, epistemic dualism asserts the autonomy of literary discourse *vis-à-vis* other forms of knowledge. *Contra* Plato, art is said to have an equivalent epistemic status to philosophy or science. This is because the two are said to exist in separate and incomparable domains of cognitive activity. Far from running on the same ticket, literature and science are thus made to look like Hillary Clinton and Emil Zatopek. One is running for political office, the other running the Olympic marathon, and the twain shall never meet.

The repercussions of dualism are dramatic and far-reaching. In one swoop, literary-critical discourse is absolved from the responsibility to defend its claims to knowledge on an interdisciplinary forum. This is because the very idea of such a forum is denied. Also denied is the compatibility of cognition-oriented goals across disciplines. Roman Ingarden, who more than anybody else has come to be associated with the doctrine of literary autonomy, is adamant on this point. In *The Cognition of the Literary Work of Art* he maintains that the differences between knowledge in science and knowledge in literature are irreconcilable. This is because the type of understanding of "a literary work of art is fundamentally different from that of understanding a scientific work."[23]

You might think this self-imposed intellectual apartheid would be prone to implosion. But as the North American or South African history teaches, once it takes root, segregation is not easy to stamp out. The times may have changed, spurred by new discoveries science and its philosophy may have moved on, but, refitted for the millennium, Ingarden's ghost continues to haunt the humanities. "The arts and the humanities do not look primarily for universals and general laws," is the two-of-a-kind dogma restated by Roger Shattuck in 1998. Instead, "they seek out the revelation and uniqueness of individual cases."[24]

The doctrine of "separate-but-equal" enjoys an enthusiastic following in the humanities. It is not difficult to see why it should exert so much allure. For starters, dualists arrogate all the epistemic rights while emancipating themselves from the rigors of cross-disciplinary inquiry. Every humanist for whom, like Aesop's Mr. Fox, scientific standards are out of reach is freed to walk away to less taxing ones. Alas, in any system of apartheid, racial or cognitive, the segregation supposed to shore up one side in the end harms both. There are matters too nuanced and resistant to reduction to be surrendered to scientists, and matters too complex and amenable to reduction to be mined by humanists alone.

Sadly for dualism, its vaunted autonomy of literary knowledge founders on the very attempts to segregate cognition in literature and science. Entrenched as it has become, the claim is profoundly incoherent. Consider, first of all, the role of specifically literary elements in the production of knowledge. Ingarden propounds that in a work of literature "much is said in similes, metaphors, and figurative or pictorial language." Such literary elements (tropes) are therefore said to be indispensable to grasping a story's cognitive content. They constitute an essential element of "aesthetically valent qualities" which participate in the "constitution of the polyphonic aesthetic value of the concretized work of art."[25]

The landmine that leaves the dualist with no leg to stand on is the relation between knowledge in literature and the way such knowledge is extracted. If the cognitive content of fiction can be expressed in propositional form, the dualist separation of the two modes of cognition – literary and scientific – loses its *raison d'être*. On the other hand, it is hard to see how Ingarden can assert that "much is said" if literary knowledge cannot be recast in propositional terms. To bootstrap out of inconsistency, the dualist would have to refrain from referring to literary knowledge in any form that would amount to paraphrasing its contents. On the other hand, if such discourse is to continue – as it has from the naissance of criticism – the autonomy of literary knowledge is an illusion after all.

One must not, of course, confuse prosecuting dualism with reducing literature to its propositional content. Literary fictions are not mere conveyance belts – and inefficient ones at that – for propositions that could as easily be expressed without the "redundant" encoding in narrative, often symbolic, and always multivalent form. Whatever else literature is, it is in part an emotional, intellectual, and experiential process unfolding in real-time. Were it ever possible to reduce an artwork to its propositional content (and I'm convinced it never will be), the *experience* of one and the other would still not be the same.

Fictions convey knowledge about people and their relation to the world not explicitly but, to a great extent, implicitly. How great an extent it's difficult to tell, of course, until subjective insights are converted into propositional form. Both types of knowledge are evaluated in confrontation with readers' intuitions (folk-beliefs) and cultural codes, which in many cases encode evolutionary dispositions. But, by the same token, there is a limit to what can be asserted on the other side. The fact that art is irreducible to plot summary and informational quotient does not establish some form of essentialism. No one, including the dualists, has ever proven the existence of a literary *je ne sais quoi* precluding the extraction of theses, hypotheses, or other catalysts for humanistic research.

With her back against the wall, the dualist has one more maneuver up her sleeve. She may stake out a minimal claim, namely that some cognitive content of literary works – or the cognitive content of some literary works – cannot be recast in propositional form. In such cases (abstract symbolist haikus?), goes the dualist, literature participates in a different type of epistemic activity. In *Literature and Knowledge* Dorothy Walsh associates it with a quasi-voyeuristic knowing "by vicarious living through."[26] Now, if the point is that by undergoing a fictional experience one can get to know what an experience is like, this is indeed a part of the story. But there is no reason to be dualistic about it. Much as real life consists of a mix of objective facts and subjective experiences, so do fiction and our response to it.

Other varieties of such indirect form of experience, mostly elaborated from the Freudian doctrine of identification, have also been proposed. Still, albeit in different guises, they all amount to one and the same thing, namely that cognitive content can somehow be extracted from literary works – the very works said to preclude extraction of propositional content. This dualist cul-de-sac turns fiction into an epistemic curiosum, one which apparently can be assessed neither by a "literary" nor by a propositional form of knowledge. On balance, like the Scylla of scientism, the Charybdis of dualism has little allure for the sophisticated voyager across *terra cognitiva*.

> *The greatest magician (Novalis had memorably written) would be the one who would cast over himself a spell so complete that he would take his own phantasmagorias as autonomous appearances. Would this not be our own case?*
>
> Jorge Luis Borges, "Avatars of the Tortoise"

Influenced by the teachings of Husserl, Ingarden's theses on the autonomy of the humanities from the type of knowledge sought by science correspond to what, in "Literary Studies and the Sciences," Livingston broadly identified as the neo-Kantian dichotomy. The term describes a composite of ideas that have long since coalesced into a leading humanistic doctrine in most institutions of learning. Its tenets, viewed through the prism of Ingarden's dualism, are familiar. The quest for knowledge is allegedly carried out by two autonomous fields of inquiry whose cognitive programs are, for the most part, incompatible with each other.[27]

The dichotomy trots out the familiar conceit of complementary epistemic islands separated by incompatible research methods. Scientists are thus said to seek objective, determinate, and cumulative knowledge, and evaluate it in terms of intersubjective criteria. Humanists pursue socially inflected, individualized, non-cumulative readings of cultural products. The *nomothetic* sciences, which favor explanations that lead to law-like predictions, are thus polarized with *idiographic* humanities. The latter, on that view, are devoted to the exploration of unique and non-recurrent facets of human life. Crudely put, their goal is to interpret symbolic and subjective dimensions of culture in ways that need not be cumulative or even compatible with one another.

The results of such laissez-faire are predictable. Research in the humanities is cultivated by virtue of being cut off from the tree of knowledge towering outside the disciplinary fence. An instructive synecdoche for this state of affairs is furnished by literary studies. Tucked away in the nook of academia carved out by this *votum separatum*, it thrives on its self-indulgent epistemic standards. Literary critics produce a dazzling multiplicity of polemical readings, and regard doing so as a legitimate form of research and a genuine contribution to inquiry. Rarely does anyone reflect on whether this array of mutually critiquing, refuting, and nullifying voices actually contributes to the explanation of anything!

There is no accumulation of knowledge to ensure that whatever is valuable in literary studies will not drift aimlessly until lost out of sight. That can happen in science too, and the work of historians documenting rediscoveries of the forgotten pioneers is immensely useful in this regard. But while one has a degree of faith that science will eventually stumble on a Mendel or a Boscovich, chances of that in literary studies are virtually nil. If the birth of analytic philosophy was, in this sense, a concerted effort to turn the discipline away from impressionistic essays and into a more rigorous *and* a cumulative vein of analysis, literary studies is in this regard not only unlike science, but even unlike philosophy.

The humanists' fears of being railroaded into a quasi-scientific system of reductions finds a piquant expression in Woody Allen's *Without Feathers*. Having enrolled in a speed-reading course, writes the comedian, he managed to complete *War and Peace* in two hours. As for the story, it was about some Russians. Allen's quip is hilarious precisely to the degree it's incongruous, going against the grain of a tradition that prohibits such reductive violence to art. Yet fear-mongers have nothing to lose by spinning the picture of incompatibility, if not enmity, between literature and science.

The idea is by now par for the course, institutionally inculcated into the mindset of arts and science undergraduates alike. It is equally widespread among the general public, who equate "scientific" with objective and "fictional" with untrue. It is, therefore, time to say once and for all that the cognitive dichotomy between the sciences and the humanities is a red herring.[28] The furore over Sokal's wacky experiment was, after all, directly related to the humanists' failure to live up to the basic standards of inquiry. These standard were applicable precisely because of the humanists' persistent ventures into domains prospected by science.

So much for the alleged dichotomy predicated, if you recall, on cultural and scientific studies being worlds apart. Speaking of the by now familiar repudiation of theory by practice, consider the nature of the experience purportedly sought by humanists. By *any* notion of knowledge there is little point in studying unique and non-recurrent events other than, perhaps, as an exercise in experiential taxonomy. Insights harvested from what is genuinely unique and singular are, by definition, inapplicable to any other context that might arise. Only the transference of experience, whether as fact, theory, hypothesis, conjecture, analogy, or any other, saves it from becoming an academic curiosum.

That said, the neo-Kantian ideology commands a great deal of influence in the university. Within the humanities, its core dualism continues to inform the types of inquiry bankrolled through hiring policies, budget rationalizations, and research endowments. Outside the humanities, highlighting the evident partition from the sciences across campuses, the doctrine clamors for equal status – *de facto* autonomy. Be that as it may, the reasons for rejecting it are legion, starting with the fact that the neo-Kantian doctrine has never commanded universal approval. On the contrary, it was invented precisely to counter the ascendancy of the new kids on the block – the nomothetic sciences.

Heinrich Rickert, one of its founding fathers, was more responsible than anyone else for the mystique of cultural studies' uniqueness.[29] Unfortunately for his ideological program, humanistic prestige continued to dwindle as the world at large simply chose to ignore it. Nothing brings it home like Matthew Arnold's *cri de coeur* from his 1882 Rede lecture, "Literature and Science." Not even Arnold's formidable oratory could halt the pattern of "abasing what is called 'mere literary instruction and education,' and of exalting what is called 'sound, extensive, and practical scientific knowledge.'"[30] The inequity favoring the ways of science over the ways of literature not only has not disappeared during the subsequent six-score years, but has become even more entrenched.

Today routine hierarchical (e.g. budgetary or honorary) decisions testify to the institutional partiality to the scientific branch of the dichotomy. "In the 'good old days,' humanists were the most important voices in colleges and universities," reminisced Henry Rosovsky, distinguished Harvard administrator and author of the influential *The University: An Owner's Manual*. "Now, prestige and money go to science."[31] Given the valorization of science and empiricism over liberal arts and humanities, one way to prop the underachiever is to bully the winner. Thus, in a triumph of spirit over reason, some humanists direct their energies to dissing science, denying that it manufactures objective, reliable, and cumulative knowledge.

This is roughly the strategy of the miscellaneous strands of postmodernism. Claims are typically advanced within the framework of rationality, even as they maintain that epistemic norms no longer apply and that rational arguments are no longer decidable in terms of truth value. Thus, with especial reference to Latour, Donna Haraway claims supremacy of social construction "for all forms of knowledge claims, most certainly and especially scientific ones."[32] Latour and Woolgar themselves do not mince words: "'reality' cannot be used to explain why a statement becomes a fact."[33]

There is no need to dwell again on the incoherence plaguing these attempts to deconstruct inquiry into a contingent amalgam of socially "fitting" worldviews. Attacks on nomothetic inquiry will never bolster the humanities. The epistemic, economic, and political hegemony of science is a fact that no amount of radical skepticism can undermine. All such skepticism can hope for is to raise doubts about certain logical foundations of scientific theories. This policy does not even begin, however, to address the supremacy of the scientific method in all walks of life.

Regrettably, many humanists work under the illusion that a higher ground for arbitration between rivals to epistemic legitimacy has been found. This is not the case. The dualist dichotomy and its judgments hail from the same wing of the academe. This resembles the wagon-circling move of Hollywood moguls who, to get legitimacy where none was forthcoming, founded the Academy of Motion Pictures and began showering themselves with Oscars. Euphemisms aside, dualism is neither an epistemologically sound nor a broadly supported framework to evaluate the institutional status of the humanities and the sciences. Its philippics for equal epistemic rights continue to be judged in terms of the dominant mode of inquiry, which, as the bottom line bears out, is anything but conciliatory.

> *The human race needs the novel. We need all the experience we can get.*
>
> Bernard Malamud, "The Art of Fiction"

While the humanities are said to be guided by idiographic hermeneutics, the facts of the matter tell a different story. Not to look too far, literary studies hardly vindicates the party line. Critics and metacritics don't deal exclusively in non-recurrent particulars; nor do they hesitate to draw freely on such paraliterary "authorities" as Marx, Freud, Heidegger, Lacan, Derrida, or Althusser. Nor can the dualist ideology account for the scientific pressures that from Hyppolite Taine (if not Aristotle) on have repeatedly been brought to bear on its domain.

The systematic research aspirations of literary formalists and structuralists are simply not compatible with the neo-Kantian doctrine. The alleged autonomy of literary criticism is further contradicted by the inability to demarcate its domain of research. Today literature and literary knowledge are routinely prospected by consilient disciplines such as linguistics, psychology, sociology, anthropology, history, or philosophy. So much for the dualist claims, and so much for the dualist variety of the permissive stance. It is time to move down our epistemological menu and look at the miscellany of views that compose the third, affirmative option.

Despite internal subdivisions, here researchers operate within the classical framework of interdisciplinary knowledge. Consequently, they judge literature's epistemic status in terms of its ability to further this type of knowledge. It is in this spirit that Walker Percy, writer and trained MD in pathology and psychiatry, insisted on "the importance of a knowledge of science to any serious writer."[34] Knowledge of science is, of course, *not* to be understood purely as familiarity with individual facts and laws. An even more important component of scientific literacy than the familiarity with individual facts and laws is the familiarity with the deep principles and the working methods that allow scientists to churn out individual facts and laws.

The alignment of literary research with the goals and principles of the sciences does not, of course, mean that the cognitive foundations of the latter are unassailable. Not all scientific methods can be justified by philosophical principles, however broad or specific. What *is* unassailable is that the rationality and coherence of science do not reside in the explicit formulation of theoretical foundations or procedural algorithms. (That's why Feynman's birds can afford to be indifferent to ornithology.) As the dead of Hiroshima would testify, if they could, scientists don't need explicit justification to dispense adequate knowledge that impacts the world, sometimes with cataclysmic results.

Indexed by difference in emphasis, the affirmative position on literary knowledge splits into a weak (illustrative), a moderate (hypothesizing), and a strong (systematic) variety. For a clear enunciation of the latter we can turn to René Girard. For Girard fiction is, among others, a source of coherent, rational, and systematic articulations of psychological "laws" of human behavior. In *Deceit, Desire, and the Novel* he proposes that writers can apprehend "through the medium of their art, if not formally, the system in which they were imprisoned together with their contemporaries."[35] Critical analysis may usefully formalize the canons of behavior depicted in a work of art, but the cognitive content is already articulated by the maker of fiction.

On Girard's view, then, literary narratives convey theses which, albeit in a less structured form, command the same epistemic status as those in the social sciences. In the best stories, woven into the plot are "those 'psychological laws' to which the novelist refers constantly but which he did not always manage to formulate with sufficient clarity."[36] Specifically, Girard elaborates a case for a constellation of writers who wrote into their novels the principles of imitative "triangular desire." Cervantes, Stendhal, Flaubert, Proust and Dostoevsky, argues the philosopher, narrated their insights in a manner constitutive of a *bona fide* psychological theory.[37]

Outside the European canon, one ought not to forget Poe and the self-styled apex of his intellectual aspirations, *Eureka*. Conceived as a tributary to the epistemological and cosmological theories of his day, this philosophical "poem" rewards the cognitive approach of the affirmative school. As I documented in *Between Literature and Science*, Poe's treatise trips to no end on factual slip-ups and argumentative sleights of hand. But it stuns even today with the audacity of its speculative vision and with the ambition to forge a working alliance with philosophy and science.

In the context it's worth noting that the heresy of the didactic, often evoked in Poe's context, does not accurately describe his views on knowledge in art. To anyone who takes the trouble to read the writer, and not his exegetes, it is evident that he never opposes knowledge as a goal of literature, but knowledge as its *sole and exclusive* goal. Poe finds truth as often in beauty as in science, which is to say that aesthetic goals are for him as important as cognitive ones. This sensible position is a far cry from the common misreading of the "Poetic Principle," which imputes to him a bias against cognition as a legitimate ingredient of literary art.[38]

If only tacitly, Girard's take on literary knowledge makes extraordinary demands on storytellers. Writers may be better-than-average psychologists, but not many can meet the challenge of furnishing systematic canons of human behavior. Another question is how much fiction would clear the checkpoint that rigorously enforced the law-formulative criteria for literary knowledge. Some apparently would, proving that literature's goals can be compatible with the basic methods and principles of science. But the goals of storytellers vary, and in many cases don't extend to quasi-scientific formulations of psychosocial regularities.

> *An idea may exist with a well-defined form and meaning in a specific science, yet be continually elaborated or reinvented by artists working with different aims and visions.*
>
> John Barrow, *The Book of Nothing*

The systematic position does not, of course, exhaust the options available to writers – and critics. At the other end of the affirmative spectrum lies the illustrative mode. Here literature does what Jesus did so well: convey and explain larger truths in the guise of stories and parables. Illustrating and popularizing lore from established disciplines, literature on this view earns its cognitive bread by clothing abstract skeletons of social-scientific theories and findings in experiential particulars. In the idiom of game theory, narratives flesh out game scenarios in psychologically and phenomenologically compelling utility and motive. The illustrative position is articulated concisely in Herbert Simon's classic *Reason in Human Affairs*. Anticipating some of the arguments from Chapter 4 in this volume, Simon says that, thanks to its formidable emotional appeal, literature can be a superlative tool of learning and acquisition of knowledge. His only stricture is that, to be meritorious, stories must be congruous with the best of contemporary theory and fact. "The scientific content," in his words, "must be valid."[39] Simon continues: "we must evaluate not only their power to rouse emotions but also their scientific validity when they speak of matters of fact," advancing an explicit *cognitive* principle for evaluating *literary* fictions.

In this illustrative – or, to fall back on his terminology, educational – role, literary works can usefully generate framing contexts to facilitate comprehension of general theories developed elsewhere.[40] To illustrate what he has in mind, let us look at an example from nineteenth-century naturalism. Only a few years after Darwin's *The Descent of Man*, Emile Zola conceived a novel cycle to dramatize the precept that heredity is subject to laws no less inviolable than gravitation. The result was the monumental *Rougon-Macquart*, built in part upon Lombroso's and Broca's theories on cranial and physiognomic signatures of human evolution.

Yet the backwardness of Lombroso's famed criminology textbook, *L'Uomo delinquente* (1876), was no secret even during Zola's times. Misusing Darwin, the author (who, regrettably, became a world authority on crime and its perpetrators) claimed that criminals could be spotted by the shape of their ears, nose, lips, or jaw, inasmuch as they were throwbacks to earlier stages of development. Instead of evolving to perfection and civilization, the criminal was said to be a biological degenerate to earlier forms of anthropoid. Evidently, Lombroso never ran into any nineteenth-century incarnation of the ever charming and erudite Ted Bundy.

In Simon's terms, *Rougon-Macquart* may be illustrious fiction, but, steeped in bad science, it falls short of the illustrative goal. The latter does not, of course, imply that narratives must necessarily be realistic. Science fiction – or at least its rational wing – is a paradigmatic class of stories parting with conventional reality while being guided by empiricism and ratiocination. As we will examine at length in Chapter 2, narratives can, of course, employ unrealistic means to illustrate quite serious theses. As demonstrated by Edwin Abbott Abbott in *Flatland*, for example, a two-dimensional storyworld can be a fantastic (in both senses) tool to model a world of four dimensions.

Abbott's celebrated novella predates by more than half a century a thought experiment independently devised by the famous twentieth-century geometer Henri Poincaré. "Let us imagine," proposed the mathematician, "a world only peopled with beings of no thickness, and suppose these 'infinitely flat' animals are all in one and the same plane."[41] It took another half-century for another mathematician, Ian Stewart, to write a story replete with thought experiments based on Abbott's and Poincaré's idea. In deference to the original, it is called *Flatterland: Like Flatland, Only More So*.

While on the subject, the illustrative role attributed to literary fictions is no different from the illustrative role with which thought experiments are tasked. What armchair experiments do so well, after all, "is give us that 'aha' feeling, that wonderful sense of understanding what is really going on. With such an intuitive understanding of the physics involved we can often tell what is going to happen in a new situation without making explicit calculations."[42] Frequent calls for thought experiments to be scripted in greater depth and detail, lest they lead astray to conceptual and/or evaluative potholes, only tighten the cognitive isomorphism between literary and philosophical counterfactuals.

While many readers sit down with a book with the expectation of learning something, one should not hang the albatross of empirical veracity on the necks of artists whose interests may lie elsewhere. Free to embark on creative paths that lead astray from being mere teaching companions for science, storytellers need not check what they write against *Scientific American* to delight *and* instruct. To take one example, misguided literary-critical praise for the science of *The Martian Chronicles* apart, its actual scientific value (in the illustrative sense) is nil. But, as Martin Gardner loves to point out, even when Mars is second home to us, "*The Martian Chronicles* will keep on stirring imaginations, arousing laughter and haunting the minds of those who have not forgotten how to read."[43]

There are stories that venture outside accepted theories and even empirical data. In their case we cross over from the illustrative to the more proactive mode of hypothesis formation. Literature "may have immense cognitive value," argues Monroe Beardsley in *Aesthetics*, "even if it merely suggests new hypotheses about human nature or society or the world, and even if only a few of these hypotheses turn out to be verifiable, perhaps after some analysis or refinement." While concurring in the main, I am somewhat dubious about the verdict on the kind of hypotheses to be found in literature. Beardsley imagines that vital insights appear only implicitly, "in the form of theses suggested by the work as a whole, or in the form of metaphorical contributions."[44] But there are counterexamples to prove that, like philosophy or science, narratives can be a source of *explicit* hypotheses aimed at inquiry.

A case in point is the metafiction of Stanislaw Lem. In *Prowokacja* (still unavailable in English), for example, the author investigates the omnipresent role of death in modern desacralized society. For his analytical base he employs the data from the methodical genocide committed by the Nazis in the occupied territories during the Second World War, as well as contemporary forms of mass murder, including (state) terrorism. Lem's attempt is one of the scarce few to integrate the Nazi atrocities into the social history of Mediterranean civilization. He also makes the case for the failure of modernity to bestow on death the cultural prominence it had hitherto enjoyed owing to its previously unchallenged Judeo-Christian roots.

Lem articulates explicit anthropological theses regarding the symbolic and pragmatic role of death in modern society. He argues that the patchwork synthesis of the ethics of evil and aesthetics of kitsch which paved the way for the German extermination juggernaut is still at work in today's culture. He dissects examples of state and anti-state terrorism, ritualized violence in art and the media, political extremism, the sanctioning of death as a national doctrine, the ultra-right turn to neo-fascism in electoral practice, and the allure of death as the ultimate cultural bastion. Backing his analysis with a welter of historical data, and couching it in the guise of a scholarly review of an anthropological monograph, Lem goes well beyond Beardsley's vision of knowledge in literature as implicit suggestion.

Books are not meant to be believed, but to be subjected to inquiry.

Umberto Eco, *The Name of the Rose*

A robust articulation of the hypothesizing role, more in tune with the cognitive ambitions and sophistication of contemporary fiction, is advanced in Livingston's *Literary Knowledge*. Surveying the field, the philosopher takes stock of sundry types of claims – or refusals to lay claims – to literary knowledge. On the way he outlines a research program better equipped to capture the cognitive potential of the stories we tell. Its goals are defined by the many ways in which "oriented readings of literary works serve to challenge and to refine, to complexify and perfect hypotheses within the other anthropological disciplines."[45]

Literary studies that put the program to action range from Livingston's own *Models of Desire*, to David Bell's analysis of Zola in *Models of Power*, to my refinement of the Turing test in *Between Literature and Science*. The recent flourish of evolutionary literary criticism even marks a whole area of literary studies that vindicates this vision. One of the most forceful expositions of scholarly faith in assimilating the biological and social sciences to advance literary knowledge – and, in turn, to advance knowledge outside the humanities – is Carroll's *Literary Darwinism*. If learning a language is like acquiring a new mind, prompts the critic, imagine learning the language of science. It then can be used "in the elucidation of literary texts, both as an end in itself – to understand the texts – and as a means of testing and refining the ideas."[46]

Do all these cognitive goings-on horn in on the human sciences? Not at all. Genesis or elaboration of hypotheses is not tantamount to providing evidence for their truth or falsehood. Not that literature cannot be a good source of evidence. Cultural anthropology would be a shadow of itself if it couldn't mine fiction for evidence about other cultures. Nor is literature destined to play only an ancillary function to more rigorous research fields. Bernard Paris, who more than anyone else has contributed to the cross-disciplinary use of cognitive psychology to study fiction, underscored this mutual benefit. "Psychology," he argued for the mimetic impulse in literature, "helps us to talk about what the novelist knows; fiction helps us to know what the psychologist is talking about."[47]

Examples of cross-fertilization abound, starting with the cross-disciplinary genre that epitomizes narrative quest for knowledge: *roman philosophique*. Surely Voltaire's *Candide* is an earnest, if fanciful, exposition of philosophical doctrines of determinism, morality, and the nature of good. In the more scientific vein, from the welter of candidates one can cite Joseph Maria Jauch's Galilean Dialogues in *Are Quanta Real?*, Ian Stewart's abovementioned *Flatterland*, Alan Lightman's fanciful *Einstein's Dreams*, Rudy Rucker's gnarly mind-twisters, and Douglas Hofstadter's debates between Achilles and the Tortoise, many of which transcend the illustrative mode and enter the argumentative.

Evolutionary literary criticism and various forms of engagement between literature and cognitive sciences – whether translation theory, philosophy of mind, authorship, intentionalism, or even artificial intelligence – offer currently the most promise of building cumulative and progressive knowledge. Locating literature within the explicitly formulated body of extra-literary knowledge identifies fiction as an integral form of the empirical enterprise. Likewise it provides a framework for evaluating it in terms of truth content and even originality. The latter is clearly tied to the constantly shifting frontiers of research, virtually always new if we're talking about integration with the sciences.

The enhanced appreciation of cognition in fiction can lead to an enhanced appreciation of literature *qua* literature. In fact, recent work in analytic aesthetics indicates that the properly *literary* value that defines *belles lettres* need include "a distinctive sort of cognitive value."[48] Fittingly, despite differences in emphasis, the three schools of affirmative criticism – systematic, illustrative, and hypothesis-oriented – adjudge the cognitive merits of fiction in an interdisciplinary court of appeal. Their appreciation of epistemic affinities between literary and scientific *discorsi* is, of course, in sharp contrast to the literary-critical establishment.

An uncompromising appeal to truth as the goal, and to scientific rationality as the principle, of inquiry is hardly paradigmatic of literary studies. Yet such uncompromising appeals are sanctioned by the epistemic failures of the current critical practices that give literary "theory" such a bad name in the broader community of truth-seekers. They are all the more urgent in that, even in these turbulent days of a disciplinary crisis of faith, most professionals seem content to abide uncritically by the canons of their work.

What does this business as usual mean? Dubbed by Livingston "megaphone criticism," it is a matter of approaching interpretation as a restatement and amplification of literary meaning. "What does writer *y* have to say about topic *x*?" is the writ that guides most interpreters in their labors. Megaphone critics do not *evaluate* textual propositions – often reconstituted with much care and bibliophilic erudition – in terms of truth or in the light of theories from other disciplines. Nor do they excoriate propositions that make no sense. Instead, critics presume to advance research mainly by "getting the message" and clarifying it for the audience (in practice, frequently obfuscating it beyond belief).

Megaphone criticism flourishes within this a-cognitive environment. In spite of a superficial semblance of rational inquiry, debates about literary meanings are conducted in an epistemic vacuum. Although elucidating the writings of John Doe – or, in the postmodern mode, Jane Doe's text – is by now ingrained into the discipline, its methodology begs a number of questions that rip the heart out of such laissez-faire "research." None are accorded the attention commensurate with their gravity. But the questions about this freewheeling kind of discourse-without-end refuse to go away.

Why and how are such exegeses valuable in the first place? How does megaphone criticism enhance the appreciation of literature? Do voluminous libraries of studies devoted to minute elaborations of canonical works really add to the aesthetics of reading? Where is the coherent and universally accepted theory of aesthetics to empower such prodigious investment of critical finesse? Do not the gargantuan proportions of these non-cumulative, and often openly contradictory, efforts undermine the "research" principles they are supposed to justify? And most importantly, how do critics evaluate the truth value of the amplified messages in the context of the regnant model of inquiry?

Once again, Beardsley hits the epistemic nail on the head. "Sooner or later . . . in talking about almost any art, a word like 'reality' is bound to crop up."[49] Sooner or later, in other words, efforts to promote the autonomy of art by banning reference to reality must backfire. Literature simply cannot but refer to the real world and real-world knowledge. Indeed, no fiction could be understood if it did not correspond in some way to actuality. This applies even to what may be the least reality-dependent literary work of our time, Luigi Serafini's *Codex Seraphinianus* (the verdict on the Voynich manuscript remains open).

For literary research, the results of such infatuation with merely elaborating literary messages can only be disastrous. The situation bears some analogy to the shift undergone by the protagonist of Calvino's "Chase." In the story, the pursued, in one mental gyration, wills himself into the pursuer. In the academic reality, those who banish literary research that looks beyond the vaunted autonomy of fiction become the banished. It is time to break with the apologetic tradition of making literary knowledge special by separating it from other forms of bringing the visible world to justice. The alternative is giving renewed consent to a perfect vacuum. For, in the same sense that multiplication by zero yields zero, critical amplification of the void can only yield the same void with which we started. Why is this conversion so urgent? I can do no better than close with the words of Alvin Kernan, one time Yale Provost, who reflects with brutal honesty on the future of our institutions and standards of knowledge:

> The universities, at least the natural sciences and the harder social science portions of them, will survive in some workable form. The stakes for a technocratic society are too high for any other outcome. But those of us in the humanities and the softer social sciences have good cause to worry about what is happening. When the dust settles, it may be that only those subjects that have some means of testing their conclusions will survive.[50]

2   Literature and modeling

He understood that modelling the incoherent and vertiginous matter of which dreams are composed was the most difficult task that a man could undertake.

Jose Luis Borges, "The Circular Ruins"

From the old-time *trivia* of grammar, logic, and rhetoric, down to contemporary liberal curricula, the study of letters has been deemed central to the advancement of learning – inordinately so, judging by the direction of cuts inflicted on today's colleges. Not necessarily metacritical or even epistemic, goals of *belles lettres* are, however, largely independent of the goals of the scholarship they spawn. But then, why take literary fiction seriously in cognitive terms? Scientists control their variables by cooking up synthetic environments in the lab. Couldn't armchair researchers "cook up" heuristic narratives, dispensing with literature altogether?

To the extent they could, they do. Synthetic squibs that attack problems by framing their salient traits augment many a humanist's arsenal, especially in areas inclined to counterfactual reasoning. In aesthetics, for example, a steady diet of oddball art, surreal societies, and fantastic forgeries garnish hypotheticals set on this or Twin Earth. Far be it, however, from downgrading narrative fiction to the foot of the epistemic ladder. Replacing *belles lettres* with Socratic dialogues, analytic vignettes, or thought experiments would be like wiping out the energy crisis by wiping out mankind: categorically missing the point.

Moreover, demoting storytelling to little more than a cognitive digest, the move would paper over all kinds of counterevidence. Among others, it would have to demote *bone fide* philosophical and even scientific inquiries that blossom into narrative fiction with a regularity that speaks for itself. From a multitude of examples, the work of Alexander K. Dewdney may be emblematic. Inaugurated as a series of worknotes on bidimensional physics, it graduated into a *Scientific American*-sponsored Symposium on Two-Dimensional Science and Technology before morphing into an original work of fiction, *Planiverse* (whose appendix tracks the project's history).

Although all narratives are steeped in commonsense logic, their cognitive engine runs on far from deduction alone. In a philosophical thought experiment the story frame is often only auxiliary, if not wholly immaterial, to the problem at hand. Underneath the narrative dress, the shape of the logical mannequin alone determines the problem – and the solution. Not so in literary simulations and models, in which the grasp of narrative conflict is oftentimes inseparable from the rich cloth of framing detail. All this is to say that ditching storytelling as a tool of inquiry may be a nonstarter for more than practical (temporal, budgetary, or even skill-related) reasons. Far more importantly, doing so would mean turning our backs on a conceptual apparatus of unsurpassed subtlety, diversity, and magnitude.

Literature is a fertile source of all manner of models: complex and simple, idiosyncratic and transcultural, self-consciously explicit and structurally sketchy, open to empirical testing and not, and so on. Rather than discuss them piecemeal, I will therefore focus on the essentials that hold for most if not all categories. A good starting point may be Alex Argyros's spirited defense of literature as a modeling factory in "Narrative and Chaos." The author cogently stipulates why a literary work can be profitably approached as a "hypothesis about the nature of the existing slice of reality or about the potential consequences of certain variations on a model of the world."[1]

Elevating *belles lettres* to the role of a cultural data bank, Argyros defends claims on behalf of fiction as a cognitive laboratory. He goes so far, in fact, as to propose that, in addition to modeling reality, narratives can actually "perform experiments on it." Inasmuch as storytelling is not a form of empirical inquiry, I take "experiment" here to denote thought experiment. This interpretation brings the author's Zolaesque thesis in line with his preceding remarks on cognitive integration across research disciplines. With the goal set, let us look at literature and modeling by way of looking at the nature of narrative representations.

Blinded by intellectual myopia, modeling is all too frequently attributed exclusively to the mathematical or experimental operations of the sciences. The reasons are partly historical, going back to antiquity and the deep links forged between Athenian axiomatic geometry and philosophical thought. Whatever the reasons, this picture is so ingrained that it trips even thinkers who ought to know better. A case in point: a recent general-science bestseller from a mathematical scientist of no mean renown. It associates modeling solely with "mathematical squiggles on a piece of paper or an electronic recreation . . . in a computer."[2]

And yet, belying this limiting vision, the book itself is smarter than the author. Chock-full of narrative models, thought experiments, typological analyses of physical interactions, and simulations of experimental results, *The World Within the World* confutes John Barrow's overly narrow view. It may, as a matter of fact, represent a paradigmatic example of bridging the techniques of fiction with the objectives of science. In doing so, this cross-disciplinary study supplies ample evidence for why narrative articulations of physical experiments, cognitive states, social trends, or even psychodramatic scenarios can be cognitively valuable.

Mindful of these principles, a more inclusive, not to say robust, view of narrative modeling is in evidence in analytical philosophy. Here, from Poundstone's *Labyrinths of Reason* to Sorensen's "Thought Experiments and the Epistemology of Laws," the art of storytelling commands respectful attention. The latter study especially brings literature to mind – and to the forefront. It construes thought experiment as a type of "experiment that purports to answer (or raise) its question by mere contemplation of its design."[3]

To be sure, experiments *simpliciter* do not aim to raise, but to answer queries. A test is normally performed once the hypothesis in need of checking has already been formulated. When the testing is over, you may indeed end up with more questions than before, but that still does not make *raising* questions the purpose of inquiry. This is especially evident in the statistical breakdown of experimental results, where analyses planned from the get-go are scrupulously differentiated from those done after the experiment. The latter are actually less reliable since, mathematically speaking, some accuracy conditions are violated by the fact that the data are no longer random and/or independent.

I think that most of my books are part of some process of self-education.

John Le Carré, *Conversations with John Le Carré*

The parallels, however, are difficult to miss. Narrative fictions routinely raise and answer questions by asking readers to contemplate the relation between their design and the meaning they transmit. From the formalist dialectics down to the psychometric empiricism of the Internationale Gesellschaft für Empirische Literaturwissenschaft (IGEL), research into literary works' affect and effect has always entailed a contemplation of their design. Much study in aesthetics is focused, for example, on precisifying the degree of intentionalism compatible with artistic design, while keeping abreast of the various circumstances in which the work may fall short of the artist's intentions.[4]

Alert to these parallels, Sorensen concludes that "thought experiments are stories," entailing by the symmetry of comparison that at least some stories are thought experiments. The mapping is partial since literature only cross-sects the class of thought experiments. Not all fictions, in other words, are instantiations of armchair inquiry: William Carlos Williams's impressionistic "Red Wheelbarrow" certainly isn't. Conversely, not all thought experiments are literary fictions. Be that as it may, implicitly endorsing the present line of inquiry, Sorensen allows that many "of the issues raised by thought experiment are prefigured in aesthetics and the logic of fiction."[5]

The prefiguring in the way designs are contemplated and related to their meaning extends beyond Edna Vincent Millay and her poetic conviction that "Euclid alone has looked on Beauty bare." Occam's razor, I venture, delineates a residual *aesthetic* dimension in all kinds of models, be they literary, philosophic or scientific. *Entia non sunt multiplicanda praeter necessitam* – entities are not to be multiplied beyond necessity – lays down a principle that shows up in all types of inquiry. Originally proposed to keep ontological speculation in check, Occam's aesthetics may not be immediately apparent in this canonical formulation. It becomes, however, almost painfully so when its precepts are paraphrased as "simple is beautiful."

Indeed, one of the astonishing points about physical mathematics is how often its conceptual compass homes in on such "soft" and "artsy" dimensions as simplicity, symmetry, or neatness. Granted that elegance alone is not enough to make an empirical theory work. Theory choice is, after all, always empirically underdetermined. Clearly, you can always think another theory than the one in hand that will account for the facts equally well. The effects of aesthetic considerations can, however, overwhelm at times. Hence Einstein's much publicized joke that if experiments came out against general relativity, it would only mean that God made an error when fashioning the universe![6]

Given these tentative parallels, it may be fair to ask how the contemplation of fictional designs compares across the spectrum of knowledge hunters. In the case of non-literary thought experiments the answer is uncontroversial. If research is going up alleys to see if they are blind, it follows that one doesn't know in advance what sort of alleys they are. By dint of constructing a philosophical or scientific fiction, the constructor posits questions in order to tease out the unknown, though often not unanticipated, answer. But the symmetry appears to break down in literature. How can a writer not know the story she is writing? If the ingredients are in her head, surely she must know it. And if not, it begins to look like a typologically novel class of ghost writing.

The dichotomy is, of course, fallacious since in this case *tertium datur*. Instead of occurrently, a writer may know the story only in outline and rely on extemporaneous inspiration to fill the blanks. She may, furthermore, harness the process of composition to jog her memory to retrieve compart-mentalized data. A serendipitous remark or even a typo may refocus her attention and lead to a fresh insight and a genuine discovery, and so forth. Compelling data indicates, in fact, that learning (or teaching oneself) through the act of composition is more a rule than an exception. So is the resultant feeling of cognitive discovery and wonder.

Generations of artists, famous and obscure, have recorded surprise at the behavior of their fictional brainchildren and at the level of their inde-pendence from the blueprints. Such surprise is expressive of revelation, insight, and learning something that was not known or even suspected before. One of America's most introspective writers professed, in fact, that the first words to hit the page "are for learning what one's fiction wants him to say."[7] Elsewhere Malamud confessed: "I can't outguess my charac-ters all the time, although God knows I try." Self-reflexively, he even made one of his creations from *The Tenants* muse: "It was as though the book had asked him to say more than he knew."[8]

Armistead Maupin, hit author of the triply incarnate (as the *San Francisco Chronicle* serial, multi-decker book collection, and TV miniseries) *Tales of the City*, seconded the sentiment. "As the series progressed," he acknowledged, "my characters took on minds of their own." Laura Brewer, reporter during the day, writer at night, posted the following reflec-tions on the theory and the praxis of the novel:

> Writing becomes more like stage directing once the characters develop a life of their own. . . . A word of caution here – they will argue with you. They will develop their own agenda, and will take you down side roads you least expect.

Across the Atlantic, William Thackeray wrote about "a thousand thoughts lying within a man that he does not know till he takes up the pen to write." Quoth Nietzsche: "The author must keep his mouth shut when his work starts to speak." The brothers Čapek corroborated that "what finally emerges from our hands is something different from what we were actually doing." In the postscript to *The Name of the Rose*, fashioned after Poe into his "Philosophy of Composition," Eco made the same point: "when I put Jorge in the library I did not yet know he was the murderer. He acted on his own, so to speak." Composing *Solaris*, Lem confessed, he had no fore-knowledge of what would befall his hero on the space station. "I had no idea, but I was soon to find out because the writing went on."[9]

The point of these parallels is not to suggest that there exists a universal discursive calculus for mining knowledge across disciplines. Leibnitz, if you recall, was looking for it with the expectation that he could settle all disputes on all things under the sun. This is, of course, nonsense. Even in mathematics, the most formal system we know, Gödel's incompleteness theorem upturns the presumption that knowledge is reducible to an algorithm. The point of these parallels is that contemplation of fictional designs is governed by aesthetic parameters not only in such "soft" areas as storytelling, but in "hard" disciplines like topology or algebra, as well.

A completely unreal world can be constructed, in which asses fly and princesses are restored to life by a kiss; but that world, purely possible and unrealistic, must exist according to structures defined at the outset.

Umberto Eco, *The Name of the Rose* (Postscript)

Tracking a problem, a novelist, philosopher, or scientist constructs a self-contained realm to play out his "what if" scenarios. Within this fictional construct things can happen in contradistinction to reality. A fictional observer can zip alongside a light beam, which, as Einstein would deduce from this science fiction, could never be (for one, his mass would become infinite). Within another fiction, a deceptor *potentissimus et malignus* can so confuse a philosopher's senses that Descartes would find a conceptual fulcrum only by means of *cogito ergo sum*. And in the storyworld of *God's Grace* a writer can exercise his moral and socio-biological imagination by making chimps talk, insect-pollinating plants pollinate without insects, and God have words with the sole survivor of a nuclear holocaust.

Storytellers typically unveil their scenarios in full narrative bloom rather than the sparse, systemized manner of scientists, although the generation raised on Borges, Lem, and Rucker has pushed even in that direction. This holds even for a full-blown illustration of an evolutionary theory, as in Charles Pellegrino's novel of punctuated equilibrium, *Dust*. Characters beset by dramatic conflicts are fiction's trademark ways of framing scenarios and scenario-specific responses. Yet, on the level of cognitive puzzles, novelists do not proceed that differently from thought experimenters in science and philosophy. All frame ingenious fictions starring Mephistophelean soul-dealers, frictionless bodies, or Buridan asses. All frame counterfactual inquiries irrespective of whether an actual experiment could be rigged up along the lines of fiction.

It is true that the entailments of general relativity were partially verified by Eddington on Principe during the 1919 solar eclipse. (Although detected earlier, it was only with hindsight that Mercury's orbital wobble was attributed to the Sun's gravitation well).[10] But no one has reproduced Einstein's armchair experiment, and no one ever will. Still, the principled possibility of empirical cross-check sets the *possible worlds* of philosophy and science apart from the *storyworlds* of literary fiction. Far from being weird planets suspended parsecs away from Earth, possible worlds are *de facto* completely self-contained conceptual universes. As such, they necessarily are internally coherent, determinate, and – consequently – consistent with any number of storyworlds.

Another fundamental difference between storyworlds and possible worlds is psychological as much as epistemic. Because so much in literary works remains indeterminate, no person (or even supercomputer) could hope to reconstruct an entire and complete possible world from literary fiction.[11] Borges's "Tlön, Uqbar, Orbis Tertius," in which a corpus of encyclopedists labor to invent another world down to the last detail, vividly narratizes the infinitude of detail needed to accomplish such a supertask. Thought provoking as "Tlön" is, "filling out" a possible world in totality is a psychological and empirical dead end.

Although the impossibility of fleshing out infinities is real enough, in practice it can be sidestepped by a ruthless pruning of extraneous details. Sieving out the infinity of parameters attendant on *all* experience, and not just supertasks (algorithms that require an infinitude of calculations), reduction saves only what's relevant. Reduction, you might say, is a technique for compacting the world to manageable proportions, ideally in the form of independent (controlled) and dependent (studied) variables. Without it neither science, philosophy, nor literature could compress the experience of the world into the intellectual orbit circumscribed by our finite processing resources. Indeed, in Mach's italics, science may be regarded as "a minimal problem consisting of the completest presentation of facts with the *least possible expenditure of thought.*"[12]

Reduction, let's not forget, is really the same thing as generalization. The trick is, of course, to make the right kind of reduction, since the task is nonalgorithmic. While undeniably true, that sort of obstacle is categorically separate from denouncing reduction lock, stock, and two barrels in the study of human affairs. And if science is our collective device to express the vast universe in a finite number of statements, literature is another. Not everyone is, of course, happy with this type of methodological association – and, more to the point, with reduction in art. In Chapter 1 we met a tangle of dualistic voices adamant that literature cannot be more than a library of idiographic experience and subjective uniqueness.

Fortunately, to balance the picture, there is Borges (with Bloy-Casares) and "An Evening with Ramon Bonavena." Here is how, in deadpan earnest, the Argentines lampoon Bonavena's oeuvre which aims to *fully* describe but a single corner of a writer's desk.

[We] learn about the ashtray – the various shades of the copper, its specific gravity, its diameter, the exact distances and angles between the ashtray, the pencil and the edge of the table, and the workmanship on the twin china sheepdogs, and what they cost wholesale and retail . . . as for the pencil – an Eagle, an Eagle Chemi-Sealed No. 2B! – what can I say? You got it down so perfectly and, thanks to your genius for compression, into only twenty-nine pages.[13]

Even Bonavena's turgid task is made possible by compression – that is, reduction.[14]

Are all narrative representations models? Clearly a generic description of the Eiffel Tower in *Paris on $9999 a Day* isn't. Nor is a typical *blazon* in Donne's metaphysically cavalier lyrics. At a minimum, then, literary models are like models elsewhere, that is, characterized by a deliberate selection (reduction) of features to further inquiry. Selective as the Eiffel Tower description may be, *Paris on $9999 a Day* does not pursue cognitive goals: no inquiry, no model. Just as not all counterfactuals are models, not all literary models are counterfactuals, either. A depiction of the Eiffel Tower slanted to further inquiry of one sort or another will have nothing counterfactual about it *per se*.

Just as artistic polyvalence is in no peril of becoming reducible to interpretative unity, the complexity of life is in no peril of becoming reducible to literary models. In the latter case, the respective roles of reality and fiction – as well as their ontological categories – would become interchangeable since it would benefit as much to study the one or the other. Can a narrative function as a model irrespective of the writer's original goals, then? *Prima facie* there is no reason why not. However, since the inquiring mind will no longer be tracking the author's intentions, neither will the model, its features determined instead by the reader/critic.

Even on this thumbnail sketch, modeling in literature appears analogous to aspects of modeling in other domains. Significantly, when Mach discusses the origins of thought experiments in *Knowledge and Error*, he makes no distinction between different forms of knowing the world. "Ideas gradually adapt to facts by picturing them with sufficient accuracy to meet biological needs. . . . Later, however, we gradually go over to continuing the process with clear deliberation, and as soon as this occurs, enquiry sets in."[15] Scratch the impression of *a priori* partition between literature and science. If anything, the similarities at the bottom of the disciplinary varieties of the knowledge hunt invite further inquiry.

In view of widespread modeling in science, a good way to shed light on modeling in literature might be to adopt science as a benchmark. Indeed, as sporadic interactions between them reveal, either realm can occasionally illumine the general aspects of their workings as well as specific knowledge claims.[16] Even as chaos-theoretic studies of complexity can help analyze the statistical (for example symmetrical) patterns of art, art and literature provide an unsurpassed source of networks of organized complexity for study. No matter what, however, the gulf between literary and scientific thought experiments *is* wide. But what about modeling in fiction and mathematics?

> *Mathematics and art are quite different. We could not publish so many papers that used, repeatedly, the same idea and still command the respect of our colleagues.*
>
> Antoni Zygmund, *A Century of Mathematics in Americana*

In a dedication to *Flatland* Abbott suggests this very tack. Arguing that humanistic inquiry ought to adopt the rigorous standards used in sciences, he draws attention to the latter's favorite modeling tool.

> Mathematics may help us to measure and weight the planets, to discover the materials of which they are composed, to extract light and warmth from the motion of water and to dominate the material universe; but even if by these means we could mount up to Mars or hold converse with the inhabitants of Jupiter, we should be no nearer to the divine throne, except so far as these new experiences might develop our modesty, respect for facts, a deeper reverence for order and harmony, and a mind more open to new observations and to fresh inferences from old truths.[17]

A more fruitful approach, therefore, may be to bypass science and look at the handmaiden that determines the form and scope of its models: mathematics. The juxtaposition may – nay, must – at first blush seem incongruous. As the proverbial queen of the sciences, mathematics should be even more discontinuous from literature than cosmology, microbiology, and other scientific domains. What could the esoteric concepts and symbols of, say, category theory have in common with westerns, sonnets, or *romans à clef*, literary categories all? Lewis Carroll apart, most intellectuals proficient in math tend to stay away from the arts and vice versa. This polarization of talent might just indicate a deeper polarization of the disciplines.

And the disciplines are polarized for good reasons. The most obvious is the immense difference in psychological motivation. The specificity of narrative models lies in depicting experiential content, if only by virtue of depicting agents in pursuit of humanly recognizable goals. Going through mental calculations and undergoing emotional states, characters end up projecting their desires onto the storyworld they inhabit (and readers onto the characters). Mathematical models, in contrast, are devoid of all such layering. Their building blocks are elements of logic, not desires and interpersonal relationships, and they are valued precisely to the extent they can be voided of subjectivity.

Perhaps intimidated by such manifest differences, there's been scarcely any commentary to date about the analogies between mathematics and narrative fiction as modeling factories; this notwithstanding the long history of relations between math and art. In the case of music, for example, the interrelations were so intimate that in the fifteenth century the art of musical invention and composition (*ars combinatoria*) was a species of mathematics. The link is actually enshrined today in the name of the leading journal of combinatorics, *Ars Combinatoria*. It specializes in such tasty intellectual stew as "Matrices with Maximum Exponent in the Class of Central Symmetric Primitive Matrices."

One must go back to Northrop Frye to find an intimation of our analogy. As a point of departure, then, I take his afterthought to *An Anatomy of Criticism*: "Literature, like mathematics, is a language, and a language in itself represents no truth, though it may provide the means for expressing a number of them."[18] Whether language in itself represents no truth is an open matter. Evolutionary psychology and adaptive anthropology place a lot of stock in genetically stored knowledge as a means of coping with the world. At least some of such hard-wired techniques can be expected to impinge on how we construct and use language.

But, far more than Frye's analogy, what brings literature and mathematics closer to each other than to the sciences is their mastermind for modeling. This remarkable capacity for thinking up things that reflect on other things goes a long way towards allaying unease about gradualistic metacognition. Just as writers of fiction are jugglers of concepts and not words (aleatorists excepted), we have it on the authority of mathemagicians that any member of their clan is not "a juggler of numbers but a juggler of *concepts*."[19] The analogies between the ways concepts are "juggled" in literature and math have even compelled mathematicians to see the latter as something of an art form – a highly specialized form of abstract art.

Thus, in liner notes to *Proof* – a drama stepped in mathematics, staged by the Hong Kong Repertory Theatre – a retired head of a math department, Siu Man Keung, asks: "Mathematics, is it not a form of art?" Indeed, replies Barrow in *Theories of Everything*, "in some universities it might be associated more closely with the arts and humanities than with the sciences."[20] As a conceptual tool, mathematics may thus be more like literature than cosmology or microbiology. Much like literature, after all, math is not a science. That's why topologists and algebraists do not conduct experiments. Even the Platonism which inclines most mathematicians to aver that they discover, rather than create, new concepts is metaphysically too wishy-washy to be of much consequence in this regard.[21]

The dispute between Platonists and creationists apart, mathematics is integrated into scientific disciplines from their nascent stages. This is so much so that many trace their birth to the rise of quantification. One can distinguish four overlapping phases in a typical process of integration: empirical, experimental, analytical, and axiomatic. The initial role of mathematics is mainly quantificatory and calculatory, historically harnessed to tabulate yields from annual harvests and predict eclipses. Progressively, however, all maturing fields of inquiry employ it for the purposes of analysis and modeling.

This powerful and not uncurious ability, almost despite its free "self," to represent the world is the source of affinity with fiction. Their unifying principle is unfettered conceptual freedom – the same conceptual freedom that separates mathematics from the sciences. No less a mathematician than Georg Cantor stated it concisely: "denn das *Wesen* der *Mathematik* liegt gerade in ihrer *Freiheit*."[22] Literature too is not restricted to the world we know. This is precisely what sets it apart from history. Its freedom to fanta-size about unreal worlds or depict agents' innermost thoughts admits much more than science – or, for that matter, history – does.

It is no different for mathematics, whose totality of logics, systems, and universes also admits much more than science can chew. Science, if you like, is interested only in the decidable part of this totality. This modeling autotelism forms an important point of contiguity between mathematics and literature. The reason the analogy is not more apparent is because the math needed for narrative and critical thinking is usually simple enough to get by with basic logical intuition. Anchored in numbers and symbols, those "squiggles on a piece of paper," mathematics appears, of course, a world apart from literary fiction and its operational units – words of a natural language. Yet even this semantic polarity is a little less than complete.

First of all, symbolic notation is only a shorthand to facilitate crunching expressions and relations of extraordinary complexity. In principle, all equations could be set down in plain English, such as that pi times radius square times length divided by two equals half the volume of a cylinder. There is even a historical precedent: up to the tenth century most Arab calculators actually wrote out numbers word by word. And let's not forget about Richard Montague's conclusion from "Universal Grammar":

> There is in my opinion no important theoretical difference between natural languages and the artificial languages of logicians; indeed, I consider it possible to comprehend the syntax and semantics of both

kinds of languages within a single natural, and mathematically precise theory.[23]

The above manifesto, which sums up the logician's lengthy study of both systems, is perhaps less surprising if you bear in mind that the origin of language almost certainly predates the beginnings of numeracy. Many of our elementary intuitions about number and quantity are likely rooted in our language instinct. Across all cultures, after all, linguistic proficiency far exceeds mathematical skills, both in complexity and universality. It's like a gift of a "mere" alphabet which comes bundled up with an ability to read any book in any library in the world, including the book of mathematics.

As far as laws of mathematics refer to reality they are not certain; and as far as they are certain, they do not refer to reality.

Albert Einstein, *Sidelights on Relativity*

At the bottom, mathematics is practically synonymous with logic – the same logic that guides narrative and metanarrative discourse. All math is, after all, reducible to properties of integers which are, in turn, reducible to the modified version of Peano's postulates of logic.[24] Mathematics, in this general sense, *is* logic. Naturally, unzipped into longhand, even relatively simple formulae and straightforward logical entailments quickly become too much to wrap your head around – one reason why mathematical terms and operations are unambiguously defined. And one cannot be said to understand anything if the premises are too complex to even tell whether they harbor a contradiction.

An illustration may be in order. "Nothing in this book is true," asserts the preface to Kurt Vonnegut's *Cat's Cradle*, innocuously enough until you strip it to logical nuts and bolts. As a preface, it is a nonfictional assertion that nothing in the books is true. So far so good, inasmuch as *Cat's Cradle* is a work of fiction. But since the preface is also part of the book, if true, it must be false since *something* in the book (namely, the preface) is true. No reason to stop here, either. If "Nothing in this book is true" is false, then something in *Cat's Cradle* must be true. Since it's not the story of Bokononism and ice-nine, which is all fiction, it must be the preface. But if the preface is true, then the same self-referential chain of reasoning kicks in. So, if true, the preface is false, and, if false, it's true. All of a sudden we're trapped in a vicious circle redolent of the liar's paradox ("All Cretans are liars": Cretan).[25]

Thanks to Alfred Tarski, we know how to climb out of this logical well. Paradoxes of this class can be a/voided by a careful separation of statements made in the so-called object language from metastatements about statements. This instantly disambiguates their circular conjunction. All the same, can one fully grasp *Cat's Cradle* without grasping the implication of the preface? Perhaps not. The understanding of Bokononism, the paradoxical and self-effacing creed central to the novel, is certainly deepened by the understanding of the paradoxical and self-effacing preface. One may debate whether or not this hangs a question mark on limits to counterfactual analysis in general. But it certainly shows that, far from in literature alone, deductions may be limited even in the case of mathematics.

Just like a maze beyond a critical size becomes practically insoluble, so does a logical problem – whether cast in words or in mathematical symbols – of greater than critical-size complexity. A canonical illustration derives from Lewis Carroll's *Symbolic Logic*. It takes the form of sorites, a kind of extended syllogism that, like its lesser cousin, invites logical interpretation of its joined premises. Forget epics, *romans fleuves*, and Victorian triple-deckers, and exercise your mindceps by deducing what obtains from no more than seven of these straightforward propositions.

1   All the policemen on this beat sup with our cook.
2   No man with long hair can fail to be a poet.
3   Amos Judd has never been in prison.
4   Our cook's "cousins" all love cold mutton.
5   None but policemen on this beat are poets.
6   None but her "cousins" ever sup with our cook.
7   Men with short hair have all been in prison.

Elementary, isn't it? Amos Judd loves cold mutton. Plainly, too much information can be as damaging as not enough, as we shall see again in Chapter 5. Even so, the point holds: the difference of language between literary and mathematical fictions, while staggering, is one of degree, not kind.

Mathematical truths are, of course, certain to the extent they are axiomatic and/or properly derived. Galileo himself was willing to stake his reputation on it. "The human intellect does understand some propositions perfectly, and thus in these has as much absolute certainty as Nature does. Of such," he added, "are the mathematical sciences alone."[26] If one is compelled to cavil with his second assertion, it is because there is a sense in which literary propositions are axiomatic and therefore certain, too. They are axiomatic by virtue of being sealed off from the world in an imaginary construct where, in principle, anything a writer wants to "go" goes. A fantasy in which Professor Zardoz squares the circle makes squaring the circle possible in that storyworld, even though it is impossible in ours (or in any possible world).

Remarkably, logical fallacy does not automatically invalidate fiction, even though it does invalidate logical reasoning from its premises. Although at a deep level all such narratives are incoherent, the reader is meant to suspend judgment with regard to unwarranted entailments in the story. Thus, unlike classical logic, from explicit inconsistencies it does not immediately follow that anything is true in fiction.[27]

Professor Zardoz has the added merit of identifying the conceptual thrust of Galileo's remarks. Stories can be illogical and, as such, literature clearly enjoys an even greater degree of conceptual freedom than mathematics. Of course, to the extent fictions aims at true propositions about the world, their representational freedom becomes radically constricted. Storytellers can say *anything* at all unless, as most do, they aim to say something relevant to us. The corollary? Certain in the former "axiomatic" sense, literature and literary models are not logically certain in the latter.

Even if today we would not predicate it as science, math indeed behaves the way Galileo paints it – providing you approach it in its formal and axiomatic guise, without reference to any subject matter expressible by the variables. Once you begin to apply the axioms and interpret the derivations, just like literature they begin to refer to the world. And – amazingly – just like literature, they cease to be strictly mathematical or certain. Calculations of infinities, for an example, do not even respect the familiar arithmetic for finite quantities. Infinity plus/minus infinity still equals infinity, so that a cunning hotelier will never run out of guest rooms in the Infinity Hotel.

Following Cantor, mathematical infinities have become open to coherent manipulations, but they still do not correspond to anything we observe in the world. Bounded by the Big Bang, the universe itself is finite in spacetime. Cosmic singularities, where quantities are expected to rise without limit, are concealed beyond event horizons. Most scientists concede, in fact, that actual infinities cannot crop up in our world. Like in particle physicists' bouts with grand unified theories, "their appearance in a calculation merely signals that the theory being employed has reached the limits of its validity and must be superseded by a new and improved version which should replace the mathematical infinity by a finite measurable quantity."[28]

Shakespeare never had six lines together without a fault. Perhaps you might find seven, but this does not refute my general assertion.

Samuel Johnson, *Life of Johnson*

To earn their upkeep, scientific theories "must approximately correspond to the way the world is, at least in their observational consequences,"[29] notes Anthony O'Hear in "Science and Art." Neither mathematical nor literary fictions are world-constrained in this way. Although in people's minds there is only one mathematical system – the one that balances ledgers and fuels undergraduate Calc anguish – in reality their number is limitless, just like the number of storyworlds. Like Boxing Day browsers, cosmologists, particle physicists, and other cognitive pathfinders routinely browse assorted mathematical constructions to see which will fit Nature.

There is no way around it: mathematical and physical existence just ain't the same thing at all. "A mathematician may say anything he pleases," joked in earnest J. Willard Gibbs, "but a physicist must be at least partially sane."[30] That said, mathematics takes very seriously its freedom to erect conceptual pyramids – including entire systems of geometry or even logic – in isolation from the world. Its truths are thus never directly, in and of themselves, propositions about reality. Bertrand Russell, mathematician himself, even quipped that math is "the subject in which we never know what we are talking about, nor whether what we are saying is true."[31]

Not to look too far for an example, the first non-plane geometries were developed in a physical vacuum. In defiance of the experientially commonsense Euclidian system, in which a triangle's angles equal 180 degrees ($\sigma = 180°$), in hyperbolic or spherical spaces the sum was simply *posited* to be less ($\sigma < 180°$) or greater ($\sigma > 180°$). No more than clever fictions spun around novel sets of axioms, Gauss's and Riemann's discoveries lay physically fallow as no one knew what to do with them. Things changed only with Einstein, who, browsing for "eccentric" manifold geometries to express the curvature of spacetime, plugged these far-out formulae into the physics of general relativity.

Here again lies the lynchpin of the modeling analogy between math and literature. Mathematical and story "worlds" enjoy an appreciably greater level of conceptual autonomy than do the sciences. Naturally, that does not mean that they are therefore useless in modeling reality. But, like axiomatic geometries or entire systems of logic, literary fictions are not *immediately* in and of themselves about reality. *The Name of the Rose* is an incomparable narrative model of the medieval mindset suspended between the Scholastic and Baconian *universi* of knowledge. But Venerable Jorge, Adso of Melk, or William of Baskerville have never existed and never will.

In this respect literature and mathematics graduate from complete strangers to kissing cousins. On the other hand, where mathematical symbols and functions are universally intelligible and contentless, literature falls back on a Babel of ethnic tongues. Does the contrast in linguistic form and degree of formalism vitiate the analogy? I don't think so. Although to a radically different degree, neither is semantically empty, if only because both are shot through with logic. Neither does it matter that variables such as dimensionless points, imaginary numbers, or idealized curves are not found in the world. Whether in Etruscan, English, or Esperanto, storytellers habitually refer to nonexistent variables such as unicorns, perpetuum mobile, or utopia.

It is no different in the case of literary "functions." Valuable as they are to the understanding not only of the story but of the real world, all metaphors belie factual states in surface meaning. That's why, *contra* Allen Ginsberg, no queer shoulders have as yet been observed even in cloning labs. Of course, as an axiomatic system, mathematics is cumulative in the strong, progressive sense. Old axioms are forever as good as new ones, and successful proofs and derivations remain valid even if the physical theories that put them to use change over time. Art has no extraneous yardstick – something like an Aesthetic Nature – to gauge distances on the road to Parnassus.

On the other hand, while the physics of Aristotle and Newton have been proven, respectively, wrong and incomplete, Poe, Virgil, and the poet of Ut-Napishtim are as "right" and complete today as they were yesteryear.[32] Literature, in this weak sense, is cumulative insofar as new art constantly augments what preceded it. This is what lies behind Dr. Johnson's adage about Shakespeare being for all ages. In another sense of "cumulative," sequels, serials, and even literary history *in toto* demand that new fiction be interpreted in the light of the old – and vice versa. This is what lies behind Baudelaire's adage about writers picking their predecessors. The understanding of Ed McBain's *The Frumious Bandersnatch* is abetted by the knowledge of his 87th Precinct procedurals, of the entire hardboiled tradition, and even of Lewis Carroll's *Jabberwocky* – whence the title.[33]

Naturally, the fact that art mutates diachronically from one style, school, or form of writing to another does not mean that it progresses in *aesthetic* terms. But if the arguments marshaled in this book are right, it makes perfect sense to consider art as progressive in *cognitive* terms. Today we know much more about people, societies, and the world at large than we did at the time of Homer, and literature reflects (though it also sometimes forges) this knowledge. To the extent that fiction contributes to inquiry, literary knowledge *is* cumulative in the same sense that scientific or mathematical knowledge is. And, in this key sense, literature is as progressive as any other enterprise directed at understanding the world.

> *Ah! – 'Ability or inability to conceive,' says Mr. Mill very properly, 'is in no case to be received as a criterion of axiomatic truth.'*
>
> Edgar Allan Poe, *Eureka*

What about the historical distinction between pure and applied mathematics, traced by Ian Stewart in *Concepts of Modern Mathematics*? Histories of course are mutable themselves, and no less an expert than Cantor remonstrated that the term "pure" should be swapped for the less wooly "free."[34] Nomenclature aside, we know roughly what the dialectic means. Free is what mathematicians do for fun, like looking for the solution to Fermat's last theorem (discovered by Andrew Wiles in 1994). Applied is what mathematics becomes in applications to grant committees, which ask, in effect, "What is its payoff to society?" Well, it helps erect bridges, design computers, or model spacetime in an eleven-dimensional continuum.

The polarization falters, of course, because free and applied math are one and the same thing. What is different is the goals set before it. In one case the discipline looks simply to extend itself father afield. In the other, the same storehouse of definitions, transformation rules, proofs, theorems, lemmas, and conjectures is applied to model and calculate things in need of modeling and calculating. Mathematics, in other words, may be generated with no utilitarian purposes in mind, or else motivated by specific social demands, like the design of Fermi's controlled pile in 1942. But even this dialectic is misleading. For, in a colossal simplification, without pure research into black body radiation, then the photoelectric effect, then quantum tunneling, there would be no "applied" hardware such as iMac G5.

Still, it is easy to recognize in the dichotomy the two orientations – often perpetuated by artists themselves – that have on occasion polarized the world of literature. There is the "applied" Marxist *naïf* or, in any case, a mimeticist. There is his counterpart, a Dorian Grey autotelist detached from the world that might hamstring the integrity of his art. As with most caricatures, both hide an element of truth because both are the limiting cases of all art. High aesthetics, of course, never impeded aspirations to reflect on one's *tempora e mores*. An ambitious aesthete could pen not only Victorian dramas, but modern anti-establishment classics, *Camp Concentration* and *334*. An angry young man could bequeath not only the socialist drumbeat of *The Iron Heel*, but the artistic vistas of *Snark* and that new book of metamorphoses, *Martin Eden*.

Motivated by specific social demands, a work of fiction can be a faithful socio-cultural barometer without ceasing to be a work of art and a work of make-believe. Vividly false by virtue of a world with only two dimensions, Abbott's *Flatland* vividly foregrounds this facility to evoke reality against all odds. Narrated by a polygon, A. Square, the first part marshals an allegorical attack on the Victorian complaisance in denying women access to education. Part Two, illustrative in the now familiar manner, elaborates the idea that gripped the late nineteenth-century intellectual elites: the fourth spatial dimension.

Transitive in the physical and rhetorical sense, illustrations of three-dimensional properties to Flatlanders invite Abbott's readers to overcome doubts about the *prima facie* surreal proposition that they, too, inhabit a world with an extra dimension. A graphic illustration of four dimensions is a four-dimensional hypercube, of which much can be learnt via such mental computations as projection, slicing, or unfolding. These are analogous to the familiar process of unfolding a regular cube into six squares shaped like a cross. And fictional illustration of four-dimensionality again is not far behind, this time in the form of Heinlein's (deservedly) forgotten story "And He Built a Crooked House."

Something akin occurs in mathematics. Its freedom to boldly go where no math has gone before is checked apparently only by internal consistency. And yet, like in Carroll's Wonderland, even here things are not as straightforward as they seem. The incompleteness theorems show that this consistency cannot be proven in systems above a certain level of complexity (starting with ordinary arithmetic). It *can* be proven, but only in a system of a higher order, and *its* consistency in a system higher still, and so on to infinite regress.[35] This production of statements about statements about statements is another trait math shares with Chinese-box fictions within fictions within fictions. Their capability for hierarchical modeling continues *ad infinitum*, limited only by the capacity to resist the $meta^n$-level vertigo.

Likewise, both can easily handle regressive statements, that is, those iterating without a stopping rule. A funny literary example is Jonathan Swift's parody from "Poetry, a Rhapsody": "So, naturalists observe, a flea / Hath smaller fleas that on him prey;/ And these have smaller still to bite 'em; / And so proceed *ad infinitum*." His lesser known next two lines, satirizing the weakly cumulative character of literature, are no less cunning: "Thus every poet, in his kind, / Is bit by him that comes behind." My favorite, however, is a Polish writer, Maciej Słomczyński, who used to write a series of detective stories under the penname of Joe Alex. Thus Joe Alex wrote books featuring a detective named Joe Alex, who in his spare time wrote books featuring a detective named Joe Alex, who . . . , etc.

Despite its modeling freedom, pure math is exceedingly useful to us. Leery of the pure–applied dichotomy, Stewart has even proposed to discard it and speak of unified mathematics and its applications instead. The merit of looking at literature in the same way is in bypassing the barren clichés of art for art's sake or mirrors of Nature. Fiction may indeed be written to create a complex aesthetic artifact, or else to model (even correct, as in *The Iron Heel*) the world. But like mathematics there is only one art – and a variety of goals it can serve. And as for the mechanics of how these goals are served, once again Frye points the way with hints of analogy between "the units of literature and mathematics, the metaphor and the equation."[36] We will return to it in Chapter 4.

There can be fantastic backgrounds, events, people, but there needn't be all of these at once. Each fantasy, obviously, must contain a body of portion of the real; the real as we know it in fiction.

Bernard Malamud, "Why Fantasy?"

Time for a recap. The biggest challenge in the discussion of literature as a tool of inquiry is to overcome the preconceptions that segregate it from philosophy and science. Aiming to dispel such preconceptions, I tried to show that the distinctions between modeling principles in mathematics – that crutch of all sciences – and in literature, while dramatic in some ways, are negligible in others. Building the case for narratives as thought experiments, I thus take the *modeling* homologies to be fundamental enough to establish literary models on a continuum with philosophy and the sciences. We will pick up the thread of analogy in the way storytellers and other cognitive bargain-hunters hunt for knowledge in Chapter 3.

Meanwhile, let us take a short but important detour to examine the nature and range of models specific to literature. Analogous to mathematics, departure from reality or from the conventions of literary realism in no way hinders the inquisitive mind. A story by Poe featuring a cosmological model featuring a giant sky blue cow and a whole bunch of rhetorical *trompe l'oeil* can be an earnest vehicle for popularizing (illustrating) the frontiers of nineteenth-century science and technology. Anti-mimetic undercurrents in fiction run, in fact, from the conspicuous, such as time travel, to the hardly remarked narrative omniscience which permits depictions of characters' innermost thoughts and states.

Not that the semantics of *what* happens in the story and the poetics of *how* the story is put together – two different levels of literary processing – can always be wrested cleanly apart. In fantasy, or for that matter in religious literature, the conceptual fabric dividing the "what" from the "how" can get pretty threadbare. Even in a seemingly clear-cut case of omniscience, a futuristic gadget or celestial prerogative may permit divination of minds – if not wholly erasing, then obscuring, the distinction. That said, equipped with the theory of truth in fiction, we can begin to sort out the relation between reality and storytelling.[37] Leaving aside all manner of narrative bells and whistles, let us focus then on the underlying modeling principles.

Broadly speaking, there are three levels of mimeticism that combine into the literary conventions of realism, fantasy, and everything else in between. Indexed by their approximation of – or, conversely, distance from – the real world, they are: logical, scientific, and psychosocial. The coarseness of the schema reflects the fact that, like the mythical Gorgon, literature will not let itself be pinned down. The *vraisemblance* of storyworlds and their denizens, be they Injuns or polygons, is an especially chaotic facet of interpretation. This is true both of the basic grasp of "what's the story" and the higher level of integration (e.g. symbolic or cognitive). Propositions about story contents are context-sensitive and can often be asserted only conditionally in terms of their likelihood and plausibility, rather than possibility in the logical or empirical sense.

The three levels of mimeticism permit exactly four (mutually exclusive and class-exhaustive) classes of narrative structures. Subsuming all theoretical permutations, they therefore subsume all types of literature currently in existence and not. Many of the genres surveyed below are familiar but, as Shklovskii was at pains to point out, defamiliarizing often brings payoffs insofar as new divisions foster new visions. Modeling techniques differ and, at the end of the day, some are more equal than others, demanding a system within which their contributions to inquiry can be mapped and evaluated. Such a framework may in turn facilitate a reappraisal of modeling in narrative fiction and, through it, of literature as an instrument of inquiry.

Preambles aside, the four modeling classes are:

1   violate no norms;
2   violate any one norm;
3   violate any two norms;
4   violate all three norms.

To no one's surprise, first-class models comprise all works conventionally tabulated as literary realism. We find here Cooper's Leatherstocking, the psycho-pathology of "The Tell-Tale Heart," the allegorical drama of *The Scarlet Letter*, the stylized erotica of *Fanny*, K-mart minimalism of *Shortcuts*, *The Deadly Sins* procedurals, and many, many more. But the dragnet pulls in more than the usual suspects. One of them is the avant-garde, heavy on experiments with dissociative narration, obscure points of view, or epistemic fragmentation. Conventionally it is set apart from the mimeticism of, say, Dumas *père* (and his ghostwriter Auguste Maquet). Yet neither violates any of the three levels of mimeticism.

Modeling realism is thus a more inclusive, because a more fundamental, criterion than standard narrative realism. It cuts across the canons of literary history and through the critical phyla of realism, naturalism, expressionism, and all other "isms." Likewise, it cuts across literary hierarchy by extending vertically from popular genres to the avant-garde. Removing the taxonomic spotlight away from narrative pyrotechnique to the modeling kit affords a better view of not only cognitive but aesthetic aspects as well. It illuminates relative postmodern finesse in the narrative department, and its conventionality in the cognitive.

Flaunting the alleged narrative impotence of its own medium, post-modern fiction by and large does not stray from home (first class) in modeling terms. No wonder that shopping for cognitive "meat" most readers avoid the postmodernist deli, fixated on novel ways to slice yesterday's turkey, and turn to nobrow or popular storytellers instead.[38] Another instructive and unanticipated insight is the appearance of robots, rockets, and outer space in the same drawer as realism. As a genre premised on other-worldly or futuristic chronotope, on no understanding is science fiction realistic. But what if theory and praxis fail to add up?

After all, if science fiction is about space, robots, and rockets in the outer vacuum – as most theorists and readers agree it is – then there is nothing other-worldly or futuristic about it. Space exploration is a matter not of the future but of the half-century long past. No need to dwell on Honda's ASIMO, Sony's QRIO, or Hitachi's EMIEW either. Industrial robots have been the mainstay of factory production for nearly a century. Likewise, rocket science, from chemical (hydrogen plus oxidizer) to scramjet propulsion, is as realistic and this-worldly as retired spacemen, who by now count in the hundreds.

Modeling-wise, a space-and-science story that does not violate logical, scientific, and behavioral norms of verisimilitude is thus perfectly realistic. Modeling-wise, *Lucipher's Hammer* by Jerry Pournelle and Larry Niven is no different from Alex Haley's *Roots*. Variations in style, point of view, or theme notwithstanding, neither epic violates logic, science, or psychology: the narrative differences conceal a common modeling bedrock. Naturally Lucipher, a stray comet that wrecks the Earth far worse than the 2004 quake-ignited tsunami, never existed. But neither did Kunta Kinte. Cut it any way you like, the black-history *Bildungsroman* and catastrophic sci-fi are the same-class modeling vehicle: different body, same chassis.

The modeling homology between the mainstream and the literature of the fantastic is no academic ho-hum. If nothing else, it ought to help redress a longstanding prejudice against non-realism as escapist and infe-rior. Although few five-star literary histories will own to such a bias, a survey of Nobel Prize winners over the past eleven decades – roughly coex-tensive with modern sci-fi and fantasy – corroborates what must be literature's worst kept secret. Compared to the less than universally lauded laureates (Pearl Buck?), there are practitioners of non-realism who ought to have got it (H. G. Wells, C. S. Lewis, Čapek, Borges, the Strugatskys), but never will since Nobel Prizes are not awarded posthumously.

It bears repeating that literary make-believe is under no orders to truck in conventional mimesis. Despite conspicuous breakaways from reality, outside of first-degree models fiction can be no less cognitively meaningful as bread-and-butter realism. Yet the double standard, set in relief by the modeling schema, is nothing new for writers who have long tried to escape guilt by association. "I write ancient mythology," griped Ray Bradbury in a 2001 interview. "I fought with them for years to take the [science fiction] label off." Shrugged Terry Pratchett: "If I'm never going to be nominated for the Booker because I'm a fantasy writer, then I don't want to win the Booker."

Even a *bona fide* litterateur like Malamud harbored no illusions about the ghetto of fantasy. With rare cynicism, he remarked: "there are some critics nowadays who feel a man can write nothing of importance unless he is dealing with some aspect of society using the method we call realism." Lem was equally adamant: "I regard myself as a realistic writer – because I tackle real issues." In this context there is nothing illogical in the *Philadelphia Inquirer* plaudits that, if he "isn't considered for a Nobel Prize . . . it will be because somebody told the judges that he writes science fiction."[39]

> *It is not licit to impose confines on divine omnipotence, and if God so willed, unicorns could exist. But console yourself, they exist in these books, which, if they do not speak of real existence, speak of possible existence.*
>
> Umberto Eco, *The Name of the Rose*

If any one of the three mimetic levels departs from verisimilitude, the narrative moves into the realm of non-realistic narration. The result are three modeling subclasses:

2a   violates only logical norms;
2b   violates only scientific norms;
2c   violates only psychosocial norms.

Logic may be too deeply fused with physics (via mathematics) to become separated in a narrative. I cannot think of a story, even less a whole genre, that would violate logic but not science, though perhaps the outbacks of quantum physics might furnish a plot or two. Normally, as soon as the logic of, say, non-contradiction goes out of the window, so does the physics in the form of the law of conservation of mass/energy. As far as I can gauge, 2a is therefore an empty set. The second class, 2b, on the other hand, is more interesting. It comprises fiction that pokes outside the borders of empirical realism. Its natural constituents are science fiction and fantasy, with four important provisos.

First of all, no time travel. Although chronomotion is habitually advertised as science fiction, this mass-market tactic is misleading. Time travel entails all manner of logical (usually cast as causal) violations, forming a distinct category of its own. Second, much of that marketing hybrid, fantasy and science fiction, is just not very good fiction. Plastic characters, adze-hewn dialogue, and juvenile psychology stretch plausibility to the point of incredulity, especially when science fiction meets the monster movie. In borderline cases such stories flip over into 3a, on which more below.

That is why a novel such as Thomas M. Disch's *The M.D.: A Horror Story* stands out from the rank and file with its crafty design and sophisticated execution. In an intertextual bow to Henry James's canonical *The Turn of the Screw*, Disch cleverly exploits the conventions of realism and the classic horror story. Where the latter depends on supernatural intrusion into the fabric of reality, the author denies such easy interpretation, setting his tale on the cusp of the natural and the supernatural. Playing havoc with critical theories of how we fill in the interpretive background, *The M.D.* is designed to hover between supernatural horror and mere statistical improbability, forever suspending readers between incompatible interpretations.

The third proviso is that some narratives conventionally accepted into the mainstream belong here. A good example may be Walker Percy. Enshrined in the Southern and Christian literary canons, neither of which is known for violations of realism, his *Thanatos Syndrome* is a wild thought experiment involving sodium reactors and illicit social engineering. Interestingly, the novel's narrator is Tom Moore, the same lapsarian MD who tangled with Mephisto in *Love in the Ruins*. Needless to say, just like sodium-reactor technology, the devil violates physics only. Čapek's *War with the Newts*, Vonnegut's *Cat's Cradle*, and Malamud's *God's Grace* are only a few of the other stories that part ways with scientific realism, while leaving logic and psychosocial plausibility intact.[40]

Fourth and finally, we may now better see why myth, classical tragedy, and classical comedy (among others) all belong in 2b rather than anywhere else. *Oedipus Rex*, to take the most celebrated example, violates only what we know of the world's physics, leaving logic intact. As a matter of fact, its fundamental theme demands a relentless application of logic insofar as the "damned if you do, and damned if you don't" ontology posits a completely deterministic world. Benign in comedy, in which Menander's twins are always reunited no matter what travails fate tosses their way, it is calamitous in tragedy, which dooms star-crossed lovers forever to stay apart.

Subclass 2c, in which only characterization is divorced from reality, is home to a miscellany of prose, beginning with Harlequins and pornography. Depending on the biological (and thus physical) possibility of the quantity and nature of sex dispensed, the latter may actually be a stowaway from 3a. It is important to note, however, that divergence from the canons of psychosocial realism need not signal lameness of quill. Morality and miracle plays or classic crime mysteries all get good modeling mileage out of deliberate stereotyping.

The *modus operandi* of detective fiction relies, after all, on the application of logic and empiricism to deduction (really *in*duction), even in such seeming out-of-this-world villainy as the "locked room" murder. On the other hand, the poverty of agents' motives – *anybody* is a suspect so long as they were physically capable of murder, even though they couldn't have done it *psychologically* – often arrests the genre at 2c, before it can cross over to first-class realism. There is a world of modeling difference, if you like, between Christie's *The Murder on the Orient Express* and Lawrence Sanders's *The Fourth Deadly Sin*, even if such distinctions may not always be immediately detectable.

The storyworlds of Hercule Poirot to Ed Delaney lie at different points on the continuum, even though the narrative transitions between them are fuzzy and incremental. At the end occupied by Lawrence Sanders's *Deadly Sin* procedurals, ambitious crime literature shades off into realistic psychological drama in which murder fuels the narrative engine. No need to dwell on Dostoyevsky and his axe murders either. In their best works Raymond Chandler and James M. Cain bridge the gap between crime entertainment and dramatic literature in stride, the latter even infusing *noir* with a detectable myth quotient.

Look at the concepts of Law and Order in crime fiction and in the physical sciences. In both cases, Law represents a set of edicts not to be transgressed, either for socially coercive or for physical-law-related reasons. (Nature's laws cannot be disobeyed and thus require no enforcement agency.) But in crime fiction Law entails Order not only in a thematic leitmotif but in a metaphysical determinism. Only the conviction of being able to control future events can lure the perpetrator to the crime. Only unforeseen developments can foil the carefully laid plans. Only the causal determinism of the genre allows the sleuth to reconstruct the history of the crime and arrest the malefactor. The aesthetics of the genre, where Law and Order triumph in the end, calls for reinterpretation in the light of the interplay between determinism and the disruptive infusion of uncertainty.

> *Hippos may be closer to whales than they are to their fellow ungulates such as pigs, so should librarians move hippo books down among the cetaceans?*
>
> Ralph Lewin, "Why Rename Things"

Such reinterpretation seems overdue in the case of Cain's fêted *Double Indemnity*, which hit bookstands in 1936 and theaters in 1944. The hero,

Walter Neff (Huff in the Wilder–Chandler screenplay), lusts after power, money, and a woman, going for all three by perpetrating a murder which he plans in expert detail. All the same, his meticulously laid-out plans unravel when he loses control of events as well as his emotions. Significantly, although Cain's protagonist moves easily in the world of crime, he's not a professional criminal. His motive for going against the law is not fixed by recidivism.

On the gut level, Cain's protagonist defies the Stoics, who taught that personal liberation lay not in defying the dictates of fate but in voluntarily settling for less even before the race got on. Far from settling for less, Walter's yen to thwart Law and Order is sparked by the very lawful and orderly nature of the world. For all the tangible monetary and sexual rewards, the act of murder seems to be a reward in itself, so much so that once the deed is done the tangible gains pale almost instantly (incidentally baffling most critics).

Pragmatically, murder is the final solution. Metaphysically, it's a gamble against the world and its uncontrollable nature. The key to Walter's defiance is in the proliferation of gambling metaphors, also salient in *The Postman Always Rings Twice*, which *Indemnity* reprises in all structural essentials. Images of the roulette, the croupier, and of crooking the wheel stress the role of control versus chance and unpredictability. Few readers will fail to link the roulette wheel to the wheel of fortune, which, in the medieval trope, determined men's fortunes irrespective of their best-laid plans.

Cain is aware that crime fiction is built around causal determinism, which assures the law's ability to close in on the perp, and metaphysical determinism, which assures that order will be restored and justice meted out. On the mimetic level, planning to commit the proverbial perfect crime, Walter is trying to beat the system and its twin institutions of law and order: the police and the insurance company. As Cain knew from an unsuccessful turn as a broker, insurance is taken out as a countermeasure to incident, bad luck, and unpredictable mishap – the losing turn of the wheel. Symbolically, his startlingly likeable – partly because foredoomed – murderer is a usurper who endeavors to play God.

In the end, Walter ends up re-enacting a deterministic pattern of tragedy and myth. His and Oedipus's fate is sealed from the start despite frantic attempts to control events and people around them. On the surface order is not restored, since neither the protagonist nor his female accomplice is brought to justice. Yet the author allows poetic justice to enact itself – Walter and Phyllis drown in shark-filled waters – highlighting the deterministic order. Naturally poetic justice, whereby misdeeds are punished by the universe, violates physics, revealing Cain's work to be more mythic and tragic in structure than heretofore allowed. Where some hardboiled critics see a first-class (1) story, and others a second-rate (2c) mystery, the novel belongs to 2b instead.

Cain is interested in retributive justice, where bad things happen to bad people as a result of a willful disruption of social law and order and the metaphysical fabric. His denouement, where just desserts are meted out to those who earn them, reinforces universal determinism. Ironically, the same determinism that pushed the protagonist to crime is now responsible for his downfall. The metaphysical edicts (and the urge to disobey them) that haunted Oedipus have become the domain of a middle-class insurance salesman, an early twentieth-century Willy Loman, an Everyman.

Moving on, third-class models also separate into three types.

3a   violates scientific and psychosocial norms;
3b   violates logical and psychosocial norms;
3c   violates logical and scientific norms.

The class 3a is dominated by much of commercially labeled fantasy and science fiction, though without chronomotion or other logical tripwires. For the most part, scientific and psychosocial veracity is a lot to ask of books and films whose future typically comes from a city-state past, science from Ye Olde Magick Shoppe, Valley-accented aliens from Central Casting, and galactic empires from a Classics Illustrated edition of *Ivanhoe*. At least in fantasy, violations of science are mandated by the infusion of the supernatural or the uncanny (to fall back on Todorov's nomenclature).

Once more, modeling flight from empirical and psychosocial norm need not equate to shoddy craftsmanship. Schematic character types can be employed with premeditation (e.g. in grotesques or allegories) to hyperbolize very real traits. In this case the arrant nonsense of the narrative vehicle can be cognitively stimulating at the (symbolic) level of the narrative tenor. At the same time, looking at the modeling principles of fiction helps unmask false pretensions to scientific accuracy, at least in the case of narratives that actually attempt to model anything. Lest we forget, much of the time 3a is really about letting loose during a few plane hours of lite entertainment.

Like 2a, and for the same reasons, 3b is an empty set. Subclass 3c, however, is far from it, principally due to chronomotion. (I assume, of course, that whisking an object from one time coordinate and injecting it into another does not violate the physics of the conservation of energy.) Still, taking liberties with logic and science, not all time-travel stories entail modeling anarchy and cognitive vacuum. Chronomotion can be harnessed to model a great deal of nonfictional problems – in a default scenario, socio-cultural effects of a future shock. Another domain is human psychology, where fiction can track the *déjà-vu* effects of undergoing a controlled experience many times in a row. Tinseltown's never-never comedy *Groundhog Day* may be more familiar, but the film worthy of the theme is Alain Resnais's *Je t'aime, je t'aime* (1968). Time travel proves equally dexterous with larger, sociographic theses, of which a canonical case is *Connecticut Yankee in King Arthur's Court*. Everyone knows the story of Hank Morgan, who, parading Yankee know-how before the medievals in the hope of enlightening them into an industrial utopia, recoils as the Dark Ages live up to the name.[41] The aging and cynical Twain's narrative about the ergodic character of history may be the answer to Leibnitz's metaphysics. From the premise of omniscient and benign deity, the German mathematician (travestied as Pangloss in *Candide*) argued that our world must be already the best of all possible worlds. Any tweaking of its parameters would only cause more pain and suffering, a lesson Twain's hero learns the hard way.

A counterhypothesis that history is evitable animates Bradbury's classic "The Sound of Thunder." Precipitated by a single misstep during a T-Rex safari, global perturbations in the historical downstream suggest a chaotic and anti-ergodic model of history. In cinema the most effective interpretation of chaos for human lives may be Kieślowski's *Blind Chance* and, from subsequent imitators, the German hit *Run, Lola, Run*. That said, generic fiction involving time travel is rarely accompanied by modeling ambitions. More often than not, degenerating into time-warp games of galactic cops and robbers, these free-for-alls where not even psychosocial mimesis is in force form the fourth and last modeling class.

3 Literature and evolution

The writer may readily feel that he is manipulating reality itself, yet safely because controlled by art.

Bernard Malamud, "Why Fantasy?"

From physics to philosophy, from jurisprudence to cognitive science, from econometrics to world politics, the academic jury is back – the intellectual and economic costs of doing away with counterfactuals would be sky high. Not only would such a ban muzzle legitimate hypotheses, like the counterfactual above, but it would stifle research, period. In philosophy alone, "definition, question delegation, drawing distinctions, crafting adequacy conditions, teasing out entailments, advancing possibility proofs, mapping inference patterns" would be greatly impaired, if not entirely crippled.[1]

All this assuming, of course, it were possible at all. Asking a humanist or scientist to dispense with thought experiments would be like asking Shaq to dispense with a dunk, a signature weapon in his arsenal. But not to worry – periodic calls for restraint, if not an outright prohibition, of counterfactual analysis notwithstanding. In history, cosmology, and everywhere in between where real experiments are too pricey or plain unfeasible, thought experiments are as likely to dry out as bathtub gin during the Prohibition. In the social sciences alone their ubiquity is sanctioned by admissions of complicity that echo from the 1960s to the 1990s: "everyone does it, and the alternative to an open counterfactual model is a concealed one."[2]

Far from an instrument of choice, counterfactual analysis is truly an instrument of necessity. To be sure, broad skepticism about hypothetical reasoning is always possible, and we will give it due heed as we go along. On balance, however, it's not likely to carry the day, for what is the alternative? Doctors of philosophy or not, we are all lifelong members of the Counterfactual Thinkers' Society. Designing scientific theories or just skyscrapers, strategizing at the Axis & Allies game board or prepping for a job interview, patronizing a Trojans dispenser or buying flood insurance, people show how ingrained the faculty for imagining states that are not is. Not to look too far, imaginary states and people are also the lifeblood of fiction. It is this genius for controlled speculation that makes storytelling such a formidable laboratory of the mind, and thought experiment one of its capital techniques. Not all writers identify it as overtly as Scott Adams, creator of *Dilbert*, whose 2001 novel *God's Debris* is subtitled *A Thought Experiment*. But few fail to identify with it. "Novels could be called thought experiments. You invent people, you put them in hypothetical situations, and you decide how they will react," is how David Lodge summarized the issue.[3]

Calling his novels none other than "experimental models," Lem insisted that in cognitive terms they "ought to be regarded . . . as *Gedankenexperimente* [thought experiments]." "In my non-assertive works," concurred Čapek, "I guillotined all concepts of happy humanity, usually by applying the method of a thought experiment." Remarking on fiction's aptitude for mind-lab genesis, analysis, and diagnosis, Percy reiterated the methodological homology between the "two branches of art and science, that is, novel-writing and psychiatry." And, on behalf of science-fictioneers, the Nebula-winner James Morrow stated that he is only "one of many writers to talk about their projects as thought experiments."

The parallels between a writer's scripting laboratory, the mental experiments of a scientist, and the universal art of getting through life by weighing "what if" alternatives are striking. In *How the Mind Works* Steven Pinker generalized them into a simile that brings out the adaptive character of literature's flair for weaving counterfactual scenarios, while holding, in Hamlet's idiom, a mirror to Nature: "Life is like chess, and plots are like those books of famous chess games that serious players study so they will be prepared if they ever find themselves in similar straits."[4] Getting from counterfactuals to "factuals" forfeits its ontological mystique when inserted into the context of evolutionary adaptation in life. Art may possess the power it does because some of its goals are common with the art of survival.

The correlation between natural selection and literature ought to be fundamental enough, of course, to permeate other arts to a similar degree. The presence of transcultural universals in any one realm of aesthetic creation should, in other words, boost the credibility of the evolution-sculpted, and thus adaptive, dimension in all art. *Mutatis mutandis*, it should also boost claims of the adaptive character of literary fictions. In this context Richard Voss and John Clarke's work on the frequency distribution in music deserves more attention than it got when first published in 1975.

The original idea, it must be said, did not seem that original at all. Art delights its consumers by mixing just the right amount of originality and tradition. Evidence for the interplay between invention and convention can be found daily at every airport, newsstand, or book-club catalogue. Genre writers habitually traffic in formulas even as they relentlessly chip away at them. Competing to stand out from the crowd, while cashing in on conventions familiar to readers, over thousands and thousands of works they end up creating endless variations on a given theme, character, or plot twist.

Even the ossified skeleton of the crime novel bears witness to this process.[5] The classical detective form first mutated into the hardboiled novel, then into the police procedural. Meanwhile the point of view evolved from the first-person sidekick of Poe into the first-person private eye of Chandler, and into the third-person objective of McBain – while the whodunit pendulum swung from the least suspect to LaPlante's prime suspect. All in order to transfix the audience anew and get legs at the sales counter.

Driven by such considerations, Voss and Clark set out to re-examine how the interplay of invention and convention plays out in music. What the physicists discovered had the makings of a headline grabber. Time and again music chosen from across the broadest geographical, cultural, and musical continuum revealed the same characteristic "spectral distribution." The term roughly describes the way sound intensity is distributed over different frequencies in a piece of music. Think of spectral distribution, for example, in terms of adjusting the equalizer to get more bass over treble. Bach and Mozart, the Beatles and B. B. King, the Bulgarian State Choir, jazz and folk songs around the world – no matter. Everything the researchers looked at yielded the same spectral pattern.

But an even bigger bombshell was in the wings. In the case of spectral distribution it is possible to calculate in advance the solution to the invention-versus-convention problem. Eerily, for every piece of music considered, its actual spectral distribution was found to be the optimum equilibrium. Given the staggering temporal and geographical distances between the sampled compositions, it is clear that at a deeper level there must be a mechanism for such spontaneous and independent musical self-organization. And the more you ponder the nature of this aesthetic invariant (i.e. spectral distribution) across diverse musical epochs, styles, and cultures, the more it looks like a prime candidate for an evolutionary trait.

The question is how we distinguish reasonable hypotheses from unreasonable ones. You might answer, "By doing experiments, of course!" That is one way of distinguishing, but scientists cannot test every hypothesis, good, bad, or indifferent.

William Poundstone, *Labyrinths of Reason*

Could natural selection hide the answer to young Amadeus's perplexed introspection about his musical ideas: "Whence and how do they come? I do not know and I have nothing to do with it"?[6] Given the proximity of music and mathematics, it is perhaps no surprise that David Hilbert, one of the greatest mathematicians in history, held that evolution was the source of insights into mathematical entities.[7]

Still, generalizations about art, math, and even more about evolution from such scant data must proceed with caution. Not all transcultural features are universal adaptations. To take the first example, artworks from disparate eras and cultures bear titles, yet art titling is hardly a trait selected for by evolution. It is certain, in fact, that the majority of our art concepts and aesthetic categories are not descendants of evolutionary adaptations of yore. This point is so crucial that, before we move any further, a decoupling of two look-alike concepts is in order.

First and foremost, literature *per se* is not an *adaptation*, in the sense of being a form of nature-selected and thus gene-codified behavior that enhances environmental fit. Novel writing and even lyrical poetry, in other words, have not been selected for as the optimum way to attract mates in order to populate the earth with one's "literary genes." On the other hand, literature is a form of functionally *adaptive behavior*. In its own way it assists in the survival and well-being of the gene-carriers and the communities who practice it.

In the jargon, literature is therefore an *exaptation* – an evolutionary by-product, a side effect, a spinoff, if you will – that enhances inclusive fitness without having been selected for by evolution for its current role. (Whether the thought-experimental component of literary fictions is an adaptation or a form of adaptive behavior only is another matter.[8]) Mozart's musical inspirations may thus be grounded in the same fountainhead of artistic creation as Melville's or McBain's knack for tale spinning. Indeed, evolutionary mechanisms may be the riverbeds that funnel more of our culture and art than heretofore allowed. These mechanisms are also the likely basis for the cognitive harmony between our stories and our environment.

After all, literary archetypes and story patterns harmonize exceedingly well with human behavioral and cognitive economy. So do the counterfactual "what if" and "if only" of literary composition. This harmony, in turn, is the likely source of literature's authority on human affairs. In *Literary Darwinism* Carroll mounts, in fact, a persuasive case for literature as a central library of behavioral data on human nature. Psychology, as he points out, is a Johnny-come-lately. For most of recorded history "our best psychologists have been playwrights, poets, and novelists."[9]

Not even a slack-jawed yokel will deny that literature contains an unparalleled record of human behavior, complete with conflicts, resolutions, and motives for these resolutions. One such unforgettable work of imagination is William Styron's *Sophie's Choice*. Equally celebrated in literary and extra-literary studies, the story is a sustained ethical thought experiment in which a concentration camp mother must choose between her two children. One will go to death, the other to live in children's barracks. Worst of all, if she refuses to make a choice, both will die.

Styron's fiction is so harrowing because its elements are credible: the horrors of the Nazi extermination, the parental investment in both offspring, and the wrenching decision to save the older child on the premise that it will stand a better chance of surviving. Subjectively we feel and understand both the mother's agony and her decision. But now we have less subjective criteria for assessing its psychological – and, through it, narrative and mimetic – truth. Sophie's choice coincides with the optimal strategy from the selfish gene's point of view. A traumatic metaphysical crisis is resolved in a way that is also biologically adaptive.

Casting narrative fiction in the evolutionary light may be just what's needed to probe the remarkable fact that counterfactual analysis, *de rigueur* in the social and natural sciences, is the very method that serves writers so well. Ex hypothesi, if you recall, literature is a subspecies of a broader category of armchair inquiry mined by knowledge-seekers from all disciplines. Scientific, philosophical, and literary thought experiments are like the Christian trinity: three manifestations of one and the same type of mental autostimulation. But how plausible is this thesis in the first place?

One argumentative stepping-stone seems to be missing, and it's the size of Gibraltar. The scientific method is anchored in the real world. Using hard, verifiable data it poses questions to the world outside, and gets answers from it. Yet in a quintessential philosophical or literary thought experiment a thinker interrogates not the world but himself. So, *where does such armchair knowledge come from?* The puzzle is big and fundamental. Fortunately, even though literary scholarship on the subject is exhausted by two entries (more on them later), the literature in other disciplines isn't. Assuming that literary thought experiments are pertinently like thought experiments *simpliciter*, we can thus legitimately seek enlightenment elsewhere.

This interdisciplinary one-size-fits-all has its downside as well as its upside. The bad news is that the philosophical arena is crisscrossed by critical flak directed at counterfactual analysis. Innocent bystanders or not, literary scholars and literary fictions may be vulnerable in the crossfire. The good news is that theses on behalf of *Gedankenexperimente* that can withstand extra-disciplinary sniping promise all-purpose protection. If they can deflect potshots from scientists and philosophers chary of armchair inquiry, they should be equally safe from ricochets from the literary-critical establishment no less.

(1) What are the evolutionary uses of humour? And
(2) Can it be learned by artificial intelligence?

Eric Idle, *The Road to Mars, a Post-Modern Novel*

The job is big, and I will do it piecemeal. I will defer until Chapter 4 the list of grievances, some imagined, some real, about thought experiments. Herein I'll tackle the dilemma that has dogged their explanatory power: the dilemma of informativeness. To get up to speed, let us begin with a related question that vexes friends and foes of counterfactuals alike. Why resort to introspections and fictions at all, when objective methods and real experiments abound? Transcending demarcations, the query bears in equal measure on literature, philosophy, and science. The fact that some of the most impressive scientific theories, especially in subjects such as cosmology or particle physics, are edifices made of fiction makes it not less but that much more resonant.[10]

Though persuasive in the operational sense, the *tu quoque* testimonials that opened this chapter sidestep rather than confront the issue. The same evasive footwork is evident in occasional appeals to the authority of science. Scientists do thought experiments, goes the rationale, and because science is a paradigm of rational inquiry, there is nothing amiss in doing them outside of science. Although both sorts of replies shore up the *epistemic* status of thought experiments, neither is equipped to establish their *epistemological* validity. Both tell us why we engage in counterfactual reasoning, not why we rightfully should.

Shifting the *onus probandi* onto the skeptic may carry the day rhetorically, but it's a pyrrhic victory at best. It fails to satisfy because it fails to acknowledge the vested interest that both the aye- and nay-sayers have in unknotting the issue. After all, just because people are compulsive thought experimenters, who more often than not get the results right, it doesn't mean that the results and the mental gyrations that bring them about can be embraced without question. To assert this with any degree of assurance we need an argument of a different nature.

Framed by natural selection, the resolution is clear-cut and compelling. Counterfactual reasoning confers a distinct adaptive advantage on its users. It alerts us to historical alternatives and future possibilities that would otherwise remain unexplored. The payoffs are simply fantastic in any environment whose instability exceeds the pace of natural selection to hardwire organisms for behavioral contingencies. Hypotheticals and, further downstream, thought experiments are thus cheap and efficient ways of dealing with the unknown. In Mach's crisp slogan, "thought experiments cost less, as it were."[11]

The *Homo* who could work out decision nodes in his head, instead of slogging down every forking and beast-ridden path, significantly bettered his odds of making it to the mating season. No need to stick one's nose in dark holes to see if it gets bitten off. If mental practice doesn't make perfect, it sure makes it mo' better. The lifestyle – technically, the life-history strategy – of simulating actions by dint of thinking about them, and expressing the results in actions, images, or words, takes feedback out of Nature's time-elongated hands and into our own.

In the twilight of the nineteenth century, William James's *Principles of Psychology* envisioned the mind as an all-purpose generator and selector of ideas best suited to deal with the world. In the twilight of the twentieth, Edward Wilson's *Consilience* fleshed out such adaptive faculties in terms of a prodigious and constantly updated library of scenarios. Not to be confused with Hollywood scripts, this technical term denotes mental coding networks – motion-picture engrams, if you like – that, processed in massive parallel, yield the decisions that we make in life. Like everywhere else, variation and fierce selection determine the degree of fit to the environment in question.

There is clearly a good deal of convergence, if not continuity, between these psychological perspectives on the subject. Either way, human minds are said to work – and exhibit adaptive behavior – using representations not tied to specific actions. Kim Sterelny called them "decoupled representations."[12] Functionally, such representations are like Wordsworth's recollections in tranquility. They are responses guided by reflection after the fact, rather than instinct-guided reactions in the sensory heat of the moment. More fine-tuned to the stimulus than the limited palette of instincts, and supporting a limitless array of responses, scenarios are a species of cognitive mapping that directs our daily truck with the world.

Now take literary fictions, those multipurpose generators and selectors of ideas recollected in tranquility. It's astounding how seamlessly they fit the mantle of considered response, decoupled from instinct-driven reaction to the contingencies of the moment. Pointedly, even though Wilson inclines towards biological determinism of life's goals, his hypothesis is logically separate from his model of scenario-selection as a technique of getting through life. The adaptive potential of counterfactuals is, as a matter of fact, fully independent of the degree to which life's goals may be "preloaded."

In *The Language Instinct* Pinker contends sensibly that, like other arts, literature is an adaptive technology "invented to exercise and stimulate mental modules that were originally designed for specific adaptive functions."[13] When one runs into his conception of artistic creation in *How the Mind Works*, however, it is with a sense of the bizarre. Art, this time around, is described as a "pleasure technology" to be indulged in for the sake of sensuous overload, the kind – in his own analogy – derived from cheesecake or pornography. Granting the pleasure factor in the consumption of art, this notion is so grossly distorted as to verge on nonsense. I'll refrain from belaboring anew the virtues of fiction as a databank, scenario builder, script editor, and modeling laboratory. But it may be worth reiterating that, whether historic or banal, all choices we make in life are acts of imagination. Picture the world iced up by nuclear winter and take the finger off the Button, opting for a quarantine instead. Picture the world in which you tell the boss off and the world in which you keep the job, and choose the one you like better. Imagining these and other "what if" scenarios has been the prerogative of storytellers since time immemorial. Bringing pleasure at no extra charge, their acts of imagination multiply alternative realities at no cost and at considerable benefit to civilization.

Given the adaptive context of the debate about art, the last word should go perhaps to Charles Darwin himself. "To avoid enemies, or to attack them with success, to capture wild animals, and to invent and fashion weapons, requires the aid of higher mental faculties, namely, observation, reason, invention, or imagination,"[14] concludes the biologist in *The Descent of Man*. The reference to imagination points again to literature and its genius for weaving fictions – fictions that help us contemplate imagined actions and their consequences.

Naturally, people use reason and imagination not only to satisfy, but to foster curiosity. Transcending the pragmatics of day-to-day survival, some of our narratives serve no other purpose than to probe the limits of imagination and kindle further explorations. *Summa theologiae* and *Summa technologiae* may be the handy landmarks, but eschatological thought has always exerted fascination on the mind, limited in its finite mental and temporal resources. It is only natural that this remarkable capacity for generating behavioral scripts, mental maps, and adaptive scenarios – in short, for storytelling – should be integrated into the evolutionary curriculum.

> *You arrive at the truth by telling a pack of lies if you are writing fiction, as opposed to trying to arrive at a pack of lies by telling the truth if you are a journalist.*
>
> Melvin Burgess, the *Independent* (London)

We are at last ready to confront the dilemma of informativeness. The sticking point is simple enough. Put the ingredients for a Greek salad in a bowl, toss them for as long as you like, and you'll still end up with no more than the same (now scrambled) ingredients. By analogy, you can juggle your thought salad as much as you like and still end up with what was there before, maybe a bit more scrambled. So, where does the knowledge come from? At no point does the inquirer input new data into a thought experiment, so the net gain ought to be a big fat zero.

In Lodge's campus novel *Thinks*, a writer thinks aloud: "I suppose that's why people read novels. To find out what goes on in other people's heads." Replies her lover, cognitive scientist incarnate: "But all they really find out is what has gone on in the writer's head. It's not real knowledge."[15] But if that is the case, why bother with counterfactuals at all? The answer is simple. We bother because the epistemic state of the armchair thinker is frequently (and demonstrably) improved by recourse to thought experiment. "Just thinking" is not so shabby a method at all. Few of us fail to be staggered by the intricacy and efficacy of mathematics, whose derivations are an epitome of getting from the known to the unknown by "just thinking."

The $64,000 question is *how* we learn from such controlled thinking. How is it that by emulating Mycroft Holmes you can improve your knowledge about things far, far away? How is it that by letting loose the reins of thought, while at the same time keeping a tight rein on them, you can improve your knowledge about things never seen, things that may have never happened, things that sometimes couldn't even happen at all? How is it that by resorting to fiction you can intellectually register a nonfictional gain? In dialectic terms, how do you get to synthetic facts about the real world by the analytic method – by thought alone?

This, as you have surmised, is the crux of the dilemma. Put this way, it makes it easier to grasp why thought experiments have at times been accused of belonging to the rhetoric, rather than substance, of inquiry. Undoubtedly, they can compel through vivid and vigorously narrated illustrations. But since they don't input new data to the mental conveyer belt, the thought-machinery can't spit out anything of interest at the other end. Ergo, concludes the skeptic, they are not a fitting tool for serious inquiry. More formally, if the analysand (what is analyzed) is equal to the analysandum (the result of the analysis), then thought experiments are trivial and therefore useless. And if the two are not equal, we must have taken a wrong turn in the mind-maze, rendering thought experiments wrong/false.

Sorensen remixes this skeptical line into a full-fledged syllogism, but underneath the philosophical robes the core dilemma remains the same. If the results of a thought experiment cannot be checked in a public experiment, then these results are unverifiable and thus useless. Conversely, if the results of a thought experiment can be checked in a public experiment, two possibilities arise. Checking the results of a thought experiment renders them superfluous if they are found to be correct – or false if not. All cases seem to spell trouble for the fellow muttering "Eureka" from his armchair.

Rhetorically and ideologically, this type of pique at experiments of the mind is reminiscent of the quasi-syllogism that, apocryphally, incited Caliph Omar of Damascus to put the library of Alexandria to flame. Either the library contains what's in the *Qur'an*, the Caliph is said to have said, and is therefore not needed, or it does not contain what's in the *Qur'an*, and is therefore not needed. In the more vernacular version, you're damned if you do and damned if you don't. If the job can be done by some other means than mental reckoning, the *Gedankenexperiment* looks superfluous. If not, the *Gedankenexperiment* looks unconfirmable, hence unjustifiable, hence useless.

So, why are thought experiments so useful? Where *does* the knowledge come from? While a proper answer will occupy the next two sections, here I will explain why they are useful even in the paradigmatic case when physical experiments are around. All else aside, thought experiments are indispensable as conceptual benchmarks for actual physical experiments. Though pooh-poohed by the doubter, the tight fit – or even, as we shall see, the lack of fit – between them can be of immense value. From the googolplex of illustrations I chose Stanley Milgram's classic experiment in behavioral psychology, in part also because of its haunting results.

Milgram's experiment involved some two score "teachers" (in reality, tested subjects) who were to reinforce classroom learning in a "student" with electric shocks. These ranged from "Slight" shocks of 15 Volts to "Severe" ones of 450 Volts. For comparison, the AAA battery delivers 1.5 Volts, a car battery 12.6 Volts, and the electric chair from as little as 1,500 to more than 2,000 Volts. Depending on amperage, wetness of skin, constitution, area, and duration of contact, etc., the lethal dose for humans can be as low as 50 Volts. The "student" victim of the lesson, in cahoots with the experimenter, writhed and contorted in synch with the administered voltage. The latter calmly instructed the "teachers" who balked at high levels of punishment to ignore pleas for mercy and keep turning that dial.

Over 60 percent went all the way to the 450 Volt limit.

The less publicized and, for our purposes, more germane part of this landmark study preceded the actual run. Sensing an opportunity to obtain valuable comparative data, Milgram conducted in effect an armchair version of the experiment with a large group of psychiatrists. After being given the details of the experiment to come, the professionals were asked to run it in their heads and predict its outcome as a percentage distribution of electroshocks. The results of their thought experiments were at staggering variance with what was later observed in the classroom.

The psychiatrists were convinced that hardly anyone would even obey the experimenter. They also felt that only a sadistic margin of 1 percent would ever deliver the 450 Volt shock. Now, putting the two sets of results side by side, the point is obvious. The contrast and the cognitive gain for the scientist were possible *only* because one of his experiments was a "dry" one. Two actual experiments might yield different results or not, but they could never yield a prediction of *what would happen if* a real experiment took place. For that Milgram needed the exercise of hypothetical thinking – an armchair inquiry.

In fact, a more general principle is at work here. Rarely, if ever, is an experiment run without *some* idea of how it's going to come out. Milgram's own actions are a paradigmatic example. The fact that he asked psychiatrists to anticipate the outcome of the experiment suggests that, in some ways, he had anticipated their anticipated outcomes. Such advance guesses are common in experiments of any complexity that, more often than not, require substantial financial and engineering investment. It is *de rigueur* for a prudent scientist to run the experiment in her head before committing herself in reality. The so-called blind experiments that often precede actual observation by testing the reliability of equipment also fall into this "test-a-counterfactual" category.

This is not to overlook cases where an experiment designed for one set of questions solves another. Roentgen owed the discovery of X-rays to a piece of cardboard smeared with fluorescent material accidentally placed next to a radioactive ore sample. But such serendipity is beside the point where the general rule is concerned. With no inkling about the outcome of an experiment, there would be little point in rigging up the apparatus in the first place. All this is to say that, far from a menu option, thought experimenting is really a *sine qua non* of experimenting. Mach concurs: "Thought experiment is in any case a necessary precondition for physical experiment." And, even more to the point: "physical experiment and systematic observation are thus always guided by thought and cannot be sharply limited and cut off from thought experiment."[16]

Deference to the German physicist in matters pertaining to the nature, validity, and utility of thought experiments is no accident. Mach, at one point professor of the youthful Einstein, remains to this day an authority on the *Gedankenexperiment* method of mental calculus. Already over a century ago he provided, in fact, a compelling – with hindsight even conclusive – solution to the dilemma of informativeness. He acknowledged in *Knowledge and Error* that there is no synthetic *a priori* knowledge in the classical sense. Knowledge about the physical world cannot be divined by thought alone. Somehow, somewhere, we must draw from the well of stored experience. But how?

Mach's formulation from *The Science of Mechanics* is as persuasive as it is concise. Not surprisingly, it is cast in terms of the evolutionary fit of thought to environment:

Everything which we observe in nature imprints itself *uncomprehended* and *unanalyzed* in our percepts and ideas, which, then, in their turn, mimic the processes of nature in their most general and most striking features. In these accumulated experiences we possess a treasure-store which is ever close at hand and of which only the smallest portion is embodied in clear articulate thought.[17]

The mind learns to build models and structures that can be continually modified and updated as new knowledge becomes available. And that dynamic knowledge base is used to plug the gaps in real-life scenarios as they unfold.

John L. Casti, *Paradigms Lost*

Mach's answer to the problem of informativeness challenges the skeptic's first premise. Thought experiments need not be redundant when followed by a physical experiment, nor false when contradicted by it. One must also bear in mind that armchair inquiry never takes place in a conceptual vacuum. The well of accumulated experience may be partly filled by evolution, but infants do not conduct thought experiments. From personal experience and general education, to mathematical or merely formal analysis, thought experimenters are aided by a host of sources that improve the efficacy of the basic innate apparatus.

Counterfactual thinkers, be they scientists or humanists, top up the well of evolution with decades of play, study, imitation, and formal schooling. Their *a priori*, if you will, does not stop with innate knowledge but extends up to the moment of armchair deliberation (more on this in Chapter 4). Evolution is, after all, a blind tinkerer who, economizing on old designs, favors those that may be only slightly better adapted. There is no guarantee, in other words, that our mental equipment is fully efficient or reliable in any given case. But no such perfection need be assumed, for, on evolutionary epistemology, (innate) nature is fully compatible with (inculcated) nurture.

Since Mach's original formulation, an imposing roster of thinkers have endorsed the evolutionary-thinking paradigm. They include anthropologists, sociobiologists, ethologists, linguists, behavioral ecologists, evolutionary psychologists, paleobiologists, philosophers, and even scholars of literature. Their work confirms in striking ways the thrust of the theory, on occasion even vindicating some of its auxiliary hypothesis. Mach held, for example, that some human fears should be instinctive, a fact he thought would be best observable in children. Sarah B. Hrdy's research in *Mother Nature* indeed points in this direction, linking infant fears of strangers to primate infanticide by invading males. Similar mechanisms have also been advanced to account for widespread fears of spiders and snakes.[18]

A seeming problem with Mach's formulation is that, taken by itself, it seems to speak of a phenotypic store of experience, acquired by an individual throughout his lifetime. Far from a Darwinian account, it looks therefore like a throwback to the epigenetic theories of Lamarck and Lysenko. A closer study of *Knowledge and Error* dispels, however, any doubt that the physicist speaks of the genotypic base to this "imprinting." And as such, in one elegant swoop Mach puts the dilemma of informativeness to rest. Genetic predispositions that have in the past tended to aid in survival are the fountain of the rough but operative knowledge used in hypothetical reasoning.

Compared to the early empiricists – exemplified by Hume's *nihil est in intellectu quod non prius fuerit in sensu* (there's nothing in intellect that has not entered it through the senses) and Locke's *tabula rasa* – the contrast could not be starker. In one way, however, things are more complicated still. The old dilemma rears up its head in another form, intimated by the title of Simon Beck's article, "Should We Tolerate People Who Split?" In it the philosopher investigates critiques of "fission" thought experiments which "split" a person and track the consequences for personal identity. Although evoked for quite different reasons, Beck's question frames the perennial perils of extravagant and rarefied thought experiments.

What is the guarantee, after all, that the intellectual fruit they yield is ripe? How can anyone be certain that the process of chasing thoughts around one's head will yield an accurate or even nontrivial result, barring an actual experiment to confirm it? The answer is simple. Given the *source* of the knowledge germinating in our heads, we can trace its *accuracy* to the same process of natural selection. To be sure, hypothetical calculus can get it wrong. Given the empirical origin of gene-coded knowledge, it is in fact inevitable that thought experiments will from time to time lead astray, especially outside the familiar range or type of phenomena. Philosophical skirmishes about people who split clearly indicate confusion at the conceptual limits.[19]

On the other hand, markedly little of such confusion is registered about hypotheticals from the familiar range of experience. This is significant, for, in this light, the apparent drawback actually bolsters the assumption of thought experiments' evolutionary and adaptive origins. After all, if the theory is correct, there *should* be less consensus about counterfactuals planted in empirically exotic domains (more on this in Chapter 4). Incidentally, Beck resolves that we should in fact tolerate people who split – or, to be precise, tolerate thought experiments about splitters.

To shed light on the dilemma of informativeness in thought experiments, let's look at the dilemma of informativeness that has plagued the lynchpin of the scientific method: induction. In one way or another, every scientist (in fact, every living organism) relies on the inductive assumption that the future is going to resemble the past. Scientists or not, we all infer from experienced to unexperienced cases, from the known to the unknown, from the old to the new. Yet already in the eighteenth century David Hume protested that this kind of reasoning (he called it the problem of induction) goes around in circles, and is therefore irrational. For what legitimates inductive reasoning? The sun rose yesterday, last Sunday, and many times before, hence we conclude it will rise tomorrow. Up to now planes have not failed to obey the laws of aerodynamics, so we infer it's safe to board them. The longer we track such regular behavior, the more confident we become about each of its subsequent occurrences. And each subsequent occurrence feeds back into the track record, which then boosts the confidence level, and so forth. The trick is that conclusions about the new do not deductively – that is, necessarily – follow from the old.

It is possible that the *full* laws of aerodynamics are: same as now until December 31, 2009, lethally different thereafter. Hokey and contrived, you will object. But how can you even argue it isn't so, other than by an appeal to induction? The problem is so central that the roll of thinkers who wrestled with it reads like the *Who's Who* of philosophy and science. Astonishingly, the answer returned by the mightiest minds is: No one knows. The riddle of induction resists all efforts to bootstrap it out of circularity. Track record (science has worked so far), uniformity of nature (all electrons are alike), and other pragmatic or causal explanations all fail since they're all grounded in induction.

It's no better one level up. Saying that predictions from the old to the new have always (or usually) worked merely turns the problem of induction into a problem of meta-induction. After all, what could justify the conviction that one can extrapolate from past electrons or sun-ups to the not-yet-seen ones? Presumably an inductive statement about inductive statements, something like: "Predicting from the old to the new has always (or usually) worked." Problem is, this new principle is no less circular, justifying not only the data but itself. Science, if you like, works on faith only!

First, it is one of the major paradoxes of the history of science, that the Darwinian theory, speculative as it must be by the very nature of its subject-matter, has been held up as a model of simple Baconian induction through the patient accumulation of facts.

Marjorie Grene, "The Faith of Darwinism"

If you believe Poul Anderson, any problem, no matter how complicated, can always be made even more complicated if you look at it the right way. Bearing this in mind, the sensible question is, why not keep things simple in the world of knowledge-hunters? Why not banish induction to the scientific dungeon? The answer is startling. We need induction, precisely to keep things simple, as a working hypothesis about the regularity of nature. Without induction, the world would become incomprehensible. It would be a mishmash of facts with no rhyme or reason, observable in minute detail yet untamed by any helpful generalization.

Much like thought experiment, induction is really a cheap and efficient way of negotiating the experience of a vast and complex world. And much like thought experiment, the pragmatic reasons for sticking with induction gloss over its explanatory dilemma. This is because, again as with thought experiment, the problem of induction is not whether it works, because it works extremely well. The problem is, why should it work at all? How is it that we can spot similarity in difference, order in chaos?

How can induction work, puzzled Quine, arguably the most influential philosopher of science of the last century, when the generalizations we make from finite data are compatible with an infinity of possible generalizations? How is it that, faced with the infinity of possible relations among the objects that make our world, we tend to converge with a high rate of success on the interesting ones? How is it that over time we tend to infer just the right kind of generalizations or theories to give us control over the environment? How is it that, trial and error notwithstanding, in the face of astronomical odds against getting things right, we often do?

Elementary. The mystery of the astronomical odds evaporates if, like a crooked Macau croupier, natural selection loads the dice in our favor. Human beings tend to get more things right than wrong because they are predisposed toward approximately correct and constantly modifiable conjectures about the way the world works. Indeed, in "Natural Kinds" Quine himself devoted a great deal of attention to such preordained correspondence. In what ought to be a familiar gambit, he pointed to innate (i.e. gene-scripted) qualities as the source of correspondence between our mentations and nature.[20]

In all this, philosophy of science finds a steadfast ally in evolutionary epistemology – the closest thing we have, in Henry Plotkin's words, to the science (as opposed to the philosophy) of knowledge. Biological adaptations, points out the psychologist, are no less than biological knowledge, and the knowledge as we commonly understand it is but a special case of biological knowledge. This simple but profound point again identifies the same source of the fit between gene-stored raw data and thought experiments of a mental reckoner. From the Darwinian point of view, there really are patterns in the world which humans are pre-equipped to ferret out.

So intimate is this harmony between mind and matter that, in Plotkin's catchphrase, when we have come to know something, "we have performed an act that is as biological as when we digest something."[21] This is what David C. Gooding seems to have in mind when reflecting on the information-carrying capacity of the laboratory of the mind: "T-experimenters must be *at home in their bodies.*"[22] And this is why cognitive gain in thought experiments is grounded in Darwinian (or, more precisely, neo-Darwinian) evolutionary theory. The interdisciplinary consensus is that the winning scenarios from the assortment available to the thought experimenter are, indeed, "those that match goals pre-programmed by instinct and the satisfaction of prior experience."[23]

Note the ubiquitous appeal to instinct and prior experience. Harking back to Mach's original formulation, biological knowledge is the conceptual serum that takes the bite out of the dilemma of informativeness. The rough and ready intuitions that bankroll armchair inquiry are really hardwired (genotypic) ingredients of our evolutionary makeup. They enhance the adaptive capabilities, and thus the survival, of members of our genus. That is why Sorensen can assert in "Thought Experiments and the Epistemology of Laws" that natural selection and adaptive pressures "have led us to develop rough and ready intuitions of physical possibility which are then exploited by thought experimenters."[24]

But the dimensions of the fit between thought and environment may be even larger, extending to the very physical structure of the universe. Laws of nature can be understood in full by a combination of very elementary concepts like counting, cause and effect, symmetry, either–or bivalence, and the like, which have a clear adaptive survival value. Since we can describe the laws of nature, and these descriptions are mathematical, and mathematics is reducible to logic and a sprinkling of axioms, it seems not so far-fetched that relatively simple adaptive mental operations can also capture the essential features of the universe at large.

Certain versions of the Anthropic Principle – those that do not invoke polyverses or intelligent design – also look like cosmological arguments for innate synthetic knowledge.[25] How so? Somewhat in the spirit of Protagoras that "man is a measure of all things," the values of some fundamental physical constants, such as Planck's, gravitational, fine-structure, and others, have been established as necessary for the evolution of sentient life on Earth. This is the *a priori*. The physical aspects of the universe, expressed as the sunny world of plants, animals, great books, and other suns in the galaxy, are the (synthetic) *a posteriori*. In principle the universe could be shaped in many other ways than it is. But only some of its potentialities, like the one we inhabit, allow for sentient observers who by definition are the product of its constants and laws.

The main issue in evolution is how populations deal with unknown futures.
Conrad Hal Waddington, *Towards a Theoretical Biology*

It may be powerful, influential and, if not exactly new, the up-and-coming paradigm for the social sciences (and, some would say, for the humanities). Yet not everyone buys the evolutionary line. In fact, the authors of the finest synthesis of sociobiology, human evolutionary ecology, evolutionary psychology, memetics, and gene-culture co-evolution to date are adamant. The "vast majority of social scientists are unsympathetic to an evolutionary perspective."[26]

This is odd because, in one way or another, harmony between the world and the mind has been the cornerstone of modern thought. No need to look further than *Critique of Pure Reason*, a philosophical classic in every sense (including Mark Twain's: a book no one reads but all wish they had). In his grand opus Kant reasoned that some truths – he singled out Euclid's geometry – must be certain because they are impressed by our minds on the world.[27] Like the philosophical rationalists, for whom innate knowledge is a *sine qua non*, he invoked a dozen such harmonized intuitions and categories of quantity, quality, relation, and modality.

Kant died in 1804, only a few years before Bolyai and Lobachevski independently worked out their counterintuitive non-plane geometries. So much for truths impressed by the mind on the world. In fact, things are the exact reverse of the *Critique*. The basic (and some not so basic) mental apparatus needed to comprehend the world comes preloaded with our genes. We tap into certain truths not because they are impressed by our minds *onto* the world, but because they are downloaded *into* our minds by the world. Just like a PowerBook is only a lump of circuits encased in aluminum unless preinstalled with OS X, the mind comes preinstalled with basic instructions on how to operate (including how to learn).

A series of recent findings in neuroscience, cognitive psychology, and artificial intelligence confirms beyond any doubt that our picture of the world is conditioned by gene-coded mental structures that make such knowledge possible in the first place.[28] Yet in other ways Kant's conception of pre-established harmony was prescient. Just as he proposed, we are equipped with innate knowledge, including knowledge about how to further our knowledge. Ironically, this allows a plausible conjecture as to why classical geometry was discovered first and why it held sway for 2,000 years. The recalcitrant parallel axiom apart, Euclid's system does harmonize with our world of medium-size things and nonrelativistic effects. Given how our minds are wired, chances were high it would be discovered first.

Pre-established harmony even informs Wittgenstein's contention that the rules of logic come to us preloaded in the rules of language (the latter known, if only operationally, to all competent speakers). Of course, taken literally, the statement is false insofar as systems of logic are innumerable.

But in a looser sense of logic as "admissible rules of transformation" it makes good sense. The underlying logic is similar because all languages share a universal grammar. This they do because the underlying reality, built in during the evolution of the language module, was similar. Categories of thought do not fall like manna on unsuspecting humans. Evolutionary adaptation and environmental fit select for patterns, theories, and relationships that correspond in practical, instrumental consequences to reality. Those patterns and theories, in turn, become mental weapons in the game of survival. Like other animals, people's odds in this most serious of games are fortified with innate mechanisms that save them from having to learn what to learn. The latter would be an evolutionary nonstarter inasmuch as, unaided, induction would proffer an infinity of theories to sift through.

Kant would have been discomfited to learn of the findings of modern neo-Darwinians. Like the basic thought processes in all human beings, it is even conceivable that his idealistic transcendentalism may owe in part to a hereditary disposition to think in certain forms. Konrad Lorenz drove the point home in a lengthy disquisition aimed directly at Kant. The way we think and intuit, he proposed, "is not something immutably determined by factors extraneous to nature but rather something that mirrors the natural laws in contact with which it has evolved."[29]

Categories of reason are, in the first instance, dependent on the central nervous system. The morphology and functionality of the brain are, in turn, dependent on their evolutionary history, and thus on the immediate, intimate, and reciprocal cause–effect contact with nature. We get an approximate but reliable enough ("satisficing") picture of the world through our senses, which themselves evolved under the pressure of natural-selection stimuli: sights of attacking beasts, sounds of growls, the searing touch of fire, and so forth. The *a priori* knowledge injected into all of us before birth is really *a posteriori* knowledge encoded in the individuals whose lineage we continue.

Through trials by fire evolution has been testing on us various adaptive solutions like a scientist tests theories.[30] More than metaphorically, living beings *are* living theories about Nature. But what sets our own kind of beings apart is the capacity for testing theories about Nature without waiting for the patient hand of evolution. Human minds possess the capacity to drum up future-oriented scripts and red-ink them in the hunt for a satisficing fit between fiction and fact. And thought experiments are the best cheap tools for imagining and *evaluating* states to see if they're worth pursuing. Concurs Dennett in *Elbow Room*: "Even an imperfect capacity to 'evaluate' some of one's own cognitive and conative states makes a big difference."[31]

Jean Piaget's research in developmental psychology (his preferred term was "genetic epistemology") led him to identify four central stages in a child's mental growth. The key of the formal-operations stage – roughly 10–14 years old – is the development of the notion of the real world as merely a subset of possible worlds. You might say that, like Eco's super-sleuth of Baskerville, the young person's mind is "not at all interested in the truth, which is nothing but the adjustment between the thing and the intellect." Instead, during the formal-operations stage it is given to "imagining how many possibilities were possible."[32]

Considering that counterfactual thinking appears to be a universal trait, it might seem to be a solid candidate for a gene-triggered adaptation. The Swiss scientist dissented. Instead of being hardwired for alternative-world brainwork, a child has to develop it from scratch through the process of assimilation and accommodation, he maintained. In the course of such active and interactive exploration, the feedback between a neonate's conceptual framework and the environment would fashion (rather than correct, as on the neo-Darwinian account) mental structures in the exploring mind.

Enter Chomsky, armed with clinical counterevidence: patients afflicted with aphasia or paraplegia. On Piaget's supposition, having missed the first "sensimotor" stage of development, paraplegics ought to develop deformed mental and linguistic representations of the world. Significantly, they do not. Exit imprinting on the world; re-enter imprinting on the mind. In fact, if one were to take Piaget seriously, the remarkable fact about thought experimenting with "what if" scenarios would be that it takes place at all. *Prima facie* there would be little point for the exploring mind to develop scenarios grounded in unreality.

> *Beauty is our weapon against nature; by it we make objects, giving them limit, symmetry, proportion.*
>
> Camille Paglia, *Sexual Personae*

From Piaget's point of view, the time and energy spent on imaginative fictions and alternative realities could be better spent on dealing directly with the world. The fact that people counterfactualize so effortlessly and efficiently suggests, instead, that the right picture of mental development is the one that does *not* leave genetic hardwiring out. Genetic presets influence a variety of individual decisions and preferences, including, as we saw in the example of spectral distribution in music, aesthetic inclinations. Aesthetics is, of course, tied to perception of beauty, beauty to perception of proportion, and proportion to perception of pattern.

Here again research confirms what artists and craftspeople have known for ages, namely that certain types of pattern – in particular symmetry –

never fail to attract us. Egyptian and medieval visual art, to choose two cultures separated by space and time, exemplify a striking preponderance for bilateral symmetry. Human sensitivity to symmetry is so profound, in fact, that it is frequently exploited for rhetorical purposes. Think of the four fundamental "Fs" of evolutionary survival: fighting, fleeing, feeding and reproduction. Primed for four disyllabic gerunds of Anglo-Saxon stock, the mind takes a while to wrap around the abrupt collapse of the alliterative symmetry.

Our predilection for the aesthetics of symmetry – reflective, rotational, translational, and dilational, in the order of importance – is well documented. Evidence accrues from such far-flung fields as archeology and evolutionary as well as development psychology. Tool symmetry of Paleolithic hominids, observed in the knapping (stone-chipping by hand) patterns of bifacial discoids, handaxes, and cleavers, is almost certainly of selective origin. So is the attraction to, and the discrimination of, symmetric images in infants as young as four months old. Reflection over the vertical axis (left–right symmetry) is very important – and apprehended most quickly – in both adults and infants. This is understandable in view of its survival-enhancing importance for facial recognition.[33]

If the evolutionary root of beauty shows in the apprehension of pattern in heterogeneity, in literary fiction it often surfaces in the form of reflective (vertical) symmetry. Palindromes, versification, rhyming schemes, repetition, foreshadowing, or even large-scale plotting or structural patterns are just some examples of this instinct for pattern and harmony. Its epitome may be a little-known miniature by Frederic Brown, entitled "The End." This short-short story (one paragraph long) is 100 percent bilaterally symmetric, so that it reads the same from the beginning to the end – or back.[34]

It is no different in everyday life. Notwithstanding large variations in judgments about physical appeal, people demonstrate a striking preference for symmetric faces. Film stars, models, TV anchors, politicians, and other public figures whose jobs depend on their looks have faces that are highly symmetric. In *The Annotated Flatland*, Ian Stewart summarizes the state of the art: "The evolutionary link between beauty and 'good genes' caused by sexual selection means that beauty is not so arbitrary a criterion as might be thought."[35]

Naturally, today's lives are paltry shadows of the millions of years in the prehistorical hominid savannah.[36] But the ability to negotiate life's twists and turns in one's imagination remains a super-effective method of avoiding trials by fire or by predator. The knowledge gained from such mental pruning of behavioral pathways can multiply manifold the more minds engage in it. It becomes even more effective if information from sundry mind-labs can be shared and traded among members of a community. This type of knowledge bazaar boosts the information gradient of the entire group.

Making the unpredictable more predictable, thought experiments are really a form of adaptive behavior to compensate for the imperfections of genetic adaptations. Swift but unswerving, instinctive responses are a maximin bet on the constancy of the environment: maximum efficacy for the minimum of fuss. But where time is not of the essence and environmental stimuli are complex, the mental calculus comes triumphantly into its own. Thought experiments raise intuitive knowledge to the level of controlled manipulation, where it can fuse with the data at hand into explicit knowledge.

Tapping into the well of innate knowledge, literature also manipulates fictive situations in order to elucidate what is true in the world of fact. This cognitive flair is exploited by scientists who label evolutionary theories after characters and themes from literature. The evocative power of fiction is excellently suited to code a particular cognitive or adaptive trait. The Red Queen hypothesis, for instance, was so called by Leigh Van Valen after one of the quirky characters from Carroll's *Through the Looking Glass*.

In the novel, alongside the Red Queen, Alice quickly discovers that it takes all the running she can muster to keep in the same place. This seems a perfect embodiment of the hypothesis, which states that continuing development is needed in order to maintain fitness relative to the systems one is co-evolving with. The literary reference sums up what's essential about the theory. In immunological terms species constantly need to mix their genetic pools anew. Stop for a moment to catch your breath, and parasites could adapt perfectly, with disastrous consequences. Like Alice and the Red Queen, all living beings constantly have to run to keep in the same place in terms of the biological arms race.

> *But now for many years I cannot endure to read a line of poetry: I have tried lately to read Shakespeare, and found it so intolerably dull that it nauseated me.*
>
> Charles Darwin, *The Autobiography of Charles Darwin*

Among the techniques of counterfactual suasion described by David Kahneman in "Varieties of Counterfactual Thinking," the most efficient may be inviting a comparison between explicit (focal) and background (dispositional) beliefs. Leading readers to examine their belief structure, literary fictions function in an analogous way. Writers invite identification with their heroes as a way of inviting a comparison between their and the readers' beliefs. In distinction to descriptively anemic vignettes of philosophy or science, literature thrives on drawing readers into a "virtual reality" where they can be someone else for a day – someone with a different angle of entry into the world.

This talent for affecting beliefs is one reason why, in *The Uses of Enchantment*, Bruno Bettelheim eulogized that the purpose of art was "to endow life in general with more meaning." Significantly, he added: "When children are young, it is literature that carries such information best."[37] As enchanted children first, discerning adults later, we follow the *peripeteia* of narrative agents whose words and actions open a window onto their motives and, through them, beliefs. These reconstructed beliefs are often enough to hypothesize reliably even about the beliefs of their authors, which can be at dramatic odds with their creations.

Rehabilitated in the rat room, Winston Smith no longer has to feign love for Big Brother in *1984*. His genuine adulation of the dictator terrifies all the more as it violates the inferred beliefs of Eric Arthur Blair, Socialist, liberal, and anti-fascist *sans pareil*. Together with other narrative techniques, such double layering (the characters versus the author) is uniquely disposed to ignite interpretive debates and, through them, a comparative analysis of one's thoughts and emotions. Brought face to face with the belief system of the protagonist, readers respond on an emotional, sometimes even visceral, level by examining the validity or fallacy of their own.

This belief-modifying potential is the grail of storytellers. When all is said and done, only the most trite poetasters harbor no ambitions to affect by what they represent. From the political agenda of *The Jungle* to the moral historiography of *Schindler's Ark*, fiction deftly manipulates the way we see the world. Once again, it needs no sophisticated theory to recognize in narrative representations a form of cognitive mapping. Literary scenarios are extensions of adaptive behavior to the human environment, whether bio-physical or socio-cultural in nature.

The interest in literature and cognitive mapping corresponds to the fact that "mazeway-building" tops any list of humans' primal (and, in that sense, primary) motivational drives.[38] It does not matter if the niche is prehistoric, with feral beasts stalking the perimeter, or information-age in character. As John Bowlby writes in *Attachment and Loss*, cognitive maps can be "of all degrees of sophistication, from the elementary maps that we infer hunting wasps construct to the immensely complex world-picture of an educated Westerner."[39]

The recent years saw a surge of interest in the human ability to work out approximate "theories of mind" and press them into service in social intercourse. It is amazing how effectively we pin a wide range of percep-tual, emotional, and rational states onto others, and then conscript these projections to calculate each other's behavior. A better understanding of minds and mental states can, of course, be sought via a better understanding of fiction. Narratives are mini-theories of mind insofar as they are mostly character-directed, and they represent human behavior with great richness and subtlety. Joel Davitz's classic *Language of Emotion* (1969) catalogues 700 terms and expressions people use to refer to emotions. A more recent *shortlist* of personality terms used in literature tops 1,700.[40]

Readers typically interpret narrative thought experiments by trying to understand the actions and thoughts of the characters that star in them. "The 'proof' of the experiment," prompts one distinguished novelist, "is if their behavior seems interesting, plausible, revealing about human nature."[41] Readers' interest is stoked, in other words, by the kind of behavioral economy that also animates our daily lives. This interest may, of course, be narrow and pragmatic (what would I do in this kind of pickle?), or broadly epistemic (how do things work in general?).

Identification in this context often starts with the identification of the characters' mental and emotional states. Why did Iago befoul the friendship of his Moor benefactor and friend? Was he gripped by the psychopathic variety of what Poe diagnosed as the imp of the perverse? Or by God-like hubris to be the master of people's fates? The fact that we shall never know the answer has never stood in the way of intense probing and conjecturing – in effect formulating theories – about the malefactor's inner states. Theorizing in this manner allows us to place fictions on the mimetic scale and evaluate events and characters in terms of their truthfulness to life (see Chapter 2).

Literature is the source of some of the most intricate experiential and creative patterns in existence. The arresting appeal of these islands of aesthetic complexity is a legacy of the times when perception of pattern or symmetry conferred a tangible advantage for the long-term adaptive economy. It has long been held, of course, that the arts are unbridled and subjective expressions of the creative spirit. As such, they are said to lie beyond systematic – not to say scientific – analysis. But evolutionary imprints on human minds, as mediated through art, are concrete counters to this thesis.

One of the most instructive ones derives from the study of a central aspect of storytelling: memory. The psychological experiment by Frederic Bartlett into how memory reconfigures over time is also a useful benchmark for what litterateurs had to say on the subject more than thirty years later. Using excerpts from a Native American ghost story, Bartlett asked his subjects to retell them repeatedly in a kind of narrative "telephone," each listener becoming a storyteller in the next iteration. It did not surprise anyone that retelling altered the tone and content of the tale. What *was* startling was that the alterations were anything but random or idiosyncratic, allowing researchers to isolate several "centripetal" factors.

First, the retellers compacted the story around the skeleton of salient events. By the same token, the narrative "meat" became variable: retained in some cases, compressed in others, eliminated in others still, or even invented *ab ovo* when it suited the teller. Finally, iterations tended to conventionalize the eccentricities of style, point of view, and rhetoric. The end-product, in effect, streamlined individuating edges into a one-story-fits-all generic commodity. For a psychologist, Henry Plotkin, the moral is obvious. Feed "a rich, clever and slightly obscure story to a group of listeners, and what comes out at the end is a rather colourless and none-too-accurate husk of a tale."[42]

How unlike the romantic ascription of grace and nuance to the smithy of oral literature by Borges and Bioy-Casares in "In Search of the Absolute." Nierenstein Souza, an unheralded Uruguayan writer, undertakes to compose a masterpiece, which is, however, nowhere to be found. Instead, his posthumous researcher is fed a gabfest of stories by the local people, none too savory or recherché. And then the epiphany hits him:

> Nierenstein took up the tradition which, from Homer down to the hearth of the peasant cottage or to the gentleman's club, takes pleasure in investing and listening to tales. The stories that Nierenstein made up he told badly, knowing that if they were worthy of it Time would polish them, as it has done with the *Odyssey* and the *Thousand and One Nights*.[43]

If Bartlett's findings are correct, the gems of our literary history are far more likely to be intentional creations by individual authors than transcriptions of oral "telephony." In general, human minds indeed display a propensity for certain types of visual (landscape) and aural (music) organization, to say nothing of a more general predilection for symmetry. This trait, captured in the title of Barrow's "Survival of the Artiest," animates the majority of the current debates about the extension of aesthetics into evolution and vice versa.

Assuming an aesthetics that enhances the chance of survival in the long run, it should be no surprise to find it thriving in those who prospered and thus passed on the predilection for certain types of landscapes or tonal preference – or, indeed, the facility to juggle "what if" scenarios. Naturally, not all of today's aesthetic categories are descendants of evolutionary adaptations of yore. Some at least are mere epiphenomena. Like the thick-end school of egg-cracking in Swift's Blefuscu, through repetition and tradition such arbitrary cultural accretions ossify into a semblance of a cultural invariant.

Literature is, and all the arts are, and even the Mona Lisa is, a practical joke – there's no woman there, and yet, people care.

Kurt Vonnegut, in the *Edmonton Journal* (2001)

Although questions raised by narrative thought experiments are critical in all senses of the word, the profession is largely mute on their subject. If the MLA (Modern Languages Association) bibliography is to be trusted, the topic that should be of interest to all theorists of literature has surfaced only twice. In 1981 Edward Davenport advanced some broad observations in a short essay, "Literature as Thought Experiment." In 1993 Alice Eileen John filed an unpublished thesis, "Fiction as Conceptual Thought Experiment." Slim though the pickings are, we need to examine what they say about literary thought experiments before we tackle the subject head on in Chapter 4.

Davenport begins on a high note, challenging literary epistemologists with his version of the dilemma of informativeness: "how can we learn about the real world by studying imaginary beings or entities?"[44] His own reply is unhesitant: by doing thought experiments, of course. Given this promising start, it is with a sense of disappointment that one scours his mini-essay for analytic pay dirt. Thought experiments *per se* get all of three paragraphs of desultory discussion. Thought experiments in art get four.

This is not to neglect intimations of several useful points. The critic notes the autodidactic aspect of literary counterfactuals, stating that Victorian novelists wrote in part to learn about their own society. He draws attention to the theory-forming (systematic/hypothesizing) role of *belles lettres*, arguing that artists' generalizations are frequently the best theories for testing against independent evidence. No less astutely, he states that where real experiments are difficult or impossible, literature is of value in elaborating the emotional and moral implications of social theories.

But when it comes to thought experiments, there is scarcely enough to cover a pinhead. "How we learn from abstractions, models, and hypothetical entities is not at all obvious," about sums up the critic's contribution. Mostly, he ventures, by virtue of "imagining certain conditions with certain laws in force and showing that certain results must follow." This gem of precision is followed by another: "A thought experiment is a kind of deduction from certain hypothetical premises." Not a word, alas, on what *kind* of deduction is at stake. Do rebus solvers perform thought experiments? Perhaps so, inasmuch as "imagining certain conditions with certain laws in force and showing that certain results must follow" covers a lot of ground, from rebus solving to scheming how not to get grounded by parents.[45]

Fuzzy thinking is in evidence throughout. According to Davenport the writer of fiction or poetry (per his disjunction, poetry is *not* fiction) "creates an imaginary world which is constructed in such a way that it will test the validity of his hypotheses." It would help to know what hypothesis Ezra Pound validated in "In a Station of a Metro." Or, indeed, how exactly his haunting, haiku-like lines – "The apparition of these faces in the crowd:/ Petals on a wet, black bough" – form a thought experiment. The only hint is another gem of precision: during the process of discovery the artist is "testing his way of proceeding against ever-higher criteria of truth and beauty."[46]

Having dished out a cliché of mammoth proportions and equally hoary, the critic asserts that thought experiments can teach us about the world even when parts of the model are defective. By any standards, such reliability is remarkable. Picture a camera manufacturer guaranteeing quality snaps even when parts of the mechanism are defective. Yet no instructions for the end-user of narrative thought experiments follow. Instead, citing Keats's ambivalence about art and death, Davenport concludes: "Keats only brings out the complexity of these ideas without coming to any definite conclusions, but this does not make the poems any the less thought experiments."[47]

On balance, "Literature as Thought Experiment" seems less interested in unraveling the nature of the counterfactual calculus than in defending mimesis from the postmodern discourse-as-the-measure-of-all-things. Rather than trace the remainder of its argumentative twists and turns, then, let us turn to John's thesis. Unstinting in nuanced interpretations of several works of fiction, its centerpiece is the delineation of what a thought experiment is. Without overlooking its sensible analytic core, it is fair to say, however, that it ends up being more useful in delineating what thought experiment isn't.

Some of the author's conclusions, for instance that readers and armchair thinkers inescapably draw on the world, resonate with what we have covered so far. But John's conception of the cognitive role for narrative fiction is draconically restricted. To begin with, she claims that thought experiments involving personhood lie outside of what literature can deal with. Moreover, stories "support questioning and reflection which is not especially structured or tidy," in which "it is difficult to discern particular, discrete *thought experiments.*"[48]

First of all, both statements testify to a complete retrenchment from her opening thesis about fictions functioning roughly like philosophers' imagined cases. Tellingly, among those imagined cases are thought experiments about personhood-splitters. Nor is it clear how, in view of what she intimates to be an almost irredeemable vagueness, the philosopher can insist that "the central feature of a thought experiment is a judging *act.*"[49] Judging unstructured and untidy – if not amorphous and perhaps even indiscernible – inquiries sounds more like an act of will than reason.

John displays an equally narrow view of what literary thought experiments can do – "clarifying some aspect of our conceptual practice."[50] This reflects her procrustean conviction that their effectiveness is limited to folk-psychological concepts of character and emotion.[51] Thus literary thought experiments can only increase our knowledge of characters but not of concepts or principles at hand. Knowledge of the latter is possible only via involvement with characters. On this fiat stories that foster little of such involvement, for example Borges's "Pierre Menard, Author of Don Quixote," are neither interpretable as thought experiments, nor even capable of contributing to knowledge. It is hard to conceive of a statement more at odds with the truth.

Moving on, John proposes that philosophic and literary counterfactuals "prompt us to imagine a scenario in which an interesting question about some aspect of the scenario is left open."[52] Successful mental manipulation, it is implied, will tease out an intuitive judgment and settle the question. Alas, this conceptual net is far too indiscriminate, hauling in all kinds of unwanted catch. One of the classic *Simpsons* episodes, "Itchy & Scratchy: The Movie," provides an amusing counterexample.

Concerned parents, Marge and Homer, contemplate disciplinary action which may decide the lifepath of Bart-the-troublemaker. The thought-balloon shows blubbery Bart waddling on the runway of a male-stripper joint, and on the Supreme Court bench as the alternative. The scene indeed prompts us to imagine a "Bart's future" scenario in which an interesting question (how will he end up?) is left open. It also teases out an intuitive judgment that discipline is needed if his future is to have an upward trajectory. But I doubt there are too many analysts inclined to defend the proposition that Marge and Homer – or the viewers – have just conducted a thought experiment.

We learn from fiction because we navigate the world using mental and emotional dispositions partly mediated through imaginative "experiments" on storyworlds. But we read narratives differently than we read analytical thought experiments. Perhaps Pinker's idea of literature as a chess library, storing shelfloads of practical and specific "game plans," is not the most helpful, after all. Shipwrecked on a desert island with a caveload of tools and some goats, you may indeed know what to do because you've read your *Robinson Crusoe*. But that's not all we get from stories.

Oftentimes literature transmits a more holistic sense of the world and the individual. In the case of *Robinson Crusoe*, Defoe's thought experiment in enforced isolation may have less to do with how to build a fire or fashion a garment out of goatskins. His principal subjects of investigation may have been more diffuse: "struggling in isolation, coping with the physical environment, being absorbed in building and managing of one's life, coming to terms with God, making intimate friends."[53] But even this is not the whole story of how we learn from the thought experiments that infuse our narratives. For this we need to open a new chapter.

4 Literature and thought experiments

Though it tells us things differently from the way they are, as if it were lying, it actually obliges up to examine them more closely, and it makes us say: Ah, this is just how things are, and I didn't know it.

Umberto Eco, *The Name of the Rose*

Thought Experiment: Imagine that you are a member of a tour visiting Greece. The group goes to the Parthenon. It is a bore. Few people even bother to look – it looked better in the brochure. So people take half a look, mostly take pictures, remark on the serious erosion by acid rain. You are puzzled. Why should one of the glories and fonts of Western civilization, viewed under pleasant conditions – good weather, good hotel room, good food, good guide – be a bore?

Now imagine under what set of circumstances a viewing of the Parthenon would not be a bore. For example, you are a NATO colonel defending Greece against a Soviet assault. You are in a bunker in downtown Athens, binoculars propped on sandbags. It is dawn. A medium-range missile attack is under way. Half a million Greeks are dead. Two missiles bracket the Parthenon. The next will surely be a hit. Between columns of smoke, a ray of golden light catches the portico.

Are you bored? Can you see the Parthenon?

Explain.[1]

Littered with scores of other thought experiments, *Lost in the Cosmos* is a useful benchmark against which to stack up counterfactuals in fiction. Extrapolating from Percy's book, literary thought experiments are acts of imagination that manipulate variables (e.g. by redirecting point of view) to alter the scenario's outcome. His first tourist group is the control group, calibrating the blasé baseline of contemporary consumers. The second is the response group, for which the dramatic variation of the experimental frame precipitates a dramatic variation in the experiential result.

Harnessing folk psychology, travel accounts, tests in reduced environmental stimuli (sensory deprivation), and whatnot, the writer illuminates existential and emotional facets of experience through the phenomenology of peril.

While serviceable, the above classification is quite nebulous. Trying to increase the analytic resolution, however, we run into problems. The thicket of definitions on record indicates that, while researchers have a good grasp of *Gedankenexperimente*, it hardly translates into taxonomic clarity or unity. James R. Brown touches a nerve when he writes: "Thought experiments are performed in the laboratory of the mind. Beyond that metaphor it's hard to say just what they are."[2] Where experts have toiled to no avail, it seems prudent to proceed via *via negativa*, instead of pushing another capsule definition. Although philosophers of science are far from reaching a consensus, there is no reason why philosophers of literature may not move forward by vectoring the latter's tugs of war. For even as any one definition fails to score a homer, collectively they put us in the right ballpark.

A general idea is that a thought experiment is a species of reasoning in the form of a hypothetical or counterfactual state of affairs, designed to draw inferences about the world.[3] The idea is adequate on the first pass, but less so on the second. "If it rains tomorrow, I'll need an umbrella" is a species of hypothetical reasoning that draws inferences about the world, but hardly a thought experiment. For starters, it exhibits no control over variables, on top of not even being inquiry directed. Still, even this general idea homes in on the core of armchair investigations: reasoning as opposed to physical testing, and "what if" possibility as opposed to actuality.

Among philosophers the leading approach is that a thought experiment is an experiment – albeit one conducted in mind.[4] Critics retort that, linguistics apart, tests are *not* conducted in mind but in the world. What takes place in mind is only thought, threatening the definition with vacuity and tautology. Other philosophers take a thought experiment to be "a process of reasoning carried out within the context of a well-articulated imaginary scenario in order to answer a specific question about a non-imaginary situation." This definition underscores the rational exertions attendant on tracking armchair inquiries. But must all germane settings be non-imaginary? In the form of a hypothetical ("What would happen if there was sentient life on Mars?"), a thought experiment can as easily direct research to an *imaginary* situation.

The "hypothetical exercise which is impossible to carry out or test in reality" fares no better.[5] Many thought experiments can be – and have been – carried out in reality. Dropping a feather and a hammer in the lunar vacuum, the crew of *Apollo 15* proved Galileo's seminal thought experiment right as both floated to the ground at the same rate. On another definition, armchair inquiry is "a process of hypothetical reasoning that proceeds by eliciting the consequences of an hypothesis," with the proviso that it "consists in reasoning from a supposition that is not accepted as true." This is not bad, although too broad. A detective's chain of reasoning, beginning with "Suppose the butler did it . . . ," may be a hypothetical but not quite a thought experiment.

Restricted to physics – though extensible to other fields – another tack defines a thought experiment as "a description of an experimental procedure as well as its outcome or possible outcomes." The latter "must be deduced by reasoning consistent with a given theoretical framework."[6] Here critics would quibble that thought experiments in ethics and aesthetics hardly ever supply descriptions of experimental procedures. However, interpreting the latter loosely, for example as a series of explicit narrative premises adopted for the thought-experimental framework, defuses the tension. Otherwise, the definition neatly implies the manipulation of variables within the field-specific inquiry. Indeed, synthesizers of empiricist and rationalist approaches to experiments in the mind assert that the latter "*are* indeed experiments, since our mind actively manipulates the circumstances and preparatory conditions for them."

On another bipartite definition, thought experiments are "arguments concerning particular events or states of affairs of a hypothetical (and often counterfactual) nature which lead to conclusions about the nature of the world." They "stand in a privileged relationship both to past empirical observations and to some reasonably well-developed background theory."[7] First, it is doubtful that all thought experiments are just arguments (see pp. 101–2). It is also doubtful that they all flow from past empirical observations – at least taken literally. Galileo's could not have, since vacuum does not occur naturally on earth. As a matter of fact, it is not Galileo's but Aristotle's theory of motion ("all bodies seek rest") that appears confirmed by daily experience and observation. And yet the Pisan was so certain of his theory that he was willing to disregard observational data if it pointed otherwise.

What about mind experiments fitting into a reasonably well-developed background theory? Broadly speaking, this is correct, if only because *all* data are meaningful solely in the context of some theory. Clearly not all hypothetical or counterfactual thinking is a thought experiment, or else daydreamers or plotting kidnappers would qualify. On the other hand, when the teenage Einstein sprinted in his mind to the front of a light wave, he did so without the aid of a "well-developed background theory" of special relativity. His mentations were carried out within the framework of Maxwell's equations for electromagnetic radiation, which his very thought experiment showed to be inadequate. At the very least, then, we need to be told *which* background theory counts.

Another reservation about "background theory" is that it disqualifies literary fictions widely mined for thought experiments. Such is the case with Styron's *Sophie's Choice*, by now the subject of a multitude of philosophical disquisitions, all part of the modern analytic canon. Skeptics scornful of armchair experiments in ethics and aesthetics will insist that this is right. Most narratives, they will point out, do not operate from the premises of a well-developed theory about the depicted events (although, as we witnessed in Chapter 1, some do). In the end, which conceptual train you'll ride on depends on which taxonomic ticket you buy.

On a more pragmatic definition, a thought experiment is a pursuit whose object is "the external world and thinking is the *method* of learning something about it."[8] This functional approach brings out the methodical, systematic way in which we move about the laboratory of the mind. But not all systematic thinking cuts the cake. A basketball coach timetabling a training regime for his team and, in the process, working out the expected performance peaks is still not a mind experimenter. The ante is upped for literary thought experiments as well. Not all narratives are thought experiments, even though all are embodied (in words, pictograms, gestures) acts of imagination aimed at the world. To qualify, stories require the isolation and tweaking of pertinent variables – of which Percy provides such a colorful example.[9]

Crucially then, the job of the literary inquirer is not merely imaginative but manipulative. Mach stresses this point in the context of another narrative, Lucian's *True History*. He notes approvingly the care with which the Roman author controlled his fantasy in order to satisfy his aesthetic and satirical ends: "It is this rejection of what is unsuitable that distinguishes the play of ideas, however free, in a literary or other work of art, from the aimless abandon of one's ideas."[10] This fits with Mach's general argument that "solving verbal or other puzzles, geometrical or construction tasks, scientific problems or the execution of an artistic design, and so on, involves a movement of ideas with a definite goal and purpose." And the backbone of the cognitive homology in the movements of ideas in literature, philosophy and science is thought experiment.

Pure logical thinking cannot yield us any knowledge of the empirical world. [p. 171]
Pure thought can grasp reality. [p. 274]

Albert Einstein, *Ideas and Opinions*

In the arsenal of research techniques, armchair experiment occupies a distinguished place. But its knack for spinning hypotheses and weeding out false inferences has not silenced all critics. Einstein's ambivalence, conspicuous in the epigraph above, reflects the suspicion of thought experiments in some circles. The suspicion escalates to outright unease as claims on their behalf climb from the context of discovery to justification. Variations of this unease are, in turn, recognizable in cognitive broadsides leveled at literature, ironically pointing toward a common methodological core. For if fiction is prone to the same charges as philosophy, it must perforce be guilty of a kindred kind of malpractice.

The ensuing précis of the central questions that stalk thought experiments does not pretend to exhaust, far less rebut, them in full. The recent eruption of the literature on the subject guarantees that the task would consume a full-scale treatise. Hemmed in by demands of space, I thus confine myself to pointing out directions which such rebuttals could take, in most cases hitching a ride on the shoulders of philosophers in the field. Needless to say, I do not subscribe to whole-hog dismissals of armchair inquiry. But as the next section makes clear, I have much sympathy with corrective critiques directed as specific areas, uses, and techniques of thought experiments.

Q: Echoing the dilemma of informativeness, Pierre Duhem and others complain that real experiments to check on thought experiments are not always possible.[11] Ironically, while rebutting Duhem, Brown skirts the same position, arguing that "a genuine thought experiment usually cannot be performed, in principle."

A: Usually impossible means that it's sometimes possible, taking the bite out of the distinction. Also, does the impossibility of cross-checks apply to the time of the formulation or in principle forever? Brown counts Galileo's thought experiments on the theory of motion as *bona fide* even though they were performed on the Moon in 1971. Besides, some armchair inquiries do lend themselves to cross-checks, even if only indirectly, for example by testing auxiliary hypotheses. Einstein's mind-race with light is one such example. It led to special relativity, which led to the empirical confirmation of the sun's gravitational "bending" of starlight.

At the end of the day, duplication is not redundancy and two experiments are usually better than one. As Quine argued in *Quiddities*, double-checking is our insurance policy on the way to getting things right – and making them stay right. When Galileo refined the idea of a controlled experiment, he may have had physical setups in mind, but the fact is that the most controlled experiment is one conducted in mind. Provided all premises are valid and all steps logically correct, the results have to be true. There is no room for observer error, faulty equipment, or other malfunctions that plague real-life men and machines.

Even though armchair investigations are typically subordinate to real experiments, simplicity and visualization can suffice to establish a proposition and/or offer a solution. Far from redundant, some thought experiments can, in fact, be so compelling that a clash with concrete experiments may only be to the detriment to the latter. To be sure, their interpretation always entails background theories and presuppositions. For this reason, indiscriminate background-trimming can be harmful when the leftovers insufficiently frame the problem. But lobbing off *excess* theoretical baggage is a priceless technique for subduing the complexity of Nature.

Solve on paper the logistics of ferrying three cannibals and three missionaries (in the canonical 1651 *Thaumaturgus mathematicus*, masters and slaves) across a river in a pirogue built for two. Remember: if the flesh-eaters outnumber the padres on either bank, the latter are stew. First of all, two cannibals go across, one comes back. Then two cannibals go across, one comes back. Two missionaries go across, one cannibal and one missionary come back. Last, two missionaries go across, one cannibal comes back and brings the remaining two cannibals in two trips. Now you can save yourself the expense of running the experiment. And if a real-life test yields less than the expected number of padres you will not conclude that your flowchart was erroneous, but that a fatal slip-up by the controller has occurred.

Q: John Norton (among others) holds that armchair experiments can be completely eliminated. This is because whatever value they have stems from rational argumentation, independent of the heuristic (narrative, metaphorical) particulars employed to flesh it out. Recasting thought experiments in the form of explicit premises and derivations should justify all of their conclusions, pulling the rug from under hypothetical scenario-weaving. Armchair inquiry is a crutch, needed only until you learn to walk right.

Although cast in a different form, this is dilemma of informativeness all over again. If *Gedankenexperimente* do not introduce new data, knowledge can come only from the data in hand, say the eliminators. Since the latter is said to be analyzable only in the form of an argument, cognitively speaking thought experiments are nothing but dressed-up arguments. The alternative, frowns Norton, is "to suppose that thought experiments provide some new and even mysterious route to knowledge of the physical world."[12]

A: As we know from Chapter 3, the evolutionary-adaptive route to knowledge of the physical world is neither new nor mysterious. A pragmatist will also argue that the heuristic component *is*, in fact, indispensable. If it wasn't, it would have been dispensed with centuries ago. Moreover, one and the same thought experiment can be – and has been – reconstructed as two distinct arguments, refuting the putative equivalence.[13] (Surprisingly, no defender of the one-on-one mapping of thought experiments onto arguments has argued that where there are two arguments there are also two thought experiments rolled up into a single scenario.)

The fact that good thought experiments are good arguments does not establish that that's *all* they are. Necessity does not follow from sufficiency. Preteen hot-rodders, having disassembled their bicycles, are sometimes left with parts which do not fit anywhere. The bike may still get you to school, but is it the same bike if it's missing all gears but one? Likewise, the left-overs from disassembling thought experiments into syllogisms might be just what is needed to achieve the desired degree of efficacy. In contrast to bone-dry analytic arguments, story-like aspects of armchair tests often activate relevant background and knowledge. The mental topology of thought experiments and arguments is not self-evidently the same.

Q: Echoing the dilemma of induction, Alfred Bloom and others believe that our beliefs determine what we direct our thoughts to, and thus what we find imaginable. Thought experiments are thus circular: they reveal what we already believe, not the nature of reality. In support, Bloom cites his study on story analysis by Chinese and American students. The target was the handling of the subjunctive – the ability to linguistically process "what if" situations. Chinese speakers apparently lack grammatical tools to reflect counterfactuals such as "If John had gone to the hospital he would have met Mary." Instead, the thought is expressed circuitously: "If John is going to the hospital . . . but he is not going to the hospital . . . but if he is going, he meets Mary."[14]

The score? US 98: China 7, in percentages of getting answers to hypotheticals about the story right. The putative conclusion? Their language stands between Chinese speakers and their ability to deal with possible worlds and, by extension, thought experiments. The inference? Language determines thought; hence mind experiments inform us of our linguistic abilities and not of the nature of reality. Slam dunk?

A: Not quite. No sooner published, Bloom's test became subject to a hail of critiques which identified critical drawbacks in the design.[15] Redesigned and retested, the disparity disappeared without a trace, turning the witness for the prosecution into a witness for the defense. In general, the Sapir–Whorf thesis ("language determines our view of the world") that stands behind Bloom's study is now under siege even among linguists.

Q: Thomas Kuhn concedes that thought experiments can correct the conceptual mistakes of a scientist. But, compelled by the paradigm-shifting paradigm from *The Structure of Scientific Revolutions*, he denies them the power to reveal new things about the world (this is yet another variant on the dilemma of informativeness). Armchair ratiocinations are just new ways of seeing the old across incommensurable paradigms.

A: There are stand-alone experiments in the mind, such as Stevinus's inclined plane, that are not aimed at finding faults in old theories. There are others, adds Brown, "where the incommensurability problem does not enter the picture (Galileo's falling bodies)."[16] There is mathematics, so fertile in modeling the world that the latter is by now assumed to be mathematical in structure. This puzzles many physicists and mathematicians to no end, since, literally speaking, math is a tautology, roughly along the lines of a thought experiment. Theorems are, after all, no more than logical derivations already implicit in the axioms and transformation rules.

As nothing new goes in at one end, nothing new should come out at the other. Yet the results of such tautological operations not only are new, but closely correspond to the world. Mathematics – a non-experimental pursuit not aimed at detecting faults in old theories – aids in learning about the world *and* attenuates observer error.

Q: George Bealer and others decry the extension of the concept to philosophy and beyond, and the consequent blurring of traditional terminology. "Thought experiment" must not be used to describe what people on the periphery of science do, for example teasing out rational intuitions about hypothetical cases. It ought to be restricted to physics,

> [where] one usually elicits a physical intuition (not a rational intuition) about what would happen in a hypothetical situation in which physical, or natural, laws (whatever they happen to be) are held constant but physical conditions are in various other respects nonfactual and often highly idealized.[17]

A: Again, "usually" implies exceptions, undermining the rule. This is not to paper over differences between scientists and scholars in the "softer" fields. Scientific – even physical – mind experiments traditionally lie at the core of the concept. But traditions can ossify and cease to reflect reality. Fiats that thought experiments take place only in physics might appeal to cognitive fundamentalists but not to researchers too busy doing them to care. Armchair inquiry is a stock in trade of all academics, as testimonials from Counterfactualists Anonymous make plain (see Chapter 3). For the sake of terminology one could, of course, pin a different label on what humanists do. But given that they use the same tool to dig for knowledge, we might as well call a spade a spade.

One thought-murder a day keeps the psychiatrist away.

Saul Bellow, *Herzog*

The conceptual and methodological pitfalls to which thought experiments in aesthetic and ethics are susceptible may owe to the scale of their evolutionary time-frame. There was much less time to develop intuitions about art and morality as opposed to intuitions about physical space, time, and elementary concepts such as cause and effect or bivalence. Still, recent work on altruistic genes in ethics and on symmetry detection in aesthetics intimates that the fault may lie not so much with our faculties, but with the lack of subtlety in accounting for how they work. Indeed, a closer look at thought experiments in the humanities – including ethics, aesthetics, and, not least, narrative practice and theory – suggests that the devil is not always as black as it's painted.

Q: Dennett identifies a bias against complexity, wherein philosophical vignettes work less like rational suasions and more like "intuition pumps."[18] They draw attention to our pretheoretic intuitions and away from hard-to-follow details, often at the cost of complexity and validity of inference. Simple yet colorful, they demand to be swallowed in one gulp, where a wise parent would advise a more careful chewing.

A: Dennett himself balances the picture: philosophy with intuition pumps may not be science, but it's "a valuable – even occasionally necessary – companion to science."[19] Not all arguments persuade by tapping into intuitions, either. Some, like the winning play in tic-tac-toe, are demonstrably rational, since algorithmic. To be sure, psychological and game-theoretic research, notably by Kahneman and Tversky, documents that people are neither wholly rational nor optimal calculators (as we'll see again in Chapter 5).[20] *Errare humanum est*, and cognitive bias toward simplification inheres in our bounded rationality – bounded by proneness to comprehension, comparison, memory, and processing errors. But in this respect knowledge-hunters in the humanities are like those in the sciences: fallible but corrigible.

Armchair inquirers typically draw on a host of unarticulated auxiliary premises. In the physical sciences Nature can often be relied on to fill in the background. But in ethics and aesthetics, in the interest of economy and rhetorical impetus, many forgo bringing auxiliary premises to the fore. Thought experiments, however, should perform better in concrete, real-life settings. Here literary fictions are ahead of the game, fleshing out their backgrounds to a much greater extent than analytic philosophy. *Belles lettres* may be ultimate intuition pumps by virtue of being vivid and picturable. Yet they owe this intuitive appeal to narrative detail and complexification, the very virtues armchair thinkers in the humanities ought to strive for.

Q: Conceding their heuristic attractiveness, Hempel argues: "intuitive experiments-in-imagination are no substitute for the collection of empirical data by actual experiment."[21] Undeniably useful for illustration, thought experiments are therefore eliminable as far as justification goes. They are simply not rational and evidence-forming enough.

A: Brown's "tiling theorem" in *The Laboratory of the Mind*, not to mention Galileo's discourse on falling bodies, demonstrates that in some cases a thought experiment suffices as evidence for empiricist reconstruction. Note that Hempel does not object to armchair inquiry *en masse*, only to asking too much of it (i.e. providing justification). Even if the future tide of opinion were to swing to his side, it would in no way mandate against humanists performing experiments-in-imagination. The question is only how much can reasonably be expected of such experiments.

Q: Applied moral philosophers, echoed by Marxists in literary studies, point to a bias towards the search for transcendent universals at the expense of concrete, "applied" specifics. As a result, thought experiments are often less than conclusive, and thus less than useful, in resolving the dilemmas they're marshaled for. The upshot of such unfettered counterfactual fancy is escapist and hyper-specialized (science) fiction, often marred by excessive jargon.

A: The point about specialization and jargon is common to all inquiry, including the sciences. The point about escapism is betrayed by selection bias. Many thought experiments in the humanities apply to concrete issues, from abortion to social contracts, and not all seek universal, value-free knowledge. Still, literature's attention to situational detail could become a model for ethics, in which conclusions are often derived from underdeveloped examples by a leap of faith that entails any number of unstated assumptions.

Q: A steady diet of bizarre cases warps our good/common sense. In 1979 Brian Barry remonstrated against the "one-sided diet of desert-island examples" in social and political philosophy.[22] In 1988 Katherine Wilkes made the same point for ethics in *Real People*. In 2001 I argued in "Interpreting Art, Interpreting Literature" that indiscriminate use of far-out Twin-Earth scenarios in aesthetics detracts from their plausibility and relevance.

A: As implied by the critiques, such shortcomings are identifiable and corrigible. Not all thought experimenters are guilty as charged, either. With regard to moral truths, Jonathan Dancy insists that an imaginary action can be framed persuasively enough to be judged as good:

> And that judgment of mine is as much universalizable, as binding on my future judgments about relevantly similar cases, as if the example had been real rather than imaginary. So imaginary cases are as effective in the argument as actual ones.[23]

But even far-out inquiries may have their role to play. When alternatives blend, the need to shake out the difference – e.g. before a policy vote – may justify an esoteric scenario that drives a wedge between them. It is thus methodologically wrong, argues Amartya Sen, "to ignore the relevance of our intuitions regarding rather unusual examples which are brought for this reason into moral arguments."

Q: Since language evolved around medium-range, familiar things like asses, torts, and falling apples, and since mind experiments rely ultimately on linguistic analysis, they will fail outside medium-range, familiar phenomena. Alisa Bokulich raises this query to the status of a fundamental difficulty for the evolutionary account. Modern theoretical physics, an area far removed from intuitive notions of space, time and matter, is strikingly successful in the application of thought experiments. If you believe neo-Darwinists, it should be anything but.

A: Physicists unaided by formalism and mathematized theory are also prone to error in judging abstract thought experiments. Bokulich herself remarks on the counterintuitive results of "The Rockets and Thread" thought experiment in which the majority of theoretical physicists at the world-famous CERN research lab initially gave the wrong answer.[24] There is really nothing odd about mind experiments working so well in theoretical physics. The further the mind strays from folk physics, the more it has to lean on formalism and theory.

Human conceptual apparatus has evolved over many millions of years in environments of evolutionary adaptedness.[25] In the process it adapted to *their* character and equipped humans with analytic skills geared to survival in *their* conditions. The ability to apprehend quantum physics and *n*-dimensional vector spaces may, indeed, seem like an extravagant largesse from normally stinting Nature. But no one understands these concepts the same way that one understands going hungry, breaking a limb, or being cheated.

This may be better grasped by contrasting rudimentary arithmetic, which has been around for tens of thousand of years, and the theory of probability, less than four centuries old. On the evolutionary account, people should fare better when faced with natural frequencies than with percentages and the entire apparatus of the probability calculus. As if on cue, research confirms (see pp. 114–15) that we deal expertly – even if not always flawlessly – with the former, but not the latter. In sum, the lesson about indiscriminately taking the mind-lab outside medium-size and familiar-type phenomena is well taken. But, *mutans mutandis*, it actually bolsters its efficacy quotient when applied *to* such phenomena.

Q: Looking inside for answers has a venerable scholastic, and then rationalist, tradition. Yet from Auguste Comte on, introspection has come under attack as a legitimate manner of getting data about the world, inner or outer.[26] Also, even if well executed, introspection may not carry us far if people's modular faculties are informationally restricted (encapsulated).

Some things in our minds could be buried so deep or compartmentalized so strictly that, like the Minoan labyrinth, they might not be penetrable to the self-investigator.

A: In *Thought Experiments* Sorensen shows that thought experiments need not involve introspection. He also points out that, historically, thought experiments preceded the concept of introspection in psychology. To be sure, concept only partly implicates usage – you can introspect without recognizing it as such by name. Still, Piaget's studies suggest that children develop a grasp of counterfactuals before introspection. Finally, in linguistics, Sarah G. Thomason provides an elegant answer to the question of why mind experiments need not be condemned as introspection. Her point that "(unlike most scientists' data), our primary data, and therefore the evidence for our theories, is inside people's heads" erases the stigma from looking inward in search of knowledge.[27]

Though the analogy with literature is apparent, it shouldn't be carried too far. The preloaded and developed linguistic structures of competent language users and the freewheeling linguistic structures of fiction writers are far from the same thing. Even though at a minimum stories are semantic and syntactic constructs, they are much more than instances of correct (or not) language use. That's why, preparing for *God's Grace*, Malamud spent a year studying evolution and anthropology at Stanford's Center for Advanced Study in the Behavioral Sciences, even though his language skills left nothing to be desired.

But that does not mean that the analogy isn't there at all. Sums up Thomason: "When linguists want to test hypotheses about the structure of a particular language, their methodology crucially involves thought experiments in a . . . literal sense: real experiments carried out in thinking."[28]

My method, to be exhibited presently in action, takes science very seriously but its tactics more closely resemble those of art.

Daniel Dennett, *Elbow Room*

New questions about thought experiments will no doubt sprout along the way alongside advances in knowledge. But all, I venture, will be surmounted by the evolutionary-adaptive account of the laboratory of the mind. That account itself will no doubt continue to evolve. But even if it ends up looking different than it does today, it will continue to underwrite the conditional power and reliability of armchair inquiry – conditional because inferential thinking will spit out true results only *if* the variables and derivations are true.

But what exactly counts as true? The question gathers urgency as we move away from the physical sciences to the biological and social sciences.

It becomes even more imperative as we pass to philosophy and *belles lettres*, all the way down to picturing in the mind's eye, daydreaming, building castles in the air, and what Mach called spontaneous hallucination. All exercise the imagination, but not all are thought experiments, because not all exercise control over the inferential process. But what counts as control?

The following five criteria help thrash out less rigorously constructed scenarios. This cognitive 'gin is, naturally, not the last word on the subject but an act of normative arson, intended to ignite debate on what is and isn't a thought experiment in art.[29] Writers are free to write as they please – though most adhere to precepts one and two (the internal ones). But, like thinking, not all writing is equal. Separating the class of narratives that deals in thought experiments from literary fictions in general is only the first step on the way to assaying their cognitive purity:

1   Clarity: Ideally, thought experiments in literature should pinpoint the independent and dependent variables – typically the antecedent and consequent actions, and causes of actions. Even as stories unfold in a dense fabric rather than isolated woof or warp of psychosocial motive, they frequently isolate proximate causes in order to minimize the causal "ripple effect." Economy and clarity of design are, after all, why writers write stories and don't run experiments in the first place. The best plots will follow alternative routes down decision trees, manipulating one factor/cause at a time, as Lem does in "*De Impossibilitate Vitae* and *De Impossibilitate Prognnoscendi*."

2   Coherence: Logical, physical/empirical, and psychosocial relations should be compatible with one another (cotenable). Anachronistic, incomplete, or ill-derived thinking ought to be exiled. This injunction is observed by most writers instinctively, and its violations are at least on occasion deliberate. Recall the part of the modeling schema in Chapter 2 that dwelled on grotesque, satire, fantasy, or time-travel, and the sundry ways in which liberties with logic and science can earn cognitive payoff.[30]

3   Relevance: A narrative identifiable with a possible world closest to reality will be most directly transferable and applicable. Hence, for all relevant scenarios and thought experiments, the least extravagant ones are preferable from the cognitive standpoint – which may, naturally, fail to coincide with the artistic. This "minimal-rewrite" rule informs countless Twin-Earth scenarios spun by philosophers and writers. The modeling classification from Chapter 2 helps detect the degree to which novels and even entire genres rewrite ground-zero rules.

4   Informativeness: Not to reinvent the wheel or design a crooked one, scenarios ought to be informed by the methodological principles and

state-of-the-art findings in germane disciplines. Unlike scientists and philosophers, writers do not have logical-empirical inspectors breathing down their neck. Novels are not, after all, position papers or even necessarily coherent sets of theses about reality. But the pseudo-science that bedeviled Zola's program of *littérature scientifique*, or the corrupt Social Darwinism of Spencer and Galton that lay behind much of *fin-de-siècle* naturalism, demonstrates where things can go wrong.[31]

5   Projectability: In the most ambitious cases writers may tease out the testable consequences of their thought experiments in search of contingent generalizations, latent implications, and even occasional gaps in extant theories. This task may be taken up by literary critics and theorists in order to advance disciplinary and – as elaborated in Chapter 1 – interdisciplinary goals.

That said, few narrative theses could be verified in a controlled setting. Unless future research in artificial intelligence, artificial life, and artificial emotion can model inner lives and social intercourse by means of computer "personoids," most literary thought experiments could hardly be subjected to test runs.[32] If we are prepared to argue for the validity of thought experiments in literature, we must thus be prepared to argue against the *necessity* of their experimental confirmation. This may go against the grain of some critiques of armchair ratiocination. But take heart from Salvati, Galileo's spokesman in *Dialogues*: "Without experiment I am sure that the effect will happen as I tell you, because it must happen that way."[33]

Let us take this a little further. Using Euclid's axiomatic method, by recombining a handful of mental Lego blocks one can spin systems (including mathematics) of unbelievable complexity. The results of such operations are in one sense trivial, insofar as they spring from the original axioms. But in the sense important to us they are anything but. The impli-cations of logical proofs, for instance, are seldom known in advance and often counterintuitive, even as they demonstrably expand our conceptual and instrumental range. So it is in narrative composition. Writers set up the starting parameters – for example endowing characters with certain attributes – and then struggle to make explicit what is already in a sense written into the tale. And if the analogy is correct, it's no wonder that they so often marvel at the unpredictable behavior of their creations.

From a skeptic's trench, this may be stretching the analogy to the point of snapping. But when it comes to *Gedankenexperimente*, it is sometimes hard to say where epistemology ends and psychology begins. This is because, on closer analysis, the cognitive machinery of prediction and explanation –

one aimed at the future, the other at the past – is not that different. This may seem counterintuitive, inasmuch as we value science precisely to the extent that it deals out predictions, in contrast to humanists' mere explanations. The subjective superiority stems from the feeling that explanations can be trivial, spurious, or circular, whereas predictions bequeath new and real knowledge that bequeaths new and real instrumental power.

Quite apart from the fact that predictions can also be trivial, spurious, or circular, this is confusion over the meaning of "new." The term can mean either "not known" – though already known in the sense of being implied by current knowledge (e.g. in mathematics) – or "not come to pass." But in either case there is a genuine sense of bettering the cognitive balance sheet, even if what we learn may be only *psychologically* new. Knowledge in fiction exemplifies the former meaning, even as science-fiction apologists plead its proficiency as a divining rod of the future. But that does not mean that literary cognition is only second best, or that good explanations are necessarily less precious than predictions.

At a minimum, a good nonarbitrary explanation is a good step towards induction and prediction, in the sense of Lévi-Strauss's dictum that "Darwin would not have been possible if he had not been preceded by Linnaeus."[34] It may be, therefore, that the glorification of empiricism in today's research hierarchy is partly misleading. If "empirical" means something like "experimental," there are forms of valuable research that fail to fall under that rubric. Euclid and Einstein were mere theorists, after all.

In contrast, if "empirical" means something like "steeped in the best scientific knowledge," then the Great Wall between theorists and empiricists crumbles, opening the door to scholars who, while mindful of science, are not experimentalists *per se*. The methodological tools of mainstream empirical psychology, for example, are at present inadequate to capture what is essential about the reading process, leaving the field open to literary critics. Moreover, much work in the social sciences consists not in gathering but in manipulating data, often by dint of armchair experiments. And in this econometrists, anthropologists, and sociologists are not that different from litterateurs.

> *When to the sessions of sweet silent thought*
> *I summon up remembrance of things past.*
>   William Shakespeare, "Sonnet XXX"

It's time to get into the psychological nuts and bolts of narratives as thought experiments. In the rationalist tradition, logic and formal analysis have long been the class achievers while storytelling played the role of an enlightening but remedial diversion. But no longer. Research into cognitive processing upturns the received wisdom on the subject. It turns out that inferences derived from constructing and manipulating mental models have often less to do with formal analysis than with narrative framing. Not only do we remember stories better than theorems, but we tend to think *in* stories, not theorems.

Nancy Nersessian, who did more work on the emergent paradigm than most, spells it out in "In the Theoretician's Laboratory." People typically process contextual information by falling back on narrative patterns "rather than by applying rules of inference to a system of propositions representing the content of the text."[35] In *The Literary Mind* Mark Turner pulls, if anything, even fewer punches. Linguistically speaking, story-like thinking, metaphorical projection, and parable precede the advent of grammar. "Parable," in short, "is the root of human thinking."

But what kind of data-tweaking fuels literary knowledge? What do the mechanisms by which mental gymnastics effect a cognitive gain look like from a storytelling standpoint? In short, where does knowledge in narrative thought experiments come from? Although geared to philosophers of science and philosophically inclined scientists, the five cognitive mechanisms outlined in *Thought Experiments* go a long way towards an answer.[36] In what follows I revisit Sorensen's quintet with a literary-critical audience in mind, sketching their narrative, aesthetic, and pragmatic analogues. I thus approach literary thought experiments as instances of mental Recollection, Rearrangement, Transformation, Homuncular system, and Cleansing, and as potentially useful tools for refining these models.

Given the lineage that extends to Plato and his Socratic dialogues, let's begin with the doctrine of Recollection. As every folk psychologist knows, most people recollect natural language better than strings of digits. Bitwise, on the keypad 843–2378 is equal to "THE BEST," yet spammers and advertisers exploit the fact that the slogan will be recollected long after the number has vanished from memory. Founded by Simonides of Keos, the ancient school of mnemonics sprang up, in fact, to aid in recollecting data that might otherwise leak from our heads like a wicker basket leaks water. Even the best thinkers, after all, are prone to memory lapses. But when they recollect, they suddenly have *more* information at hand.[37]

In Chapter 2 we ran into sorites, a chain of interlocking syllogisms wherein the predicate of one becomes the subject of the next. The chain can be long, so long that it can make your eyes sore – so you end up with "sore-eyetis." Taught in this way to people with zero interest in logic or Latinate terminology, the pronunciation and meaning fixate (transfer from short-term to long-term memory) much more easily.[38] Evidence from neuroscience and psychology corroborates that humans are disposed towards human-interest information, not abstractions and numbers. In cognitive science the fledgling research in artificial emotion follows the recognition of the hitherto neglected emotive component of recollection. At a minimum, emotions are lasers that etch data deeper into the tissue of memory.

Can recollection be explained in terms of memetics, whereby the fittest meme burrows in the mind, reprogramming it to become its advertising agent? Perhaps, especially if most memorable – which for Darwin meant shortest and easiest – includes most resonant emotionally. Anthropological data indicate, in fact, that, on top of being efficient information conveyers, stories outclass rivals in facilitating information storage. Their role in human subsistence is studied in Michelle Sugiyama's "Food, Foragers, and Folklore," which tracks how the practical information about consumable resources is disseminated in the stories of foraging tribes. Strung into a narrative, data about plants and animals are recollected more vividly than informationally equivalent but disjointed series of data-points.

Because stories are remembered better and longer, story-like thought experiments should outperform others in retaining, indexing, and retrieving knowledge. Contextualizing information, the narrative form fosters good memory and good recollection – first steps toward good thinking. Indeed, most preliterate societies employed their own Johnny Mnemonics: professional memorizers charged with storing prodigious amounts of data in mind. Oftentimes such data would become organized by bards into verse, as in the notable case of Mohammed's *Qur'an*.

Medieval troubadours were thus apt to recite *chansons* of credulity-defying length thanks to the latter's high mnemonic quotient. Human-indexed relations between narrative agents and events helped them memorize and then reproduce massive amounts of information. Evolutionary predisposition to symmetry further aids in grouping and organizing diffuse facts. Repetition – whether in the form of a rhyme scheme, alliteration, refrain, chorus, allusion, periphrasis, or any other – is none other than a form of translational symmetry. Its mnemonic quotient, detectable in the propensity to recollect, is even higher for verse than for narrative prose, while both are vastly superior to digits or nonsense syllables.[39]

Since raw experience supplies an undetermined (or underdetermined) picture of the world, the recollecting thinker needs a mill to refine coarse experiential grain into flour. "We achieve this by varying the facts in thought," prompts Mach in *Knowledge and Error*.[40] The twin keys to success in this respect are mental husbandry and a Greenpeace ethic. Thought experiments enrich the thinker by amassing and storing atoms of experience, and then recycling the content of memory. Like a nugget which acquires sparkle from being polished and fitted, the recollected data is mentally polished and fitted into new contextual frames. The cognitive value of these mental gems rises.

Literature works in an analogous way. Recollection in tranquility was, after all, the rallying cry of generations of Romantics who set their azimuth on the Preface to *Lyrical Ballads*. By recollecting and refitting events and characters into new narrative frames, subtly or not so subtly different from the ones in which they had prefigured, writers offer insights into the nature of these narrative building blocks, and through them the world. Data redux, in other words, are useful, but data redux-plus are more useful still. Wordsworth's advice is not just to re*collect* but to re*frame* old experiences in light of the new – typically in light of new knowledge.

Even when facts don't change, they may reveal their full meaning when re-examined in pensive tranquility. Like hypertext, recollected data can encompass substrata of information accessible to a well-placed mental cursor. *Romans à clef*, for example, are contrived to jog memory so that readers can recollect public events and identify flesh-and-blood prototypes in the dramatis personae. Following the complex detail of a novel-size thought experiment and ferreting out its implications calls, of course, for an alert mind and a long attention span. Here, once again, recollection proves handy by redistributing mental assets over time. Notes Sorensen: "We can only attend to so much while perceiving. Our ability to replay old experiences lets us borrow attention from the future."[41]

A dramatic illustration of the power of recollection is Sidney Lumet's classic *Twelve Angry Men*. The twelve jurors acquit a man from the charge of murder when, among other things, they realize that the eye-witness's account is untrue. One of them recollects that the witness rubbed the bridge of his nose during testimony, a meaningless fact at the time. Later on, in the light of other discrepancies, the recollected gesture convinces the panel that the witness suffers from poor eyesight and could not have seen the accused. Thus in one sense the juror did have the requisite fact at his disposal. In the more important sense, however, he didn't – not until another juror's (Henry Fonda's) dogged questioning awakened his recollection.

The reprocessing of old experience can occur at the level of an entire plotline. Many literary works reframe archetypal scenarios in search of novel insights in novel contexts. Cain himself re-enacted the working-class love triangle from *The Postman Always Rings Twice* in a middle-class setting in *Double Indemnity* (and in *Serenade*). In cinema the very same scenario was reinterpreted by Pierre Chenal in *Le Dernier Tournant* (1939), Luchino Visconti in the unacknowledged *Ossessione* (1942), Tay Garnett in *The Postman Always Rings Twice* (1946), Bob Rafelson in the 1981 remake of Garnett, and Lawrence Kasdan in *Body Heat* (1981). In fact one interesting avenue for literary inquiry is to investigate different emotional, rhetorical, and aesthetic effects of scenarios based on the same narrative structure – or, if you will, gaming conflict.

Creativity, as has been said, consists largely of rearranging what we know in order to find out what we do not know.

George Kneller, *Art and Science of Creativity*

Rearrangement covers situations where, like Lumet's twelve angry jurors, we may both possess the required information and at the same time lack it. This time, however, the hitch is not in failing to recollect, but in failing to draw the necessary conclusions. The problem is widespread and widely acknowledged. As a rule, prompts psychologist James E. Alcock, people have "considerable difficulty organizing information into a format that is amenable to correlational inference."[42] They don't, if you like, think "scientifically."

To take the first example, uninstructed intuition is not at all reliable when it comes to estimating probabilities, judging the import of apparent coincidences, detecting principles of organization, and discerning the degree of randomness – or, what comes to the same thing, discerning the degree of patterning. The thinker may have all the ingredients in hand in the form of raw data but, because they are so chaotic, he may fail to grasp their significance. Failing to extract latent inferences, in the operational sense he thus does *not* have the information. Ordering or reordering the data, on the other hand, can render them user-friendly and tease out the solution.

On the Rearrangement model a (literary) thought experiment performs like the Newton handheld organizer was supposed to. Its operative function is task simplification – in other words, streamlining kludgy input for easy access. This function is made salient in "Ecological Intelligence," one of the most effective examinations of mental algorithms' fit with the theory of evolution. Its author, Gerd Gigerenzer, investigated how people handle data about frequencies of events. Broadly speaking, such data can be expressed in two informationally equivalent ways. *How* they are expressed, however, makes all the difference.

In the probability calculus (technically, Bayesian inferences), expected returns take the form of a probability function. In natural frequencies, on the other hand, they are expressed more intuitively as "one in x number of cases." From medical diagnoses and O. J. Simpson's murder trial, to AIDS counseling and expert-witness reliability in forensic cases, the researcher compared what happens when statistical information is rearranged into a more facile form. In each of the above cases frequencies of events were initially expressed in terms of the probability calculus. Disturbingly, few individuals, including trained professionals, could handle them with any degree of ease or success.

For most people, hacking through the formulae for base rates, hit rates, and false positive percentages proves a formidable obstacle. When rearranged into natural frequencies, however, that same information begins to "talk," resulting in a vastly superior performance. To put it plainly, people classify information and make predictions better when the information is put in plain language. In our case, the plain language is the language of natural sampling, whereby people update event frequencies (speeding fatalities, hits by falling apples, mishaps on Fridays the thirteenth, and such like) from experience.

Conversely, when data are *not* rearranged to facilitate comprehension, human processing capacities become stretched to the limit – and beyond. The best case in point is Alan Dershowitz, star lawyer advising the O. J. Simpson defense team. During the criminal trial, having manifestly misunderstood the statistical correlation between wife battering and wife murder, the legal expert dismissed it as negligible, on the order of 0.1 percent. Such a low probability might indeed lead one to conclude that the husband could hardly be the killer.

Rearranging the information makes the startling truth come to light. The likelihood of a wife beater being a wife killer is shockingly high – one in two. Expressed in natural frequencies, the reasoning is easy to follow. Of 10,000 battered women, on average one is killed by her husband every year. Among the remaining 9,999, one is murdered by someone other than a husband. Thus two women are likely to be killed every year, one of them by her spouse. This gives the probability of one in two, or 50 percent, that a battered, murdered wife has been killed by her husband (and not 0.001 percent as claimed by Dershhowitz).[43]

Rearranging statistical evidence from the laboratory, the clinic and the courtroom, Gigerenzer demonstrates time and again that "natural frequencies can make human minds smarter."[44] You can, indeed, get something out of nothing. This is because, when human minds come into play, information is not an independent quantity. Crucially, research shows, it depends on how it is represented. Our throughput channels are perforce limited, and any technique or trick that can simplify the problem is at a premium. Many of us grasp this instinctively, in many cases systematizing, schematizing, and standardizing information far beyond the requirement of logical satisfiability.

Well attuned to the power of literary rearrangement, in Part Two of the "Essay on Criticism" Alexander Pope enjoined his contemporaries to write "What oft was thought, but ne'er so well expressed." A rearrangement of old truths that rationalizes their meaning and facilitates their grasp can be as fruitful, the writer intimated, as original thought. Pope's adage itself was, of course, only well expressing what was oft thought – and done – by countless predecessors. For millennia before *The Dunciad*'s mock-allusions to Homer and Virgil, alluding to resonant motifs allowed writers to convey structural, emotional, or aesthetic information with a minimum of narrative outlay. The myths, archetypes, and public symbols in question were connotative shortcuts to shared literary knowledge.

> *We organize our experience and our memory of human happenings mainly in the form of a narrative.*
>
> Jerome Bruner, "The Narrative Construction of Reality"

Let us briefly review the narrative homologues of four methods of Rearrangement: shortcutting, chunking, deformation, and angle of entry. The essence of *shortcutting* is that, instead of wrestling with an intricate problem, you begin with a drastic simplification. Having vanquished the featherweight, you then upgrade the insights to the originally intractable task. Scaled-down models, in other words, are a good way to sink your teeth into a problem before reintroducing complexities shed during the cognitive shortcut. Dealing with a simplification of the more convoluted but analogous problem can help unravel the latter.

Another variety of cognitive shortcutting is stretching things to their limit. Instead of framing costly and time-consuming scenario forecasts, it pays to extrapolate their best or worst case in order to evaluate their consequences. Technology may, for example, create means of engineering violence out of human nature through a universally enforced medical procedure. Would such a somatic makeover be invariably beneficial? Instead of tracking intermediate social states, focus on the best-case scenario. If a model of humanity socially engineered to refrain from war and murder begins to behave like a dystopia, you have your answer.[45] Far from outmoded genre conventions, utopia and dystopia are thus indispensable cognitive shortcuts for literary thought-testing of boundary conditions of social policies.

The concept of *chunking* involves breaking a problem into smaller bites which can then be digested separately with greater ease. It rose to prominence in the 1960s and 1970s when Herbert Simon looked into simplifying decision-making in organizational routines, focusing on the compression or "chunking" of information. Information is not processed (short term) and retained (long term) in discrete entities but as psychologically meaningful chunks of input sequence. Those appear to comprise from five to seven elements, irrespective of whether they are numbers, phonemes, words, etc.[46] In the 1990s a greater appreciation of chunking even led to a revolution in bioinformatics and library science (search engines) and the rise of the science of data "usability."

Herding data together for easier access and associative retrieval has a straightforward equivalent in plot structuring. Chapter divisions or "threading" devices such as flashback or foreshadowing facilitate cognitive processing by chunking heterogeneous story material into coherent groupings. This is, of course, only the tip of the iceberg. Writing can be organized by meter, verse, sentence, stanza, paragraph, scene, episode, act, chapter, and even sequential instalments of entire books. Such a multivolume *opus* can even span half a century and more than fifty novels, as in the case of McBain's 87th Precinct.[47]

Chunking and cognate types of internal ordering are the drill sergeants of literature. They transform verbal chaos into organic, disciplined art. How central these integrated levels of organization are to grasping even the basic flow of thought becomes apparent when this invisible scaffold is removed. A textbook example is the "stream of consciousness," pioneered by Eduard Dujardin in the 1880s. Notwithstanding the high degree of control exercised in these verbal experiments and in subsequent editing, modernists who embraced it held that it approximated the natural flow of thought.

In contrast, most readers found this programmatically uninterrupted and undigested flow *un*natural, if not downright obscurantist. This is because chunking verbal diarrhea into discrete syntactic units boosts not only the narrative logic, but even such basic elements of story processing as the grasp of the story line. Significantly, the operative term here is not brute complexity but degree of organization. Highly digressive and thus immensely complex, the storylines of the *Arabian Nights* or *Childe Harold's Pilgrimage* are nonetheless immediately understandable – if not exactly easy to recollect.

The *deformation* strategy resembles shortcutting in that the cognitive boost also owes to the simplification of a problem. "Since much of explanation is a matter of reducing the strange to the familiar, a thought experiment can illuminate by systematically varying a plain phenomenon into one equivalent to the vexatious one," observes Sorensen.[48] The obvious advantage of the familiar is that it can be used as an intellectual cross-pollinator, or at the very least a memory flogger. Stuck with the new, fertilize fallow intellectual ground by falling back on the old. Confronted with Escher's *trompe l'oeil* staircase, deform it into the ascending and descending halves in order to understand the source of the illusion.

All literature, no matter how realistic, deforms reality. We do not even need Borges's pedantic Ramon Bonevena to appreciate that the fullness of experience can never be rendered in print. Selecting aspects of experience to write about, authors perforce simplify (deform) the totality of experience. But just like a dieter remains the same person when ten pounds lighter, the essence of an event can be preserved – and even made more salient – by trimming the contextual fat. Conceptual deformation helps thinkers get a better grip on knowledge, and its effects radiate upward, helping organize what we know, what we know that we know, and so on.

The narrative technique that directly maps onto the *angle of entry* is the point of view. Approaching a problem from different angles frequently fosters different perceptions. These, in turn, foster cognitive Gestalt shifts, quite in the manner of the perceptual shifts studied by psychologists early in the twentieth century. Viewing humanity through the eyes of a Lilliputian or a sentient ape on a planet with a half-buried Statue of Liberty are but two iconic examples of a shift in perception precipitated by a shift in perspective.

Selecting a particular angle of entry into the story, writers funnel our perception and, consequently, our understanding of characters and events. From the "innocent eye" of Huck Finn, through the composite "we" narrator of Faulkner's "A Rose for Emily," down to Kurosawa's *Rashomon*, in which differences in point of view literally yield different versions of reality, art generates insights by tweaking perspectives. Brecht's *Verfremdungseffekt* is, in fact, a cogent theory of how an estranging point of view inclines the spectator to see things anew – and more deeply.

Naturally, the four methods of Rearrangement are not disjunctive. They even overlap with Recollection insofar as the latter is often enhanced by rearrangement. A similar overlap is evident between the angle of entry and the third cognitive mechanism: Transformation. Moving from real-life experience to hypotheticals allows us to gauge, grade, and fine-tune responses in ways that we can transfer back to real life. This is again salient in fiction. Projecting themselves into the lives and motives of narrative agents, readers can fathom their own *hypothetical* beliefs and desires, and project them back to better understand the fiction. Emotional identification, felt by everyone who watched *Bambi*, is a concrete manifestation of transformation from hypothetical to real.[49]

> *Jeffrey discovered that he was internally debating with himself, holding full conversations between warring segments of his imagination.*
>
> John Katzenbach, *State of Mind*

On the Homuncular model, learning is effected by virtue of a cognitive auto-prompter. Decades of research in the neurosciences and cognitive psychology bring home the lesson that much of our knowledge is compartmentalized over different areas of the brain. These areas do not necessarily "communicate" well, or even at all, with one another. Hence the idea, as Gilbert Ryle put it, of *le penseur* communicating with himself in order to jump-start the process of discovery. Emblematically, the armchair thinker pushes information through his brain by saying things aloud and listening to what is enunciated. When thoughts boomerang back, they simulate an external trove of information that, one hopes, will trigger the right kind of association.

The precept is familiar to all writers who habitually edit their prose by stepping back in order to see it better. Clarity of thought rarely comes from a state of enlightenment while fingers whisk across the keyboard. It is a matter of organizing one's arguments so as to make them intelligible to others. Often it is only in the course of putting thoughts down on paper – or struggling to verbalize them – that one realizes how thin the understanding of an issue is. Writing things down and then reading what's on the page or saying it aloud and listening in are two familiar ways of bootstrapping the mind into a better understanding and, when appropriate, changing what you think.

The fact that various parts of the brain don't always communicate or cohere perfectly has repercussions not only for cognition but for a wider range of human behavior. One of the most significant is that, in the normal course of their running, diverse brain modules can pursue cognitive or behavioral strategies that may clash with each other. When such incompatible impulses bottleneck in the executive chain, they may even give an appearance of irrationality. Certain types of self-defeating behavior can be traced, it seems, to homuncular subunits fighting for the steering wheel.

Poe's short story "Imp of the Perverse" is a brilliant treatment of such a self-defeating split between facets of the narrator's psyche. It may be worth noting that, unlike science and philosophy, fiction tolerates and even embraces irrationality. It is also worth noting that Poe's far-sighted fiction appeared a hundred years before the social sciences began in earnest to model human beings as less than monolithically rational calculators and strategists. It shows again that, as far as generating and/or complexifying hypotheses go, we have much to learn from the theorists who work in the medium of art.

Storytelling is a form of cognitive autostimulation. Among the research programs in literary studies that explore these homuncular properties, the most promising emerge from two different levels of discourse analysis: semantic and pragmatic. Semantically, two of the crucial tactical means at the writer's disposal are the metaphor and simile (to a lesser degree also metonymy and synecdoche). In a hallmark of cross-pollination, mental categories from one domain are used to elucidate others. The metaphorical tenor projects partially onto the vehicle, and vice versa – so that stormy seas can be employed by Petrarch to capture some of the characteristics of love.

Metaphor typifies the variety of cognitive processing whereby thinkers yoke concepts from disparate semantic fields, that is, those that did not previously "communicate" with each other. No new data enter the loop, yet the result of such internal cross-pollination is often a deeper understanding. In *Metaphors We Live By*, George Lakoff and Mark Johnson coherently argue, in fact, that, far from being a disciplinary trope, metaphorical understanding and expression power all cognition. Evidence from priming and gesture studies in psychology, historical semantic change, sign language, discourse analyses, and language acquisition backs their claims up.

The conceptual framework in terms of which human beings think and act does appear to be fundamentally metaphorical in nature. Crucially, it is not that our thought processes are *expressed* via metaphors, but that they *run* on metaphors. Rational thought evolved in parallel with our brains and bodies, making metaphor "a neural phenomenon."[50] Encoded in primal metaphors – themselves rooted in the course of human evolution – the linguistic fossil record yields more instances of such homuncular cognition than Scheherazade had stories.

On a different level of discourse, namely literary pragmatics, a popular technique of autostimulation is feeding writing into the very neuroprocessor that wrote it – in effect, teaching yourself through writing. Writers' testimonials from Chapter 2 make teaching yourself through writing all too clear. Another instance of a homuncular system is a feedback loop composed of the author and the critic. Communication occurs via a gamut of reader response, from elaborate criticism to the basic "buy or not buy" decision on the part of readers. That communication is internalized and fed back into the loop in the next book, and so on.

Intrinsic to the reading process, this reciprocity between individuals who have not previously communicated with one another relies on reflexive intentions. Simplified somewhat, the author's intention to communicate by means of the work is identifiable by readers as reflexive, that is, intended to be recognized as having been intended to be recognized. In game-theoretic terms it can be modeled as a tacit, nonfinite, two-person, non-zero-sum bargaining game of incomplete and imperfect information.[51]

Finally, the fifth and last psychological mechanism of cognitive gain from "mere" thinking: Cleansing. In this capacity *Gedankenexperimente* rid users of incoherence, contradiction, or overall irrationality in belief systems. In *Knowledge and Error* the ever-obliging Mach offers this epigrammatic nugget: "Knowledge and error flow from the same mental sources, only success can tell the one from the other. A clearly recognized error, by way of corrective, can benefit knowledge just as a positive piece of knowledge can."[52] Kuhn's much-reprinted "A Function for Thought Experiments" goes so far as to claim that their "sole aim is to eliminate confusion"[53] through such mental purging.

Although mental cleansing receives star billing from Sorensen, in the literary context it is probably less important, inasmuch as it can be subsumed as a special case of the first four mechanisms. Few writers venture to write with the express purpose of clearing away the cobwebs from readers' mental gearboxes, although some thought experiments of the cleansing variety can be found in embedded fictions. Interpolated in larger narratives, such more or less autonomous thought experiments may indeed be of the "put two and two together and get five" variety. Often they thin out into parables – like the story of the invention of chess – at one end and philosophical *contes* at the other.

Naturally, some narratives do aim to improve – and often do improve – one's grasp of logical relations between events and characters. Classical detective fiction in the Poirot mode is salient in this respect, insofar as so much of its narrative currency is spent on futzing around with timetables, alibis, and logical causality of a particular sequence of criminal moves. But, in the main, cleansing of contradiction is neither a widespread nor even a typical mechanism behind literature in general, and literary thought experiments in particular.

> *Reason is, and ought only to be the slave of passions, and can never pretend to any other office than to serve and obey them.*
>
> David Hume, *A Treatise of Human Nature*

Any one of the five cognitive mechanisms may manifest itself more readily in a certain type of mental calculus or a certain type of task-solving, than another. This gives no grounds, however, for taking them to be domain-specific evolutionary adaptations.

Mainstream psychologists approach the mind as a general problem-solver, the processes of which extend over multiple domains. Evolutionary psychologists, such as David M. Buss in *Evolutionary Psychology* (1999), insist that human psychology is innately channeled and problem-specific – in short, massively modular. This is because general solutions may fail to guide organisms adaptively, and even if they work they may lead to costly errors or be nontransferable from context to context. In short, where most psychologists see a one-size-fits-all processor, evolutionary psychology favors a swarm model. The swarm comprises not only "peripheral" modules for perception or language, but "central" faculties handling any manner of higher functions: reasoning, belief formation and attribution, and – significantly – foresight and planning.

Note, first, that evolutionary modules must be general to some extent, or they would utterly fail us during the paleontologically recent change in environment from the hominid savannah to the urban jungle. Being partly general in nature still leaves plenty of room for specific expressions of environmental response – and for a degree of modularity. Chomsky has consistently argued for such a limited-modular theory of mind, whereby some faculties are run by mental modules, each devoted to handling its own range of stimuli and tasks. This compartmental model, elaborated by Jerry Fodor, resembles a mental federation whereby our cranial assembly of heterogeneous modules is like the United States – pursuing several agendas while remaining united under a central authority.

Oddly enough, although modularity lies at the heart of the schism, one finds as much vagueness as dogmatism in discussions of its central notion: module. All the more reason to commend the careful anatomy of both schools conducted by Richard Samuels in "Massively Modular Minds" (2000). His distinction between modules as systems of representations and predispositions, and modules as cognitive mechanisms is particularly useful. Simplifying, the cognitive modules (the author calls them Darwinian) are computational processes that go after problems on their own. The former (Chomskian) modules are more like public libraries housing answers to problems that may befall the librarian (the general processor).

The distinction leads Samuels to conclude that, polemics aside, no argumentative or experimental evidence favors either theory of mind-architecture. While some modularity is undeniably a feature of cognition, the modules in question may be more like wings of a library, each devoted to specialized knowledge and indexed for instant retrieval, but under the aegis of a head librarian. In fact, a hybrid of the modular and the central-processor models of the mind elegantly resolves the rivalry which splits the field. And the split is real enough. Fodor and Chomsky, two main proponents of peripheral modularity, proceed with restraint when it comes to the grand picture of the mind. In a display of disciplinary boosterism, evolutionary psychologists show no such restraint.

On their view, in the course of natural selection, the mind developed mental "modules" designed to handle specific adaptive challenges. How specific? Postulants multiply modules for self-identity, other minds, logic, countability, language, physical forces, objects and shapes, social and family relations, social status, sexual behavior, parenting, eating, dress, learning, cheating, travel, combat, flora and fauna, resource acquisition and husbandry, disease evasion, architectural structures, spatial relations, rigid-object mechanics, friendship, theory of mind, grammar acquisition, pursuit of truth, fear, tool manipulation, facial recognition, mate choice, sexual behavior, social exchange, natural frequencies inference, semantic inference, and many, many others. Many indeed: the most outspoken advocates see in our heads a confederation of hundreds or even thousands of domain-specific modules.

What is the upshot for our five cognitive mechanisms of literary mind experiments? The case for nativism (innate predisposition) for a language module appears iron clad. In fact it was the success of Chomsky's picture of a "language organ" that led to generalizations about a mental philharmonic of special-purpose modules. Although evidence for domain-specific modules is often ambiguous – and although, on occasion, Cosmides and Tooby (1987) strike a conciliatory note – most evolutionary psychologists profess massive modularity. Few acknowledge that domain-general processes are no less efficient in evolutionary terms, so long as they combine low-budget circuitry with passable efficacy.

Many putative adaptive modules are, for example, explicable in terms of associative learning. Edward Thorndike's old-time Law of Effect – actions with a positive outcome are likely to be repeated, while those followed by a negative outcome will be eliminated – is both general (domain transcendent) and compatible with natural selection. In short, the range of "candidate theories about the architecture of the human mind is larger than one might think from reading the work of evolutionary psychologists."[54] Recollection, Rearrangement, Transformation, Homuncular system, and Cleansing are, therefore, simply advanced as general models of how armchair experimenters in particular, and human beings in general, sieve thinking into channels that focus attention, organize perception, recollect data, and generate suitable inferences and conclusions.

Literary fictions work on us by working on our beliefs. The familiar inability of many readers – including literature scholars – to articulate clearly and concisely what they learned from reading doesn't prove that they learned nothing. Articulation of what is learnt is a meta-process categorically distinct from learning itself, which frequently manifests itself on the behavioral level, through action rather than formal analysis. Children continuously acquire, modify, and apply information about moral behavior, which often they could not articulate. Similarly, at the creative end, writers need not start from a clear and cohesive set of precepts to construct a cognitively valuable story.

But even if in literature the process is more diffuse, instinctive, and incomplete than in philosophy or science, the structure and global strategy of the thought experiments all three employ are not always that different.

5   Literature and game theory

There must certainly be some mistake in this matter.

Laurence Sterne, *The Life and Opinions of Tristram Shandy, Gentleman*

Exploring methods that have proven their efficiency abroad, several studies lately have focused on the gaming element in literature. Unfortunately, the net outcome of this interdisciplinary outreach is to perpetuate the misuses of game theory in particular, and social-scientific work in general. Having entered the canon in the Norton edition of *Tristram Shandy*, Richard Lanham's "Games, Play, Seriousness" is a quintessential example of what passes for integration of literary and extra-literary inquiry. Authored by a scholar known for discerning work in the field, for more than a generation the essay has vaunted its allegiance to game theory. In reality, it epitomizes the laissez-faire interdisciplinarity typical of literary studies.[1]

Although Lanham professes to examine what light "a body of knowledge called 'game theory'" can shed on "the game sphere of *Tristram Shandy*," he is profoundly ignorant of the very tools he has chosen. So much so, in fact, that in the end he does not avail himself of game theory at all. With the single exception of Anatol Rapoport's *Fights, Games and Debates*, his ruminations are based on sources at best peripheral to the field. More oddly still, Lanham tries to discredit game theory altogether, concocting fiats that are methodologically and factually false. With "conflict as it occurs either in ordinary life or in imaginative literature," alleges the critic, game theory "cannot deal at all." This after boasting of his complete lack of "competence . . . to explain game theory even in its simplest outline [*sic*]."[2]

To reiterate from Chapter 2, modeling always entails making limiting assumptions about the state of affairs under investigation. Belittling its analytic and modeling powers, Lanham dwells on the fact that game theory – in implied contradistinction to literature – cannot describe *all* parameters of a situation. This schoolboy error is exemplary of the kind of pretensions lambasted by Borges (this time working alone) in his "On Exactitude in Science." In the story a College of Cartographers also pipedreams about a map of the empire of the same scale as the empire, coinciding with it point for point – with predictable results.

Lanham's blunder is all the worse that, already in the foreword to the book that served as his primer, Rapoport argues that "the formal mathematical approach has a bright future in all areas of knowledge, including behavioral science"[3] And the evidence bears him out. To date game theorists have successfully applied their findings to problems in jurisdiction, criminology, sociology, the military, the legislature, political science, accounting economics, advertising, sports, biology, psychology, agriculture, international relations, management, behavioral science, and, not least, literary studies. Clearly, this Norton-bankrolled failure to do justice to the interdisciplinary study of conflict should not dissuade literary critics from mining it with more vigor (and rigor) than up to now.

Lanham's caricature of game theory merely as a source of "some beguiling metaphors" is mirrored in his misrepresentation of its usefulness. Ignorant of the myriad applications, he concedes only that "one of its principal contributions to *literary* conflict is in rendering us self-conscious about it." Furthermore, finding fault with the assumptions of rationality typically made with respect to players' behavior, he dismisses them altogether. Having thus rejected the very body of knowledge that was to inform his interdisciplinary venture, the critic unveils the real source of his gaming concepts. These are "philosophers of play [who] cover a very wide spectrum and hypothesize irrational players, moving from there in great leaps to a universe of existential absurd."[4]

Although game theory has little to say directly about the existential absurd, it can contribute to the analysis of some of the paradoxes that underlie existential angst (see pp. 148–50). More to the point, Lanham's hostility to the assumptions of rationality is once again misguided. Game theorists who study rational conduct work side by side with researchers, who, in the words of Thomas Schelling in his classic *Strategy of Conflict*, examine players "in all their complexity – with regard to both 'rational' and 'irrational' behavior."[5] Even the former affirm that, while their chief interest lies with rational players, it extends to cases where one "deals with an opponent (or opponents) liable to more or less irrational behavior."[6]

In general, stuck with the paradoxes of coordination intrinsic to the Prisoner's Dilemma, game theorists are well aware of commonsensical as well as strategic problems with the rationality postulates of classical decision theory. Blinded by Rapoport's qualified critique of those postulates, Lanham ignores critiques of his mentor's views, published *nota bene* before our critic interred game theory lock, stock, and barrel.[7] Grounding one's judgment of a body of knowledge in a single source can, of course, hardly result in an informed opinion. And, in Lanham's case, examples of misinformation abound.

The critic asserts that game theory tries to "above all make the contending parties aware of . . . the self-pleasing ingredient in conflict." This is simply wrong. In some bargaining situations the lack of communication or the ability to conceal one's utility can actually better the payoff. Lanham's confloption reaches its zenith when he pulls the rug from under his own two feet, tacitly adopting the rationality principles dismissed earlier on. He complains that "practically no one has considered the novel [*Tristram Shandy*] as a *game* in Rapoport's sense of the word."[8] Yet Rapoport takes a game to be "idealized as a struggle in which complete rationality of the opponents is assumed."[9]

After decades of such rampant confusion, it's time to set the record straight. What *is* game theory, then? It is a theory of decision-making involving more than one agent (player), where the results (outcomes and payoffs) of players' actions (moves) are at least to a certain degree interdependent. In literary studies, it can model the reading process as a tacit game between the author and the reader.[10] Equally, game theory can assist in the analysis of story contents. It can model and rationalize characters' actions, the motivations for these actions, as well as their consequences. It can explain strategic choices by exploring links between agents' moves and the structure of the plot. It can even tackle interpretive questions, such as whether the inner calculations of a Hamlet can account for his actions.

Research in literary studies and game theory can even prove of benefit to the latter. If nothing else, it can help social scientists profit from the wealth of lore about human behavior transmitted in fiction over the ages. In fact, argues Nigel Howard, "they should continually be testing their theories against this." Tipping the scales in literature's favor, he even contends that, if some normative postulate "doesn't make sense to Shakespeare, perhaps it doesn't make sense!"[11] Fertile as narrative fiction is for game-theoretic exploration, no assumption need, naturally, be made about the latter's universal applicability. On the contrary, its validity should be judged only *a posteriori* when the narrative proves analyzable, especially if one can suggest a solution to the conflict.

> *Paradoxically, it has turned out that game theory is more readily applied to biology than to the field of economic behaviour for which it was originally designed.*
>
> John Maynard Smith, *Evolution and the Theory of Games*

Connections between game theory and evolution are numerous and intimate, crowned by the flourishing of a novel discipline, evolutionary game theory. Assuming for modeling purposes infinite populations, continuous time, complete mixing, etc., the discipline studies the evolutionary dynamics of population genetics. Of course it makes little sense to treat impala or gibbons as rational decision-makers. Hence, in a crucial break with economic behavior, evolutionary game theory approaches environmentally stable solutions (so-called attractors) as survival strategies sustained by evolutionary forces. The payoffs for the players (organisms) are assumed to reflect their degree of environmental fitness.

Apart from the study of biological equilibria – the most famous of which, John Maynard Smith's Evolutionary Stable Strategy (ESS), dates back to 1982 – game theory has been used to prominently study the evolution and stability of sex ratios. Recently biologists also applied evolutionary game theory to develop a genesis model of animal communication (mostly through analysis of signaling and other communication games). Fight–flight (hawk–dove) stimulus response, territoriality, cheating (free riders), and a bevy of other behavioral evolutionary responses have all by now been successfully subjected to game-theoretic analysis.

Ironically, of late evolutionary game theory has become of intense interest to social scientists (economists, sociologists, psychologists, anthropologists), to say nothing of analytic philosophers. This is, first of all, because game-theoretic calculus can, as it turns out, be profitably applied to other dynamically changing systems, such as culture. Second, the rationality assumptions of *dynamic* fitness are quite frequently better suited for the modeling of social systems. And finally, this dynamic orientation of evolutionary game theory aces classical game theory, in which iterated games were of only limited significance.

Given the deep connections between game theory and evolution, and given the deep connections between evolution and thought experiments, game theory is also deeply connected with the latter. The connections between it and thought experiment are, of course, much more direct. Take any thought experiment involving interactions of actors in any social drama. It could be an econometric counterfactual designed to tease out the implications of various levels of taxation. Or it could be a far-out scenario of Malamud's *God's Grace*, where a sole survivor of atomic annihilation interacts with irascible God while trying to jump-start civilization with a posse of talking chimps.

Game theory is a perfect tool to analyze multiplex decision modes in either case: rational taxpayers or the unlikely group of the meek who inherited the earth. Surprisingly, it can even analyze God's dealings with his creation. In *Biblical Games* (1980) Steven Brams pioneered a mathematical analysis of the strategic behavior of the Old Testament God, partly amenable, as it turns out, to game-theoretic inquisition. Malamud's novel even anticipates the contemporary turn to game theory in ethics, itself more and more inclined to acknowledge the genetic roots of morality. As Robert Wright sums up decades of such research in *The Moral Animal* (1994): "people tend to pass the sorts of moral judgments that help move their genes into the next generation."[12]

Game-theoretic analysis is, therefore, a good way of getting at literature as thought experiment. Effective as it can be, it offers of course no Ariadne's thread to safely navigate through textual indeterminacy. The latter is exemplified by questions of (un)reliability inherent in all fiction, typically exacerbated in first-person narration. Filtered through the protagonist's mind, story elements often become tainted with her strategic considerations. Furthermore, the identification of conflicts and players, as well as the enumeration of their strategic choices, preferences, and outcomes, may meet with less than unanimous approval.

But that is precisely where game theory comes into its own. Formally foregrounding its analytic assumptions, it invites critics to examine the latter for alternative constructions of events. Put another way, game theory offers an exact format, language, and method to forge comparisons of even the most personal – as well as interpersonal – dimensions of character and plot. Another source of its suitability to literary studies is the simple fact that a majority of narratives are amenable to this type of analysis. Not merely authors who avail themselves of game-theoretic ideas, but all those whose characters interact with others constitute a rich field for analysis of conflict and cooperation.

Naturally, many novelists intuitively employ any number of game-theoretic principles, to the extent that such principles are part of the innate psychological equipment. In that sense, bringing those tacit procedures to the surface in the form of an explicit analytic framework can provide literary theorists with better access to the deep structures of human behavioral economy. Literary theory built on game-theoretic procedures can thus provide not only tools for analysis of fiction but a neutral frame for intertextual comparison. Its potential in literary studies is enormous, and its as-yet scarce applications can only grow.

Given that almost any narrative could be fruitfully explored by these means, their applicability extends from Vonnegut's evolutionary *Galapagos* to, indeed, *Tristram Shandy* and beyond. From the beheading game between Sir Gawain and the Greene Knight and the tit-for-tat verbal skirmishes between Chaucer's Miller and Reeve, to Jane Austen's elaborate parlor "games" of love and social prejudice, and the strategic hide-and seek of espionage games in John Le Carré – the sky is the limit. The main contribution of game theory is to make explicit the psychological motivations and utilities agents resort to, and, when possible, suggest a solution to the interaction (game) in progress.

Afforded a more precise way to evaluate the characters' behavior, literary scholars ought to be better poised to complexify and enrich their studies. As intimated by Howard, they could even complexify and enrich some of the game-theoretic models employed. To be sure, literature is more than just narrative prose. For this simple reason no one should go scouring haikus or valedictions for archetypes of games, fights, or debates – or, for that matter, thought experiments. But most stories, whether cast in prose or verse, are riddled with complex characters and motivations. And as such, they are sure to yield a spectrum of interactions, from zero-sum conflict at one extreme to full cooperation at the other.

More than any time in history mankind faces a crossroads. One path leads to despair and utter hopelessness, the other to total extinction. Let us pray that we have the wisdom to choose correctly.

Woody Allen, *Side Effects*

This is not to say that some narratives are not paradigmatically suited to game-theoretic analysis. Some may even be written with that very analytic framework in mind. *Fail Safe*, best remembered from Sidney Lumet's 1964 screen version, is only one novel among many that tackles a topic tailor made for the game-theoretic machinery – a superpower struggle for military and political dominance. And the topic is all the more important since, decade after nuclear decade, it refuses to go away. After all, only a few years into the new millennium it is clear that the more things change, the more they remain the same.

Wars proliferate, while belligerent chieftains who masquerade as presidents, premiers, prime ministers, or ayatollahs remain as near-sighted as ever. Weapons trade remains the mainstay of national economies, strategic thinkers still promote peace by readying for war, and the global outlay on armaments in any one year far exceeds, gulp, US$1 *trillion*. Few studies bring this state of affairs home like Jonathan Schell's *The Fate of the Earth*. Capped for the millenary edition with a new essay, "The Unfinished Twentieth Century," it examines the genocidal after-effects of the most likely nuclear-exchange scenario. "It may be one of the most important works of recent years," wrote Walter Cronkite for the jacket, adding almost as an afterthought: "there still may be hope to save our civilization."

Afraid that the Ecclesiastes's sun that also rises might be made of runaway neutrons, Schell takes literally Camus's precept that the duty of his generation consists in preventing the world from destroying itself. There is no mistaking the dread with which the author eyes the beast in our civilization. Inking disarmament and non-proliferation treaties, the beast stockpiles A-, H-, and N-bombs, playing political chicken with one finger on the button. Why else would the US try to rattle Russia with the son of the moribund Star Wars ballistic missile system? Why else would Putin ratify START II only conditionally, keeping his nukes ready in case Bush, in a spur-jingling moment, begins to rocket laser-shield satellites into orbit?

Fail Safe and *The Fate of the Earth* don't take to task the madness so much of individuals, but of a group – an organization. They dissect the *genius tempori* of the period when humanity teeters on the brink of a nuclear cataclysm in the name of political and military posturing gone awry. Both reflect the absurdity and paranoia of all ideological confrontations and model the essence of group (ir)rationality, which applies with equal force today. As documented by the Coalition to Reduce Nuclear Dangers, after decades of lip-service to world peace and two Strategic Arms Reduction Treaties, the combined number of American and Russian strategic warheads alone sits at well over 13,000. Given that just one is needed to vaporize a major city, there are not enough cities on the planet to feed these bombs. This is not counting tactical nukes, which are the mainstay of current research and development.

As was spelt out in the 2001 Nuclear Posture Review, the US doctrine calls for a replacement of the triad of ICBMs (Intercontinental Ballistic Missiles), "boomer" subs, and strategic bombers with a new nuclear triad. These are offensive strike systems (including the old triad delivery platforms), active and passive defenses (including SDI, or Star Wars), and a wholly revamped infrastructure (including the new Pentagon). Lest they be accused of peace-mongering, Bush's hawks spell out the essence of the "new" posture: "Nuclear weapons play a critical role in the defense capabilities of the United States."[13]

The announcement trails in the wake of a disturbing trend marked by the American withdrawal from the Anti-Ballistic Missile Treaty, the failure to ratify the Comprehensive Test Ban Treaty, and failure to act fully on the Strategic Offensive Reductions Treaty with Russia. Not to put too fine a point on it, the new nuclear posture effectively abrogates the American responsibilities set in Article VI of the Nuclear Non-Proliferation Treaty. Price tag? Almost $7 billion for atomic weapons research and manufacture in 2005 alone – far in excess of the average annual outlay during five decades of the superpower arms race.

Having apparently won the Cold War, today the US is rapidly "developing earth penetrating nuclear weapons (bunker busters) and low-yield nuclear weapons (mini-nukes), one-third the yield of the Hiroshima bomb," reports David Krieger, President of the Nuclear Age Peace

Foundation. At the same time it is "demanding that other countries – including Iraq, Iran, North Korea, Libya and Syria – refrain from following its example."[14] This atomic hypocrisy knocks a few more teeth out of the Nuclear Non-Proliferation Treaty, and further dims the prospects of ratification of the Comprehensive Test Ban Treaty.

Response to the threat of these low-yield, target-tailored atom bombs has been swift. In the main, it has been limited to individuals rather than worldwide protests like during the 1970s opposition to the "industry-friendly" N-bomb. Not that it makes the hypocrisy any less apparent. "The U.S. government insists that other countries do not possess nuclear weapons. On the other hand they are perfecting their own arsenal. I do not think that corresponds with the treaty they signed," notes Mohamed el-Baradei, 2005 Nobel Peace Prize winning director-general of the International Atomic Energy Agency.

All of a sudden the doomsday clock is ticking again.

John Kerry: "By pursuing new, 'usable' nuclear weapons designs, this administration underscores to every rogue regime in the world the value of nuclear arms."[15] Edward Kennedy: "It is wrong for this administration to start developing new types of nuclear weapons that have no plausible military purpose and that can only encourage even more nations to go nuclear." Al Gore: "This administration has rejected it [the Comprehensive Test Ban Treaty] and now, incredibly, wants to embark on a new program to build a brand new generation of smaller (and it hopes, more usable) nuclear bombs." Rose Gottemoeller, Energy Department: "people abroad will interpret this as part of a really enthusiastic effort by the Bush administration to renuclearize. And I think definitely there's going to be an impetus to the development of nuclear weapons around the world."

> *It is a wholesome plan, in thinking about logic, to stock the mind with as many puzzles as possible, since they serve much the same purpose as is served by experiments in physical sciences.*
>
> Bertrand Russell, "On Denoting"

Although outwardly *Memoirs Found in a Bathtub* looks nothing like *The Fate of the Earth*, both could have sprung from the same pen. A brainchild of the Cold War hysterics, Lem's book came out in 1961, barely a year before the Cuban missile crisis.[16] Reflecting the time when both superpowers were readying themselves for a nuclear slugfest, with the fate of the Earth hanging in the balance, it is replete with matters foremost in everyone's mind: espionage, the balance of power, global rivalry, and the in(s)anity of the military mindset. It models the perfidious – because not irrational – madness embraced in the name of brinkmanship, mutual assured destruction, containment, linkage, Desert Shield, Nuclear Posture, and other slogans for doctrinal and military confrontation.

Although unique in Lem's *oeuvre* – he hasn't written anything like it before or after – *Memoirs* is typical of his abiding concern for our civilization. With a little help from game theory, I intend to throw fresh light on the acute paranoia of strategic power games represented in the novel.[17] A key difficulty resides here in textual indeterminacy about agents' beliefs and preferences. Unlike laboratory models or quantifiable real-life settings, storytellers don't provide sufficient data to hazard a numeric foothold on characters' value systems. In fact, skilful authors "often conceal certain essential motivations of their characters in order to reproduce the mystery we often feel in real life as to why people behave the way they do."[18]

One can thus hardly expect to work with cardinal utilities or expected-value calculations. One way out is to assume strictly ordinal rankings in which players' choices are ordered according to the preference (utility) of outcomes, with no numerical values attached to payoffs. This is, indeed, the route I take below. In the process I investigate aspects of individual and group rationality which, not coincidentally, spell out the same warning for the new millennium as they did in the heat of the Cold War. Survival of our species is, after all, no more than a working hypothesis. But what if the hypothesis fails the test?

Riveted by our propensity for strategic madness, Lem is forever reassessing the peril of the power games we play. Tellingly, even as he reduces nuclear-age ideologies to absurdity, he refuses to take political sides. The Third Pentagon may be buried under the Rockies of Ammer-Ka, but its bureaucratic mannerisms are unmistakably East European. A philosopher rather than ideologue, Lem models an institutionally universal type of situation instead of a politically specific one, keeping its warning fresh in our millennium. Throwing their weight around the globe, commanders-in-chief of the Pentagon we know, the Second Pentagon bankrolled by the Nuclear Posture, and the Third Pentagon from Lem's fiction might even be sane and rational. But the antagonistic process into which they might draw us all can limit effective strategies only to MAD (mutual assured destruction) future.

Perhaps with game theory in mind, Andrzej Stoff interprets *Memoirs* as the sum total of the "rules that determine the functioning of its world."[19] The rules of the Pentagon's spying game, and the socio-political – perhaps even ontological – world they foster indeed turn out to be one and the same thing. Ambling aimlessly through the subterranean labyrinth, the nameless hero chronicles with incredulity and terror its self-devouring madness. One by one, the bizarre rules that govern his world are revealed to this nuclear-age Quixote in encounters with its various functionaries. Is it possible that this monster was born of rational war on an ideological enemy?

Like the stations of the Cross, his progress is marked by visits to various parts of the Building, of which the following are the central ones:

1   The office of Commanderal Kashenblade, who destroys Agent's entrance pass and cryptically alludes to the protagonist's Mission.[20]
2   The tour of the Department of Collections, in effect a spy museum.
3   The office of an odd old-young spy in golden spectacles, who discourses with the protagonist on the universal principle of Cause and Effect and, apparently misreading his intentions and identity, commits suicide.
4   The chapel where Agent witnesses the funeral service for the old-young spy, receives a report from a monk spy, Brother Persuasion, and meets Father Orfini.
5   The office of Major Erms, who gives Agent a copy of his Mission – or does he?
6   The Department of Codes, where Captain Prandtl lectures the name-less protagonist on the nature and ubiquity of codes and ciphers.
7   The Archives, where Agent samples the monumental spy-library database.
8   A bathroom, where Agent meets a pale-faced spy, who, explaining the Building in a frustratingly incomplete and enigmatic manner, only confuses Agent further.
9   The doctor's office in the Medical Section, where a seemingly sponta-neous drunken party turns out to be an elaborate setup staged by Dolt, Sempriaq, and other *agents provocateurs*.
10 Same locale, where Agent again meets Father Orfini, who proposes to him a bizarre secret pact in which betrayal is a condition *sine qua non*.
11 The bathroom again, where Agent discovers the body of the pale-faced spy, who has (presumably) committed suicide, and where Agent (presumably) does the same.

The picture that emerges from his quasi-Brownian ricochets off the Pentagon's spy corps is as warped as the mock-scholarly reconstruction by the future archeologists in the book's introduction. Following the bizarre meeting with the Commanderal, Agent concludes, for example, that the *modus operandi* of this bureaucratic Moloch is based on a random system of operations. As if that wasn't enough, whatever he glimpses of his Mission contains a verbatim account of his chaotic wanderings in the Building.

Everything is there, down to the faithful rendition of his innermost thoughts and emotional states!

The Pentagon's prescience is not only at odds with the randomness that governs its ops, but quite simply out of this world. Indeed, no literal interpretation could make sense of elements that defy any, literary or scientific, realism. The Building's omniscience aside, "machines to change night into day and vice versa" are as absurd as "counterfeit atoms and electrons."[21] Much like Picasso and Braque warped, amputated, and reconfigured their canvas to highlight what would otherwise remain unremarked, Lem distorts to amplify the effect of his verbal *Guernica*. From time-travel jibes and (lost in translation) archaic orthography in the introduction, to the allegorization of the Building, the Mission, and the nameless protagonist as Everyman, the realism of spy fiction shifts in modality to the 2b grotesque.

> *Though this be madness, yet there is method in't.*
> William Shakespeare, *Hamlet*

In a central scene the protagonist is offered a secret pact. He knows he is going to be betrayed, and is encouraged by his collaborator, Father Orfini, to betray him in return. Entering the pact not out of strategic motives but with sincerity, Agent can fill the prescribed *form* with authentic content – even though it will have exactly zero impact on the course of events.

This mad, mad world mimics the ontological roller-coaster of Borges's "The Lottery in Babylon." The universal lottery inverts the relation between Order and Chance, gradually substituting one for the other so that the train of events remains completely intact yet its nature is altered profoundly. This leads to paradoxes like that of a thief who steals a ticket which credits him with a burning of his tongue, which also happens to be the penalty fixed by the legal code for the theft of a ticket. Thus some Babylonians can argue that "he deserved the burning irons in his status of a thief; others, generously, that the executioner should apply it to him because chance had determined it that way."[22]

Much as in Borges, in the Pentagon form also dominates content. As Lem revealed in *Fantastyka i futurologia* (*Science Fiction and Futurology*), he dreamt up this radical concept while reading spy memoirs. He wrote:

> It occurred to me that a spy who works notoriously for both antagonistic sides may, after a certain period of his activity, be no longer certain whom he is deceiving and whom aiding; acts of patriotism or betrayal are then differentiable only statistically (according to whom he has respectively more – or less – harmed or helped by means of his reported information).[23]

Totalizing the concept of intention, *Memoirs* models communal attitudes in order to highlight paradoxes of rationality in a situation gone strategically mad. What lessons for group and individual rationality hide in the autarchic fortress of the Last Pentagon? The Building's idiosyncrasies come to the fore in confrontation with the outside world, which intrudes upon it in the person of the anonymous narrator. Even though the Building interacts with Agent through various functionaries, all present a monolithic front as if united against him by virtue of a common strategy. This is a key point in the novel that models aspects of group rationality that depart in intriguing ways from the established wisdom on that subject.

Memoirs provides a dynamic illustration of a community that, by dint of its military and strategic conditioning, ought to be a paradigm of hard, calculating rationality. Through the analysis of the Mission Game, I question this assumption as well as the postulates commonly accepted in social, decision, and game theories, particularly regarding the transfer of individual to group rationality. To get up to speed, we may begin with the related problem of individuality. Why should the Building's staff be indistinguishable in their actions and attitudes? How can such uniformity be sustained over time and inevitable changes in personnel, well documented in the novel?

Replacement and rotation in the Building are the order of the day because of so many deaths that are a staple of its counterintelligence ops. During his brief foray, Agent himself witnesses numerous executions and suicides. Besides, just like the pale-faced spy before him, he himself is a newcomer, drafted to augment the Pentagon's spy corps. Although Stoff finds little evidence to suggest Agent's arrival from the outside, the text leaves no doubt about it.[24] *Memoirs* opens with talk about an entrance pass without which Agent could not have penetrated the underground fortress. The meal tickets he needs to obtain corroborate his status as an outsider to the Building's structure. Besides, the infiltration of the Building by the Anti-Building's agents attests not only that the Outside exists, but that it must have means of repeated access to the Pentagon.

I propose that social groups and institutions that undergo large turnovers of personnel can maintain their character owing to the convergence of reciprocal expectations. Every member of the group expects what everybody else expects everybody else to expect. In such a climate, the expectations – and consequently the behavior – of every new inductee adapt to the expected behavior of other recruits. The result is an unwritten social contract whose tacit terms are embraced willy-nilly by all new arrivals. Paradoxically, the rationality of individual conduct may be dominated by the (expected) behavior of a group *without suspending the individual rationality of each person concerned.*

This surrender of individual preferences and the attendant feeling of powerlessness or inevitability is a result of the convergence of expectations. What is experienced by individuals is not even the outcome, but the expectation of the outcome. Emerging from the reciprocal expectations of expected expectations, this subjective perception of its inevitability grows into the certitude of a self-fulfilling prophecy. The I-guess-what-you-guess-what-I-guess-what-you-guess-I-think *esprit du corps* effectively denies any individual the power to thwart it. The widely studied difficulties attending coalition-formation are precisely what safeguards the relative stability of the Building, just like they do in many real institutions and traditions. Once such a tacit and reciprocal equilibrium takes root, it can be changed only through explicit collusion – hence the second matrix below is an example of the Collusion Game.

The above conclusions are far from banal insofar as they suggest that some social-scientific assumptions about the compatibility of individual and group rationality may be incomplete. You may be rational in desiring a certain outcome, and in believing that a certain course of action may be the proper way to secure it. At the same time, you may be rational in *not* pursuing this course of action. This apparent contradiction is a result of the strategic consideration of the convergence of reciprocal expectations. This only superficial irrationality hides at the bottom of the herd instinct, whereby people occasionally feel compelled to actions which they both do not want to perform and are essentially free not to perform.

All this casts a different light on the notion of optimizing rationality. Interpersonal analysis, involving multiple or even group agents, depends on the so-called utility function which maps agents' inchoate preferences into an ordered and consistent form. This daunting task is made possible by the theoretical fiction of a *rational* agent. Although no more than a heuristic idealization, useful things can be learnt from the analysis of a being who knows what he wants, has well-determined goals and preferences, is capable of evaluating any set of alternatives, and always optimizes his profit. A rational agent is also assumed to be perfectly informed and able to process properly all data at his disposal.

But even if agents had perfect access to perfect information – that is, if they knew all the rules of the game they were embedded in – their conduct might not be fully explicable according to the classical postulates of rationality. The moment the rules become too vast or complicated for an individual to grasp in entirety, for practical purposes the situation becomes not unlike a freeform game. In freeform games players may observe, or fail to observe, rules which were in force at different stages of the game, in essence giving them the power to make the rules up as they go. Rationality is at least partially indexed not only by the quality but also by the *quantity* of the available information.

> *But to know one's own desires, their meaning and their costs requires the highest of human virtue: rationality.*
>
> Ayn Rand, "Causality vs. Duty"

At about the time of *Memoirs*, a prominent game theorist advised:

> Rationality is a collection of attributes, and departures from complete rationality may be in many different directions. Irrationality can imply a disorderly and inconsistent value system, faulty calculation, an inability to receive messages or to communicate efficiently; it can imply random or haphazard influences in the reaching of decisions or the transmission of them, or in the receipt or conveyance of information; and it sometimes merely reflects the collective nature of a decision among individuals who do not have identical value systems and whose organizational arrangements and communication systems do not cause them to act like a single entity.[25]

Even today, rationality is all too often approached as an attribute strung evenly alongside a one-dimensional axis, with perfect rationality and absolute absence of it at either pole. Yet rationality is a more compound, complex, and heterogeneous kind of animal. The ramifications of this simple postulate extend to just about all spheres of human life, from systems of jurisprudence that lean heavily on precedent (like the American), to school test evaluations and personal relationships, down to counterespionage or superpower nuclear-arms diplomacy. The best way to imagine the difference is to look at threat situations.

Many standard attributes of rationality can become drawbacks against an opponent impervious to punitive threats by virtue of a genuine or feigned inability to act rationally. Children, madmen, fanatics, or nuclear doomsday machines cannot be threatened as effectively as agents with a certifiable ability to hear, comprehend, and act freely. Conversely, threat efficacy rises as a function of perceived irrationality. A hardened al-Qaeda operative known to hold his life in contempt can threaten to detonate explosives strapped to his belt with more credibility than a timid civil servant. That's why Melville's Barnaby the Scrivener, an unobtrusive man all his life, is dubbed a harmless crank and not a revolutionary when one day, enigmatically, he refuses to obey instructions.

The power of game theory lies in its power to analyze the strategic basis of such paradoxes of rationality, which, despite all appearances of illogic or madness, can be tactically perfectly sound. Let us remember that, far from being an inherent attribute, rationality is really a function of one's ability to make decisions. As such it can be, to some extent at least, manipulated at will. And, as a matter of fact, in an astounding number of situations it is. Many bargaining processes, including arms, border, or hostage negotiations, can serve as examples of such manipulation – in effect cheating at the rationality game.

Ideally, a rational agent is expected to maximize his knowledge by keeping communication channels open. Yet a unilateral disruption of communication can clearly be of advantage. Kidnappers who, after threatening to kill the hostage unless their demands are met, publicly sever contact with the outside render themselves impervious to counter-threats. Worse, in this way they effectively shift the responsibility for the victim's life onto the blackmailed party. Ironically – and *contra* Lanham – if phone lines get cut accidentally, it makes perfect sense for the kidnappers to fix them, only to cut them in full view of the negotiators.

How could the underground Pentagon degenerate to this point? How could it become imprisoned by commands not given and rules not enforced by anyone – in short, by strategic thinking run amok? As in real life, one of the decisive factors is physical isolation. Apparently the Pentagon ceased to function "in the seventy-second year of its retreat from the world."[26] Left to itself, the giant organism had deformed only gradually, by a series of micro-steps imperceptible until their accumulation. Naturally, there was nobody at the helm of the process. The Building evolved toward its homeostatic equilibrium simply through the stochastic multitude of interactions among its lower-order elements: departments, sections, and individual agents.

In *Science Fiction and Futurology* Lem himself advanced a condensed analysis of aspects of experimental sociodynamics. Dissecting the atrocities of the Nazi occupation of Poland, he identified several key elements, among them isolation, psychological stress, permanence, and presence of an antagonist, that can contribute to the gradual erosion of group rationality. His arguments about "sociodynamic transformations linked to the incidence of critical points in group instability"[27] indicate that, spread over time, the presence of these catalytic factors can precipitate the type of degeneracy depicted in the novel.

Perplexingly, the presence of apparently normal, sensibly acting and interacting individuals does not automatically entail the rationality of their communal macrostructure. Not that this paradox is anything new. It has been known at least since Condorcet's 1785 work on nontransitive preferences – for example voters who prefer a Republican to a Democrat, a Democrat to an Independent, but an Independent to a Republican.

Neither is it a theoretical and thus dismissible matter. A perfect embodiment of this very problem occurred in the pairwise runoff in a 1980 US Senate election between the conservative D'Amato and the liberals Javits and Holtzman.[28]

Clearly, rationally individual choices can lead to unreliable and undesirable collective choices. Indeed, Martin Shubik argues that one of game theory's most important findings may be the realization that "a concept of individual rationality does not generalize in any unique or natural way to group or social rationality" – in fact, it "may not even be consistent with it."[29] Whether the nuclear scenario is that of *Memoirs Found in a Bathtub, Dr. Strangelove, The Day After, By Dawn's Early Light,* or the Pythonesque *Whoops! Apocalypse!,* rational thinking can lead to military postures in which human actions, free in principle, fall victim to the edicts of strategically preferred outcomes.

Mad logic generates its own inertia, which perpetuates itself without volition or design, simply out of tactical impotence. Thus, in the Pentagon plans are still planned, schemes schemed, and plots plotted – in fact, their production reaches a Rabelaisian feast of information, with documents "everywhere, on every level of the Building . . . millions and millions of them."[30] To Lem's readers these reams of datapoints shuffled from one desk to another were as satirically adroit as familiar. Run by self-aggrandizing paperistocrats, the state bureaucracy was a ship drowning under his own weight. Truth being stranger than fiction, it would take Jerzy Kosinski to exploit this informational glut. A years-long paper trail of petitions and cross-references buried the truth so deeply that it eventually earnt an exit visa from iron-curtained Poland to the Outside.

Just because the information-processing capacity of even a super-spy must, perforce, be limited, in some situations a senseless paper profligacy can be quite sensible. For a human agent the presence of a cornucopia of information may be as, or even more, damaging than too little. This is true even on the level of logical satisfiability – absence of pernicious paradox, inconsistency, or self-contradiction. Remember Vonnegut's and Carroll's mind-twisters from Chapter 2? Unable to verify satisfiability for a given set of propositions, and thus ignorant of their implications, one cannot be said to understand them.

The arguments often heard that because of the human element, of psychological factors, etc., or because there is – allegedly – no measurement of important factors, mathematics will find no application, can be dismissed as utterly mistaken.

John von Neumann and Oscar Morgenstern, *Theory of Games and Economic Behavior*

Throughout his Kafkaesque trials, Agent loyally clings to the belief in his Mission. Without it, the summons to the Pentagon and all subsequent events would seem to be spurious and arbitrary actions of a bureaucratic python choking on its own tail. Allowing that the ranking may initially seem counterintuitive, I construe Agent's preferences in his interactions with the Building as follows.

BEST	Building provides Mission (M); Agent pursues Mission (P)
2nd BEST	Building provides Mission (M); Agent does not pursue Mission (−P)
2nd WORST	Building does not provide Mission (−M); Agent pursues Mission (P)
WORST	Building does not provide Mission (−M); Agent does not pursue Mission (−P)

The point requiring comment is Agent's second-worst outcome. It states that, in the event of the Mission being denied to him he would still try to pursue it. There are at least four plausible interpretations of this situation. Agent tries to pursue *some* mission in the absence of indication that *the* Mission – his Mission – exists. Conversely, his behavior is designed to force the Pentagon to supply him with a mission – he repeatedly states his belief in its existence, hoping it will be taken into account. Furthermore, Agent's persistence can be explained as a search for reasons why he has not been given a mission. In fact, his efforts to discover its contents are a natural reaction of making sure that there indeed isn't one.

    Now the Building's preferences in this conflict:

BEST	Do not provide Mission (−M); Agent pursues Mission (P)
2nd BEST	Do not provide Mission (−M); Agent does not pursue Mission (−P)
2nd WORST	Provide Mission (M); Agent pursues Mission (P)
WORST	Provide Mission (M); Agent does not pursue Mission (−P)

The assumption of partial conflict is the only plausible one, even though the opening scenes, where Agent in vain seeks a spying cell ready to receive him, may imply a coordination problem instead. The latter would suggest cooperative motivation, reducing the game to harmonizing the players' moves. *Memoirs* fails, however, to corroborate such a scenario. Very early on Agent meets Major Erms, who is in possession of Agent's Mission. Had coordination been the problem, the game would have been over at this point. Instead, despite multiple encounters with the major, the protagonist never receives anything but vague evasions concerning the undertaking for which he had ostensibly been recruited.

The Mission with which Agent is to be entrusted is the central symbol of the novel and the center of his quest in the netherworld. Allegorically capitalized throughout, the Mission is Agent's *raison d'être* in the Building, as well as – at least in his mind – the *raison d'être* for the Building itself. Only unshakable belief in the Mission can account for his refusal to leave the Pentagon while knowing the location of the exit.[31] Whatever torments, whatever tribulations he endures, Agent clings to the hope that "that thrice accursed Mission"[32] must exist.

But what about the Building's preference that Agent should not cease to pursue the Mission? Every time the nerve-racking "monkey business" becomes too much to bear, it offers him "spiritual comfort"[33] to restore morale and faith in the quest. Despite incontestable textual evidence, it is not easy to offer a universally plausible interpretation of the Building's motives. For one, the novel is sparse in the account of its intentions *vis-à-vis* Agent. Moreover, Agent is not only the protagonist. He is also the narrator of the memoirs and, as such, a potentially unreliable source of information about the Building.

One plausible hypothesis is that, as a neophyte to the spying business, Agent does not initially merit an integration into the Building's structure – hence the pretence of an important Mission he must pursue. Alternatively the Mission may be only a decoy inasmuch as Agent is scheduled to be an unwitting catalyst, a microscope through which the Building can study the behavior of its agents. Evidence in support is the drunken party in which Agent takes part because Dolt needs "a suitable actor"[34] to test another agent's reaction. By far the simplest and perhaps most convincing explanation may be the Building's uncertainty about Agent's – or anybody else's, for that matter – loyalty. Paranoiacally suspicious, the Building could never attain certainty that Agent has not been turned even before entering the premises.

The most arguable point in the Building's preferences may be the greatest utility in not providing Agent with the Mission he so hungers for. The outcomes where Mission doesn't exist are the Building's best and second best, whereas providing a Mission yields in either case a worse result. The reason why the Mission – or rather any Mission – is not desirable is that it would undermine the minimax strategy against the Anti-Building. The equilibrium solution to zero-sum games is a strategy that guarantees to one player a minimum payoff and prevents the other from maximizing his payoff beyond the same value, *irrespective of the moves one's opponent might make.*

Since in a zero-sum conflict both players are motivated to minimize the other's gains while maximizing their own, the minimax/maximin strategy is considered a solution to the conflict. Locked in a spying duel, both the Pentagon and its Communist counterpart perpetuate the hostility which has long since lost relevance beyond their precincts. The Cold War ideologies pitch the Building against the Anti-Building into a conflict in which they occupy wholly antagonistic positions, exactly the situation that justifies the use of the minimax strategy. Any distinction between the Building and its Communist counterpart is, of course, artificial because of a mutual takeover by *n*-tuple agents whose loyalty – definable only as the degree to which they have been unmasked – is more virtual than real.

Who is to say whether the Building is not, in fact, the Anti-Building? Refusing to help despite Agent's repeated pleas, raising his hopes only to dash them next, offering pacts in which betrayal is a *sine qua non*, the Building's actions are indistinguishable from its mirror image on the other side. Because of interpenetration and a pervasive inability to distinguish friend from foe, the only reasonable assumption is that any course of action, any Mission the Building might cook up, is already known to the adversary.

In an artifice of Machiavellian proportions, the Third Pentagon finds itself in a spot where, in order not to betray its purpose, *it must have no purpose at all*. The Building, therefore, routinely operates on a random basis, completely refraining from using pure strategies (its pure strategy, if you like, is to play randomly all the time). Bizarrely, despite outward marks of dissipation and irrationality, the Building's strategy of avoiding commitment to agents and missions is actually sensible as an extreme variant of Hamlet's "method in madness."

> *We are going to do Matrix Two and Matrix Three simultaneously. We are essentially going to make one giant movie that will be cut in half.*
>
> Joel Silver, *JAM! Showbiz*

Before drawing the two matrixes for the Mission Game, I must encourage readers to resist the feeling that this sort of analysis may be too arcane for them to understand. The concepts employed here are relatively simple game-theoretic applications that ought to be intelligible to anyone willing to stay the course. All the same, you may prefer to skip the matrix and return to it later, armed with the insights from the analysis.

A few words about notation. For simplicity's sake, BEST, 2nd BEST, 2nd WORST, and WORST are denoted respectively as 4, 3, 2, 1. Thus the top-left box entry "2,4" means no more than "2nd WORST, BEST." The rankings are strictly ordinal, meaning that the numbers merely express the relation "is preferred to," and must not be taken to have any absolute and comparative value. From the fact that alternative 2 is preferred to 1, it does not therefore follow that it is *twice* as attractive – it could be preferred just a shade more, or a million times over.

In the case of strategies, M denotes the existence of the Mission, and −M its absence. Similarly, for Agent's moves, P denotes his pursuit of the Mission, and −P no pursuit. Thus for every one of the Building's moves, Agent has a pairing countermove. In the matrix the Building's payoff comes first, followed by Agent's payoff. Thus a strategy pair "2,4" is to be read as follows: if Building provides Mission (plays M), and if Agent pursues Mission (plays P), the result for the Building is 2nd WORST, and for Agent BEST.

Since Agent is initially unaware of the Building's moves, theoretically one could model the players' actions as simultaneous. Their preferences – analyzed in the previous section (see pp. 140 and 141) – are reflected in Figure 1.

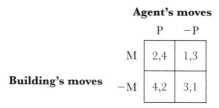

Agent's moves

	P	−P
M	2,4	1,3
−M	4,2	3,1

Building's moves

Figure 1 Mission Game matrix

More properly, however, the situation should be depicted as a metagame where the Building makes the first move, with Agent's response contingent on the Building's play.[35] The game tree for the Mission Game, which represents the complete sequence of the players' moves and responses, is shown in Figure 2.

The game tree does not include information sets. Even though in the beginning Agent has no idea of the Building's opening move, the following days make it plain he will never get to see his Mission. Similarly, despite his attempts to confide in various functionaries, from Major Erms to the Admiradier, the pale-faced spy, and the doctor from the Medical Section, none of them is of any help, taking advantage instead of his naiveté and sincerity. On top of that, after his bizarre lecture session with Captain Prandtl, Agent comes to suspect the presence of unfathomable layers of codes and ciphers in every aspect of the Building's life, nixing his chances of straight talk with anybody in the Pentagon, and thus of discovering his Mission.

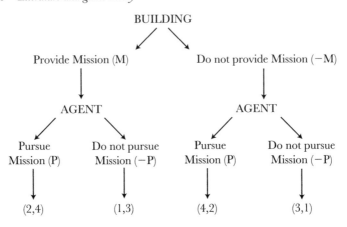

Figure 2 The game tree for the Mission game, which represents the complete sequence of the players' moves and responses

All this allows Agent to reconstruct the Building's opening move (Do not provide Mission), making the omission of information sets harmless. It also simplifies the analysis, which otherwise would have to include two games, one in which Agent knows and the other in which he does not know the Building's choice. To distinguish moves from strategies, the matrix of the 2×2 game can now be expanded to a 2×4 metagame in which the Pentagon has two strategies and Agent four – two replies to each of the Building's moves. Agent's four choices, completely describing his contingencies foreseeable from the Building's opening move, are given in Figure 3.

(P/P)   Pursue Mission regardless
(−P/−P)   Do not pursue Mission regardless
(P/−P)   Tit-for-tat strategy: pursue Mission if it exists, do not pursue if it does not
(−P/P)   Tat-for-tit strategy: do not pursue Mission if it exists, pursue if it does not

Agent's moves

		P/P	−P/−P	P/−P	−P/P
Building's moves	M	2,4	1,3	2,4	1,3
	−M	**4,2**	*3,1*	*3,1*	*4,2*

Figure 3 The 2 × 4 metagame

The matrix is quite persuasive. The Building should never play M, since all M choices are dominated by −M. This means that, for all cases where the Building plays −M, its payoffs are better than when playing M. Since the Building is rationally "bound" to choose −M, Agent's best option is to play either P/P or −P/P, which dominate (guarantee better payoffs over) his remaining options. In both cases the payoff for Agent is second worst (2), as opposed to worst (1) in the case of the other two.

However, between Agent's two strategies, P/P and −P/P, the former weakly dominates the latter. This means that, while the payoff for Agent is in both cases the same (2nd WORST, or 2), in the event of the Building changing *its* strategy, the Agent does better if he sticks to P/P. The strategy pair 4,2, then, emerges as the solution to the game. The equilibrium can be regarded as stable since neither player profits from a unilateral change of strategy (defection). Since the actual choices made by the players in the novel coincide with the solution to the Mission Game, it suggests the – however counterintuitive – *subjective rationality* of both players' moves.

> *I John Faustus of Wertenberge, Doctor, by these presents, so give body and soule to Lucifer prince of the East, and his minister Mephastophilis.*
>
> Christopher Marlowe, *Dr Faustus*

Halfway through the book, grasping at straws, the protagonist joins an apparently spontaneous evening of revels, only to discover it was another choreographed episode in the ubiquitous spying game. Frustrated and lost, he is then offered a chance to enter a pact with another agent.

The Collusion Game (see Figure 4) models what follows between Agent and Father Orfini. Recall that the institutional convergence of reciprocal expectations leaves any individual powerless, doomed to solitude and frustration, unless he's willing to take the risk of forming a coalition with a like-minded agent. The choices which Agent and Father Orfini confront are Collude (C) and Not Collude (−C). The Collusion Game matrix involves only two players as secrecy is essential to forestall the Building's knowledge of the pact – a precondition for the potential success of any collusion.

Agent's moves

		C	−C
	C	3,3	1,4
Orfini's moves			
	−C	*4,1*	**2,2**

Figure 4 The Collusion Game

Although the matrix is drawn for Agent and Orfini, the strict symmetry of the payoffs is independent of the identity of the players, suggesting that the matrix models, in fact, any pair of the Building's agents. Second, the game *is not strictly competitive*. In fact, the matrix explicitly recognizes the possibility of collusion between players in the 3,3 payoff, 2nd BEST for both. The high ranking of such an outcome is borne out by Agent's dogged attempts to confide in various functionaries and induce them into cooperation. Orfini's explicit and the pale spy's implicit offers to form a pact – both actually keep their rendezvous with Agent – also suggest a preference for coordination rather than solitary ops tacitly enforced by the rational insanity of the Third Pentagon.

The game captured in the matrix is, of course, the Building-specific variant of the Prisoner's Dilemma. Its seeming incongruity lies in the fact that in the case of collusion between players their respective payoffs are only second best. Should not the payoffs be highest, reflecting the greatest desirability of such an outcome? Two heads are better than one, and the examples of Agent, Orfini, the pale-faced spy, or even Prandtl ("he wanted to tell me something, but couldn't – or wasn't allowed"),[36] intimate that the desire to confide is widespread in the Building.

Alas, *Memoirs* makes it painfully obvious that there is not a single instance of successful collusion. The fear of the Building's ubiquitous and all-knowing eye makes the cooperative outcome not necessarily the most preferred one. Trying to tear down what he sees as a veneer of deceit, the neophyte agent seeks, of course, someone who will side with him rather than with the Building. The reason his efforts are doomed to failure is not even because coalitions are formed only to be denounced, but because the formative phase can hardly take place. As with the Mission Game, to understand *Memoirs* is to understand the origins of such a strong anti-coalition prohibition.[37]

To collude or not to collude? That is the question that any agent must be asking himself, inevitably followed by questions about the loyalty of the other agent. Is he a double, a triple, or even some indecently higher number – an undeclared sextuple, an over-zealous septuple, or worse? The implicit injunction not to collude is evident in the offer of a two-person coalition extended to Agent by Orfini – the event modeled in the payoff matrix. After days of vain efforts to find a fellow conspirator, Agent should jump at the deal. Yet, whether because he discovers that their talk has been bugged, or because the scales finally fall from his eyes, Agent concludes that he has been again betrayed and chooses to miss the rendezvous.

In the Building's newspeak world, where treason is loyalty, there can be no successful collusion unless agents form a *binding agreement* or an *effective set*. Let's look at these conditions in turn. Most cooperative solutions presuppose free communication between players and the ability to form binding agreements. But to reach an agreement one must communicate, and to communicate one must first render one's meaning unambiguous. Good luck, where "truth is but another way of lying,"[38] where everyone's speeches, jokes, confessions, fits of rebellion, silences, and even deaths are supercoded for fear of playing into the hands of the enemy.

The formation of an effective set runs into its own obstacles. The demands that (1) the new coalition be sufficiently *strong* to implement its agenda and (2) the players be *properly motivated* (for all players the payoffs in the new coalition should be better than the old) cannot be met. The condition of strength founders since, against the enormity of the Building, a two-person coalition cannot enforce any change of policy. Quite the reverse – the Building's staff are, in effect, a grand coalition to which individuals must accede in order to wield any, however minuscule, power. Naturally, bargaining power lies in players' threat leverage and their value to the coalition, both negligible in this case.

Old-timers like Orfini entertain no illusions when it comes to maverick outsiders like Agent: "You'll cooperate all right, if not now then tomorrow."[39] So much for two-person coalitions. The Building's vastness and random ops make it equally invulnerable to the formation of larger coalitions, even if only because they could never ascertain when their membership changed from subcritical to critical. Moreover, for n players, the formula for the number of subsets is 2^n, yielding $2^n - 1$ nonempty sets. For its own security, the growing coalition would have to control all subcoalitions that might form within itself. Without binding agreements, this is an impossible task in view of the exponentially driven solution for any high value of n.

What about the second condition, proper motivation? Let's begin with the two intuitively sensible provisos laid out by Von Neumann and Morgenstern. A new coalition must be Pareto optimal (there is no other payoff in which all players simultaneously do better) and individually rational (each player could obtain at least as much by not colluding).[40] The payoff from the Building's grand coalition should thus be at least equal to agents' 2nd WORST outcome of 2. That means that there is little inducement to risk an even lower payoff (1) by entering a two-person alliance only to be duped by the other player. The threat of being left out in the cold by a treacherous partner is all too real. It is strong enough to drive the old-young spy and the tall officer to suicide, and the Building is rife with (self-)executions of agents who miscalculate their alliances.

To recap: because the conditions of Pareto optimality and individual rationality cannot be met, the players in the Collusion Game are not properly motivated. Because the players are not properly motivated and do not command the necessary coalitional strength, they cannot form an effective

set. Because they cannot form an effective set or arrive at binding agreements, the highest utility of 4 cannot represent successful collusion. In the
Collusion Game the preferred payoff is thus associated with the situation
where the other player colludes, leaving his fate, as it were, in the hands of
his partner. For these reasons, collusion yields only the second-best value of
3, while the second worst (2), although not very attractive, at least offers the
relative appeal of security.

The paradox in the Prisoner's Dilemma resides in the difference
between the payoffs obtained independently and the payoffs players could
get by coordinating their moves. Although each spy has a minimax strategy
which guarantees a minimum payoff (not a very attractive one), there is a
cooperative outcome which secures a higher payoff for both. Yet as long as
the players cannot enter into binding agreements, its appeal is illusory
since a defection will always provide one with a better outcome at the
expense of his partner. In our case, although the only stable outcome (2,2)
yields lower payoffs than the cooperative (3,3) the latter is fool's gold.
Whether one enters a coalition with pure intentions or not, in either case *it
is always better to defect.*

Even on multiple iteration the cooperative strategy does not come out
on its own. Even if one player signaled his preference by sticking to the
cooperative C, the other could always do better by denouncing the naïf to
the Pentagon's execution section. Such a defection bolsters one's status as a
loyal agent but further reduces the chance of collusion between any pair of
agents. In fact, since inside the Building everyone's loyalty is in perpetual
flux, there is little chance of reciprocal altruism since only death can halt
the unmasking of camouflage. To enter into a binding agreement one
would have to somehow step outside the Building. Inside, only death is
"something that no amount of subterfuge could ever alter,"[41] in keeping
with the hardboiled dictum that "Dead men don't tell lies."

> *The absurdity of life, which actually has nothing to do with either society or behavior within
> society, cannot be denied or eradicated.*
>
> Albert Camus, *L'Etranger*

There is a symmetry between Agent, who has to assume that all his moves
are known to the Building, and the Building's position *vis-à-vis* the Anti-
Building. Where the Pentagon plays randomly against its Communist
counterpart, the hero intuitively follows the same course while searching
for the Mission. And yet, no matter what he does or doesn't do, his tactical
resistance ends in defeat. Agent's suicide is thus not only a termination of
his contest with the Building. It is also a means of quitting the game which
he is condemned to play on the Building's terms.

Unless the Third Pentagon changes its strategy – and the matrix suggests no inducement to do so – Agent's payoff will always be second worst. His suicide and the corresponding change to the (3,1) outcome, instead, indicates a dramatic change in his preferences. The corresponding drop in the Building's payoff intimates that his suicide is born as much of despair as of revenge. It is this sense of play and experiment that led Ewa Balcerzak to describe Lem's fictions as "philosophical treatises" that model social scenarios and run "multifaceted analyses on these models."[42]

Convinced in the pathos of his solitude that he is facing an inimical world, in reality Agent is facing only himself. In this he resembles others of Lem's Hemingwayesque heroes from the 1960s: scientist Kelvin from *Solaris*, astronaut Bregg from *Return from the Stars*, Navigator Rohan from *The Invincible*, mathematician Hogarth from *His Master's Voice*, and to some extent even pilot Pirx and Tichy. Existentially alone, all start out by viewing the world through anthropomorphism-tinted glasses. All but the Agent undergo an epiphany, as a result of which they abandon the atavistic belief in the order of things, where Man is at the center of a universe whose meaning can be read out in its workings.

Agent's journey echoes the tireless labors of human cultures to justify the unjustifiable and find meaning in the meaningless. The deep need to domesticate the Cosmos (evident in theism, animism, totemism, or other forms of religious personification) is never more apparent than when he seeks Someone to ask, "What do you want me to do," and refuses to accept that "There will be no answer."[43] In its own way *Memoirs* captures the Beckett-like absurdity of the Game of Life. Amid other meaning-seekers whose experience may be identical in its fruitless lack of cooperation and aggravating search for a higher reason, the game must be played out in isolation.

Lem's novel is relentless in painting spymasters condemned by rationality to existential solitude. Every man is "infernally alone" in a quest for the Mission, a lifelong task that makes "no sense, no sense to anyone."[44] Played out in real time despite frantic attempts to cast a glance ahead, the Game of Life may be the only one that, irrespective of interim tactics, always ends in the same immutable outcome. Agent's frustration is the reaction of a man who tries to outfox the imagined Builder of his fate, refusing to believe that he carries it in his own hands (in a yellow folder).[45]

An allegorical Everyman, Agent misconstrues the Building's randomness and indifference as a metaphysical bias toward his life. Nothing, of course, could be further from the truth. Far from an imposition from God or Big Brother, at its heart lies no more than an evolutionary mean of daily transactions conducted by its inhabitants. Infinitely vast and complex, the Building is like Borges's library, filled with seekers on a mission to explain the world to the minds trapped in it. Indeed, the vast espionage library, the museum filled with spying *accoutrements* past and present, and the gallery exhibiting severed human hands out of a warped celebration of history, all symbolize this teleological autonomy of human thought.

It may be human nature, allows Lem, to search for meanings in the external world, whose constants signify nothing. But that doesn't make the labors of the Department of Codes any less demented. Its deconstructive paranoia dictates that, since everything contains inexhaustible strata of meaning, everything is in a code. Like a typical Department of Literary Deconstruction, it never stops to reflect that *il n'y a pas de hors-code* means just the opposite – if everything is indeed in code, nothing is. No matter how grand the design or how noble the illusion, equating reality with one's perception of it amounts to solipsistic folly.

The position of the inquiring mind *vis-à-vis* external reality is a permanent fixture on Lem's landscape. "The [scientist] who succeeds proves himself an expert puzzle-solver," wrote Thomas Kuhn only a year before *Memoirs* in *The Structure of Scientific Revolutions*. As if in response, in the only scene where we see a larger group of the Building's functionaries, there is "no conversation, not even about the food; they were busy solving puzzles instead."[46] To make sure the analogy is not overlooked, one of Lem's super-spies actually comments on the etymology of the Roman word *speculator*. It turns out that the scholar-explorer and the scout-agent are both rooted in the figure of an information-seeker.

John Chadwick, a cryptologist involved in deciphering the Linear B script, captures the epistemic bond between spies and researchers: "Cryptography is a science of deduction and controlled experiment; hypotheses are formed, tested and often discarded."[47] And yet, while comparable in method, the ontological orientations of a scientist and espionage agent are profoundly at odds. The former takes for granted that his object of inquiry is intentionally neutral, even if only because research, as one prominent astronomer put it, is "best done by believing that realism is true, even if in fact it isn't."[48]

On the other hand, the information a spy seeks is not only of human origin, but may have been tampered with to thwart him. In *The Decipherment of Linear B*, Chadwick again underscores this: "There is an obvious resemblance between an unreadable script and a secret code; similar methods can be employed to break both. But the differences must not be overlooked. The code is deliberately designed to baffle the investigator."[49] In contrast, the "code" of Nature is not. There is a world of difference, in other words, between unlocking Nature's secrets and outwitting an opponent – who could be a writer of fiction – in an interpretive game of wits.

This difference lies at the center not only of *Memoirs* but of *The Structure of Scientific Revolutions* as well. The latter's legacy is a metaphor of revolutionary science that, in an almost Freudian stereotype, sweeps away the parental authority of the old. But Kuhn's case study – the replacement of Ptolemaic cosmology by the Copernican – is actually atypical. More often than not, new theories not so much overturn as supersede the old, revealing them as limiting cases of more general laws. Where the philosopher saw catastrophic (*pace* catastrophe theory) ruptures between paradigms split by bolts of scientific lightning, old and new theories are more like adolescents growing into adults, with much continuity and kinship between them.

All too many humanists tried to buttress the edifice of constructivism with what they read into young Kuhn's theses. To set the record straight, here's mature Kuhn on truth and knowledge in his 1992 Rothschild Lecture. It is said, he writes, that

> power and interest are all there are. Nature itself, whatever that may be, has seemed to have no part in the development of beliefs about it. Talk of evidence, or the rationality of claims drawn from it, and of the truth or probability of those claims has been seen as simply the rhetoric behind which the victorious party cloaks its power. What passes for scientific knowledge becomes, then, simply the belief of the winners. I am among those who have found the claims of the strong program absurd: an example of deconstruction gone mad.[50]

Casting a different light on Kuhn's own theses, this unequivocal rejection of anti-realism has wide repercussions for any sophisticated theory of knowledge, including knowledge in literature. Grounding science, philosophy, and literature in the world outside our windows, it underlines the contrast between two visions of the world and inquiry. The first is a moderately realistic belief in understanding mind-independent reality, one empirical step at a time. The other is a form of constructivism that argues for a plurality of community-relative interpretive paradigms. Few statements capture its cognitive upshot as colorfully as Paul Feyerabend's public recantation of seriousness of purpose in the introduction to *Against Method*, and a wish to be remembered only as a "flippant Dadaist."

In the days when the nuclear ghosts of Khrushchev and Kennedy are poised to rise again, the contrast between these two visions makes, to my mind, the strongest case for literary scholarship in which realism, objectivity, and rationality are refugees no longer.

Conclusion

From the amoeba to Einstein, the growth of knowledge is always the same: we try to solve our problems, and to obtain, by a process of elimination, something approaching adequacy in our tentative solutions.

Karl Popper, *Objective Knowledge: An Evolutionary Approach*

The working title for this book – *Mining the Mindfield* – contained a *double entendre*. First of all, it evoked the process of prospecting the mindfield – that is, the breadth and depth of our mental faculties. As such, it was expressive of the search for the source of our talent and propensity for creating imaginary worlds, different from the world we know, yet so useful to the understanding of it. The answer, as you know by now, is twofold. The immediate source of this talent and propensity is thought experiment, and the underlying one is evolution.

But, equally, *Mining the Mindfield* evoked the image of the minefield of contemporary literary criticism. Even in the best of times, it is not an easy territory to traverse in pursuit of a methodological overview and a cognitive appraisal. Today the inherent difficulty of the terrain is aggravated by factions who, armed with various theories of knowledge, snipe at truth and reason. Yet traversed it must be, for there are richer intellectual ores in narrative fiction, and more effective ways of interpretively "mining" them, than are dreamt of in current critical philosophy.

The task is timely, inasmuch as literary studies of the last generation or so seems to have been caught between a rock and a hard place. One side of the critical arena is occupied by postmodernists of all ilks and stripes celebrating their break with classical inquiry. On the other side of the bleachers sit the skeptics who need convincing that literature is capable of more then airy-fairy subjectivity. In some ways it is hard to blame them, as science has indeed come a long way since Arnold's and Snow's Rede lectures. Douglas Hoftstadter and Stephen Hawking are living examples of scientists who are also popular writers, Pulitzer winners, and multimillion-copy bestsellers.

Yet the same skeptics have no trouble accepting the cognitive credentials of inquires that, stripped to essentials, are so much creative fiction. The Delphi method of futurological forecasting, for instance, relies on imaginative guesses to tackle issues too obscure, complex, or interdisciplinary for any one expert to handle. Instead of committee proceedings – potentially biased by bandwagon mentality, status bullying, unwillingness to be seen as flip-flopping, etc. – the method solicits opinions without hoping to decide the truth of the matter. Grounded solely in the expertise and imagination of the think-tankers, Delphi forecasts merely seek consensus in areas deemed inexact to begin with.[1]

This is not to cast aspersions on futurology. We do need to predict the shape of the future, even in its vaguest outline. My point is only that the above account is also an accurate account of what some writers do when elaborating their "virtual-reality" scenarios. You could say, in fact, that *Of Literature and Knowledge* is a book-length defense of this very point. Hence, on the one hand, it delineates a constructive alternative to the fuzzy epistemology of literary-critical revisionism, abolitionism, and dualism. Hence, on the other, it aims to jump-start a science-consilient program of literary research.

Doubters will not, of course, be silenced easily. Grouching that writers and critics misrepresent science whenever they have something to say about it, they may actually have a point. John Updike's well-received *Roger's Version* illustrates what and how much lies at stake. Laboring to overcome Wayne Falke's critique of the Rabbit novels, in which Updike "told us what we knew, not what we should know,"[2] *Roger's Version* situates itself on the border of theology and science. Searching for a compass with which to triangulate God, Man, and the world, a graduate student designs a computer program to comb the values of physical constants for regularities that might reveal the Divine Design.[3]

Much of critical interpretation focused on the novel as a remix of *The Scarlet Letter*. To be sure, Updike has been recycling Hawthorne's romance for decades, notably in *A Month of Sundays*. This time around Chillingworth returned as a Christian theology professor, Roger Lambert, Dimmesdale as a born-again micro-whiz Dale, and Hester embodied partly in Esther, partly in Verna. Hardly anyone, however, commented on the vital link with science symbolized on the cover by a detail from Michelangelo's Sistine Chapel – God's finger reaching to Adam's – displayed on a desktop terminal. The computing and cosmological dimensions were of little interest to megaphone scholars.

The oversight is all the more conspicuous in that Updike's preface credits Paul Davies, Fred Hoyle, Robert Jastrow, Martin Gardner, and other scientists and philosophers of science whose work went into his own. Rehashing their theories – at times so poorly paraphrased as to smack of a lecture room – Updike tries to bring his cosmological speculation in line with scientific findings on the subject. Equally important, he tries to draw attention to the fact that he tries. Not that the invasion of science into domains long held to be beyond its sway is anything new – not, at least, outside the humanities. For today's astrophysicists and biologists, grappling with etiological and even theological entanglements of universal creation comes with the territory.

In *Roger's Version* the big idea is a search for patterns among physical constants. This, states the writer, is to be attempted "not in its content so much as in complexity, at a level that would yield graphical or algorithmic clues to an underlying design, assuming there is one."[4] A moment's reflection prompts that such a program could never be vindicated. Even if one could establish some fixed relation for cosmic constants, it would only prove the *necessity* of physical and biochemical conditions for the Creation – not their sufficiency.

Studies of the complex dynamics among patterns exhibited by physical constants are nothing new under the sun. And, predictably enough, in the case of *Roger's Version* the scientific verdict on its science is not flattering. A computer expert, Eric Weiss, even reviewed *Roger's Version* with its central research idea in mind. Charitably he concluded that, while the author captures "many of the outward . . . signs of computing, he fails to communicate . . . its intellectual content and concepts."[5] Pulling fewer punches in *The World Within the World*, John Barrow – mathematician, astronomer, and bestselling author himself – shrugged off Updike's scientific pretension as simply garbled.

Seeing how badly literary fiction fares in the extradisciplinary court of inquiry, literary scholarship cannot remain a matter of restating and refining literary insights because, under the microscope, these can turn out to be so much nonsense. To better the ratio of sense to nonsense, humanists need to undertake no less than a paradigm shift. They need to move away from dualism-led megaphone criticism and become answerable to the basic facts and methods of all inquiry. Getting one's science right is as vital as redeeming literature from those who would deconstruct it or relativize it into nihility. But either way there is little excuse for pretending that humanistic *research* can go on like before.

> *I hate relativism. I hate relativism more than I hate anything else, excepting, maybe, fibreglass powerboats.*
>
> Jerry Fodor, *Behavioral and Brain Sciences*

In conclusion, some things bear repeating. First, the cognitive orientation in literary studies does not nullify appreciating stories as aesthetic artifacts. Interactions with literature owe much to symbolic understanding, emotional epiphany, or sheer entertainment value. The axiological goals of traditional scholarship must, in other words, be pursued with proper vigor, especially amid the inundation of mass-market brain candy. The task is Herculean since, as a socio-cultural institution, literary studies is losing its capacity to function under the astronomical amount of print that perniciously clogs the system. More books, after all, have seen the light of day since *The Catcher in the Rye* than in all previous history combined.[6]

That said, interpretive and polemical interpretation must not be confused with systematic *research*. Without a sound framework for evaluating claims to knowledge, literary studies will only perpetuate its image of a clearinghouse for all kinds of irrational beliefs. A failure to appeal to the factual state of affairs can only lead to such odd developments as the discipline's infatuation with psychoanalysis. After libraries of conclusive reports on factual errors, scientific missteps, and falsified evidence in Freud's theories, the only place (save the analyst's couch) in which psychoanalysis is still in vogue is a department of literary or cultural studies.[7]

Decades of rampant mistreatment of literary fictions as case studies for the anachronistic and incoherent brood of psychoanalytic doctrines did not impress on its professors that, as a cogent research discipline, it is a dead end. This despite clinical diagnoses of psychoanalysis as a placebo. This despite an aesthetic straitjacket into which works of imaginative fiction have to be forced in order to endure "interdisciplinary" scholarship in the neo-Freudian or neo-Lacanian vein. This despite conclusive scientific studies best summarized by Frederick K. Goodwin, past director of the American National Institute of Mental Health: "there is no real evidence that it works."[8]

Few things could convey the shakiness of literary studies' credentials as sharply as being lumped in with pseudoscience. Under the heading of "Research by Literary Interpretation," here is how a recent interdisciplinary bestseller characterizes such laissez-faire practices: "Pseudoscientists frequently reveal themselves by their handling of the scientific literature . . . They focus upon the words, not on the underlying facts and reasons." And worse: "In this regard the pseudoscientists act like lawyers gathering precedents and using these as arguments, rather than attending to what has actually been communicated."[9]

In any body of thought, be it a system of logic or literary epistemology, internal consistency suffices to have its axioms accepted as correct. But the situation changes if that same body of thought aims to say something sensible about the world. With empirical accuracy as the goal of inquiry, from the googolplex of consistent systems only a few will pass the correspondence test with reality. Of course, not even empirical soundness guarantees correctness. Experiments checked and rechecked a hundredfold might overlook hidden variables while confirming those we already know – as it was with approximating gravity by means of the Newtonian equations.

But even if, in principle, experimental accuracy does not establish truth beyond the wildest skeptical doubt, in practice it will be the baseline if our criteria are to be fundamentally empirical. Robin Fox captures this consilient ideal eloquently in "State of the Art/Science in Anthropology":

> Humanistic insight and scientific objectivity are not and should never be opposed: a devotion to humanistic values will lead to a more insightful science, and an equal devotion to scientific values will lead to a more convincing humanism. We are equal partners in the task of achieving a better understanding of mankind.[10]

In this context one must take note of the paradigm shift among both the apologists and the debunkers of postmodernism. Clearly, we are in the midst of the changing of the guard. Anaphoric titles such as *After Poststructuralism: Interdisciplinarity and Literary Theory* (1993), *After Postmodernism: Reconstructing Ideology Critique* (1994), *After Postmodernism: Education, Politics, and Identity* (1995), *After Postmodernism: An Introduction to Critical Realism* (2001), *After Poststructuralism: Writing the Intellectual History of Theory* (2002), and *After Poststructuralism: Reading Stories and Theory* (2004) make clear that literary scholarship today is all too aware of the need to redraw the cognitive maps sabotaged by ideology.[11]

On its passé tenets, human beings are not agents driven in part by evolutionary instincts and in part by moderately rational and intentional attitudes towards the world. Instead, each one of us is like Locke's blank tablet – subject to a totalizing rewrite by ideology, imprisoned by race, sex, social status, and inculturation, and reducible to their amalgam. One answer to this reduction of individuals and societies to constructions of power comes from the study of evolution, which documents the myriad ways in which we are preprogrammed to do things independently of cultural specifics. To varying degrees the individual claims of this ever-developing body of knowledge are, of course, all open to revision. But its core facts and methods provide a "sufficing" stepping stone to more knowledge.

An elementary component of science, evolution is also an elementary component of cognitive literacy. That's why, between Darwin and Derrida, I prefer to bet my money on evolution. That's why the burgeoning field of literary evolutionary studies impinges on the understanding of literature, fiction, and art. That's why, if serious about knowledge, we must cast away all versions of Sidney's "poet nothing affirmeth" with everything it allegedly stands for. Only ill-guided appeals to disciplinary autonomy – themselves rooted in nineteenth-century romantic-idealist aesthetics – could pin this cognitive bracket onto literary propositions.[12]

To rejoin the epistemic lists, literature scholars must put themselves in the unfamiliar, although historically not new, context of forging links with the mainstream of social-scientific research. Understandably, no transfer of scientific theories and methods to humanistic inquiry can take place without a degree of sometimes painful readjustment. But, as I argued in *Between Literature and Science*, theories and methods drawn from the social sciences can only lead to new research opportunities. Science is an "ever so fallible, heterogeneous, and daily outdated body of knowledge. But scientific research and its methods are the best means of learning about the world. And as such they deserve our respect and critical – in both senses – attention."[13]

This is because literature, philosophy, and science are inseparable manifestations of the same human instinct to interrogate the world and help negotiate the experience of living in it.

Notes

Introduction

1 See Donald Brown's synthesis of the so-called Universal People (1991).
2 See Gottschall (2003, 2004).
3 An entertaining account of mondegreening comes from Pinker (1994: 186).
4 For a detailed analysis of the fiction–nonfiction distinction, see Swirski (2000a). For background, see Currie (1990).
5 Livingston (1990: 24).
6 While conceding that the line is not clean, Szabó Gendler (2000) attempts to distinguish between hypotheticals (which *could* for all we know obtain), and counterfactuals (which could *not*). For our purposes nothing rides on the distinction; hence I use these terms interchangeably.
7 Poe (1987: 252); for a full analysis of the science and philosophy of *Eureka*, see Swirski (2000a). Subsequent quotations from Calvino (1968); Malamud (1997: xiv); and Percy (1997: 360).
8 Poundstone (1988: 132).
9 Mach (1976: 136).
10 Sorensen (1992a: 3).
11 Heil (1995: 23). See J. R. Brown (1991a: esp. 28–32), for a contraposition of counterfactuals in science and philosophy.
12 Such views are expressed, or at least detectable, in Shapin (1984); J. R. Brown (1991a); Gooding (1994); Nersessian (1993); Hacking (1993); McAllister (1996); and Souder (2003).
13 The prominent, if not sole, exception is Nancy Nersessian; see also Chapter 4.
14 See the discussion of relativism in Chapter 1.
15 Although the foundational contribution, Von Neumann's minimax solution for two-person zero-sum games dates back to 1928, the discipline was not established until the publication in 1944 of Von Neumann and Morgenstern's *Theory of Games and Economic Behavior*.
16 Standard introductory sources on Lem are Swirski (1997, 1999, 2006b). I wish to thank Joseph Carroll for his penetrating and pertinent comments on various parts of the book, and my research assisstant, Selina Lai, for her diligent help.

Chapter 1

1 Lyotard (1979: 84).
2 For analysis, see Swirski (2000a: ch. 2). Revised here, the central portion of this chapter appeared previously in Swirski (1998c).
3 Goodman and Elgin (1988: 153, 24).
4 The extent to which Goodman continues to enter debates about postmodernism can be gleaned from his recurring presence throughout Hacking's *The Social Construction of What?* (2000).
5 Grosz (1993: 209). Cf. Judith Butler: "I do not understand the notion of 'theory' . . . why not simply call this operation *politics*, or some necessary permutation of it?" (in Rabaté 2002: 1–2).
6 Goodman and Elgin (1988: 161).
7 Goodman and Elgin (1988: 162).
8 Grosz (1993: 209).
9 Goodman and Elgin (1988: 163).
10 Rorty (1992: 141); Carson, quoted in Hershbach (1996: 12); Polkinghorne (1992: 149); Machery, quoted in Levin (1993: 21).
11 Jameson (1991: 218); Eagleton (1996: vii); Harding (1986: 113).
12 Sorman (1989: 354; my own translation from the French). Cf. Laudan: "The displacement of the idea that facts and evidence matter by the idea that everything boils down to subjective interests and perspectives is – second only to American political campaigns – the most prominent and pernicious manifestation of anti-intellectualism in our time" (Laudan 1996: x).
13 Gross *et al.* (1996: 108).
14 Miller (1988) and Laudan (1996) delineate pragmatic alternatives both to positivistic scientism and to unabashed relativism.
15 Sokal (1996: 62). Exhaustive web coverage can be found at www.keele.ac.uk/depts/stt/stt/sokal.htm. The entire affair is the subject of *The Sokal Hoax: The Sham That Shook the Academy* (Editors of *Lingua Franca* 2000); it includes a number of subsequent commentaries. Perhaps the most accessible and shortest, though no less devastating, account is M. Gardner's "Alan Sokal's Hilarious Hoax" (2000).
16 Held (1996: 202).
17 Published in Europe as *Intellectual Impostures* (Sokal and Bricmont 2003).
18 See, for example, Livingston (1988).
19 Carroll (1995: 436).
20 Far too many to cite, and even less to summarize; from a series of by now classic and unanswered (on the level of specific argument) refutations one can select Elster (1983); Siegel (1987); Livingston (1988); Fox (1992); MacDonald (1992); Levin (1993, 1995); Gross and Levitt (1994); Patai and Koertge (1994); Carroll (1995); Sokal (1996); and Crews (2001, 2002, 2006).
21 Crews (1993: x).
22 *Republic* (Plato 1999: 832).
23 Ingarden (1973: 164).
24 Shattuck (1998: 59).
25 Ingarden (1973: 157, 152).
26 Walsh (1969: 129).
27 An early but effective critique of the neo-Kantian opposition is Bunge's *Causality and Modern Science* (1959).
28 Miller (1987) and Laudan (1996) record the epistemological confusion perpetrated in the name of this alleged dichotomy.

29 For the background on nineteenth-century neo-Kantianism, see Schnädelbach (1984).
30 Arnold (1885: 69).
31 Rosovsky (1991: 539).
32 Haraway (1991: 184).
33 Latour and Woolgar (1986: 180). In *Paradigms Lost*, Casti cites one of the celebrated scientists of our time, Freeman Dyson: "There's a whole culture of philosophy out there somewhere with which we have no contacts at all . . . there's really little contact between what we call science and what these philosophers of science are doing – whatever it is" (Casti 1989: 47).
34 In Lawson and Kramer (1985: 26).
35 Girard (1965: 3).
36 Girard (1965: 25).
37 See Livingston (1992a).
38 I am thus in disagreement with Weissmann (1996). For more on the cognitive dimension in Poe, see Swirski (1996b, 2000: chs. 2, 3).
39 Simon (1983: 32).
40 In a cognate sense of "illustrative," La Caze (2002) argues for the role of the image, analogy and metaphor – as opposed to strict logical argument – in cognition.
41 Poincaré (1952: 37).
42 While the homology is mine, the words are J. R. Brown's (1991a: 7). Among his classes of thought experiments, the mediative especially performs the same role as the literary brand of scenario-cum-analysis.
43 M. Gardner (1990: 42).
44 Beardsley (1958: 429–30, 430).
45 Livingston (1988: 260).
46 Carroll (2004: 36). For evolutionary studies, see also Cooke and Turner (1999); Storey (1996); Koch (1993); Argyros (1991); and Dissanayake (1992).
47 Paris (1998: 233).
48 Stecker (n.d.: 6).
49 Beardsley (1958: 5).
50 Kernan (1991: 5).

Chapter 2

1 This and the next quotation from Argyros (1992: 667).
2 Barrow (1998: 29).
3 Sorensen (1992b: 6). *Thought Experiments* defines them similarly as "experiments that purport to deal with their question by contemplation of their design rather than by execution" (Sorensen 1992a: 6).
4 For an update on the various models of intentionalism and a defense of moderate intentionalism in art criticism, see Livingston (2005).
5 Sorensen (1992b: 6).
6 Will (1993).
7 Malamud (1997: 19). Next quotation in Malamud (1991: 115).
8 Malamud (1972: 84).
9 Thackeray (1991: 170); Čapek, quoted in Matuška (1964: 127); Nietzsche (1996, vol. 2: 245); Eco (1984: 28); Lem, quoted in Bereś and Lem (2002: 80; my own translation from the Polish).

10 It might have been verified five years earlier had not the Freundlich expedition to the Crimea, set to confirm general relativity, been interrupted by the onset of the First World War.
11 For background and analysis, see Swirski (2000a: ch. 1).
12 Mach (1960: 586).
13 Borges and Bioy-Casares (1976: 29).
14 For a comprehensive analysis, see Swirski (2001).
15 Mach (1976: 120).
16 See Swirski (2000a); also Elster (1983); Bruce and Purdy (1994); Fox (1996); Hollis (1994); MacDonald (1992); Moser (1989); and Ortiz de Montellano (1991, 1992).
17 Cited in Abbott (2002: 7).
18 Frye (1957: 354).
19 Stewart (1975: vii). For the background and metaphysics of mathematics, see Hersh (1997); also, Barrow (1999: 83–107).
20 Barrow (1991: 235).
21 For a lucid treatment, see J. R. Brown, "What Is Platonism?" (1991a: 53–8).
22 "The *essence* of *mathematics* lies in its *freedom*" (Cantor 1883).
23 Montague (1974: 222). Compare this to Winograd: "The idea is that language and thought can be modelled by such things as formal logic. But I think that that is grossly oversimplified. What people actually do has very little in common with formal logic, and what's missing is the social dimension" (quoted in Waldrop 1985: 44). In this case, the logical and pragmatic approaches may be rendered compatible by the evolutionary account; see Lakoff and Nuñez (2000).
24 Although Peano's work was later found to be incomplete, Russell and Whitehead showed in *Principia Mathematica* that his five proposals can all be defined in terms of logical constants (a further rider is that one must accept – as most logicians do – the axioms of infinity and choice).
25 The modern canonical formulation of this self-referential paradox is "This sentence is false." Of course, the liar's paradox need not be self-referential; cf. the conjunction of these sentences: "The other sentence is false" and "The other sentence is true."
26 Galileo (1953: 103–4).
27 For analysis, see Swirski (2000a: ch. 1).
28 Barrow (2000: 52). An early and ardent exposition of the conceptual and modeling freedom in the field is Sylvester's famous "A Plea for the Mathematician" (1904).
29 O'Hear (1992: 390).
30 Cited in Jaki (1966: 118).
31 Cited in Barrow (2000: 165).
32 Poe's tales are not prone to be found wrong or incomplete; his cosmogonic theory from *Eureka* already has been. See Swirski (2000a: chs. 2, 3).
33 McBain's art is discussed in Swirski (2006a: ch. 3).
34 See, for example, Dauben (1979: 132).
35 In "Some Philosophical Implications of Mathematical Logic" John Mayhill proposed another analogy between mathematics and art: "The analogue between Gödel's theorem and aesthetics is something like: There is no school of art which permits the production of all beauty and excludes the production of all ugliness" (Mayhill 1952: 191).
36 Frye (1957: 352).

37 For a detailed analysis, see Swirski (2001). In what follows I implicitly reject conventionalism (reduction of knowledge to linguistic conventions) and its attendant attempt at reduction of all conditions to logical necessity (and possibility).
38 For nobrow and popular literary cultures, see Swirski (2005).
39 Malamud, quoted in Weinberger (1983: D04). Bradbury, quoted in Booth (2001: E13); Pratchett, quoted in Horton (2002: D10); Malamud in "Why Fantasy?" (1997: 47); Lem's final quotation from Bere's and Lem (2002: 129).
40 For full analyses of Čapek and Malamud's novels, see Swirski (2005: ch. 4; and 1998a, respectively).
41 It's not clear if Hank's experience is a dream vision following a blow to the head or a result of an actual removal to the sixth century (in the former case, the violation would be only physical). The Strugatskys develop the same thesis by means of a Not-Quite-Twin-But-Close Earth scenario in *Hard to Be a God*.

Chapter 3

1 Sorensen (1992a: 15).
2 Tetlock and Belkin (1996: 4).
3 Lodge (2001: 61–2). In the next paragraph: Lem, quoted in Bere's and Lem (2002: 129, 343); Čapek, quoted in Matuška (1964: 129); Percy (1977: 361); Morrow, cited in Goldstrom (2000).
4 Pinker (1997: 542).
5 On the subject of genre fiction, see Swirski (2005). On the modern transformation of the hardboiled paradigm, see Swirski and Wong (2006), and Swirski (forthcoming).
6 Cited in Jacques Hadamard (1949: 16). I focused here on music; in *Aesthetic Judgment and Arousal* (1973) Gerda Smets published the results of her pioneering "bioaesthetic" study directed at discovering epigenetic rules in visual abstract art, crowned with a similarly startling and reproducible convergence.
7 Basic numeracy seems a good candidate for an evolutionary invariant. Some animals exhibit rudimentary intuitions for small numbers (roughly up to between four and seven). Documented in the case of food items or the number of young, they detect differences and initiate action accordingly; see O. Koehler (1951); Ramsey (1978).
8 For more on exaptations, see Gould and Vrba (1982). A great deal of caution with regard to adaptations is argued by Sterelny (2003: esp. 101–5). Being a form of knowledge, on Plotkin's terms literature should be an adaptation, a conclusion that strikes me as far-fetched.
9 "The Deep Structure of Literary Representations," in Carroll (2004: 109).
10 On this point, see Barrow (1998, 1999). The dilemma of informativeness was notably rehearsed – if not formulated – by Kuhn (1981). The most compelling answer from the evolutionary standpoint is formulated by Sorensen (1992b).
11 Mach (1976: 136).
12 Sterelny (2003: 41).
13 Pinker (1994: 427).
14 Darwin (1981: 372).
15 Lodge (2001: 42).
16 Mach (1976: 136, 149).
17 Mach (1960: 36). Where, following Mach, I seek to supercharge the cognitive battery in evolution, Kuhn and Brown seek it, respectively, in paradigm-busting

reconceptualization (seeing old data in new light) and the Platonism of abstract categories (universals).

18 J. B. Watson and R. R. Watson reported in "Studies in Infant Psychology" (1921) that darkness, animals (e.g. snakes), and humans do not elicit innate fear responses. These findings have been intensely critiqued by generations of psychologists; for early examples, see Thomson (1968: 363–5).

19 Even the short sample of debaters cited by Beck (1992) includes Baillie (1990), Johnston (1987), Kitcher (1979), Lowe (1990), Parfit (1984), Seddon (1972), Wiggins (1967, 1976, 1980), and Wilkes (1998).

20 It is no accident that, going beyond the sense warranted by thought experiments, Quine conceived of philosophy as continuous with science.

21 Plotkin (1997: xvi).

22 Gooding (1993: 285).

23 Pinker (1994: 113). Plotkin's entire chapter "Behaviour Without Thought" (from Plotkin 1997), contains a spirited defence of instinct as knowledge.

24 Sorensen (1992b: 15).

25 The argument extends to the Weak and the Strong variants; see Barrow and Tipler (1986).

26 Laland and Brown (2002: 94).

27 Kant also declared that logic of his time was so developed that it left nothing to study. All that was known in Kant's day is an elementary fraction of modern logic.

28 See Shreeve (2005) for coverage of this research. In *Consilience* Wilson discusses an example of such "prepared learning" with regard to snakes (Wilson 1998: 86–7).

29 Lorenz (1975: 184). The term "satisficing" (two sentences down) was introduced to psychology by Herbert Simon, the economist from Chapter 1 who advocated the illustrative role for literature.

30 Peter Munz argues this point in *Philosophical Darwinism* (1993). According to Popper, scientific theories themselves are driven by natural selection. The anthropomorphism of Nature "testing" designs is, of course, strictly metaphorical.

31 Dennett (1984: 37).

32 Eco (1983: 306).

33 For more on variation, see Simpson and Oriña (2003) and Gray *et al.* (2003). For a lucid account of knapping and symmetry, see Wynn (2000). Symmetry in children is discussed by Bornstein and Stiles-Davis (1984); and Uttal (1996). Some experimental setups with infants, which involve measurements of their average attention spans, open themselves to skeptical interpretation. For more on ideal physical characteristics in humans, see Buss (1994).

34 The story is reprinted in M. Gardner (1979: 42).

35 Abbott (2002: 76).

36 On the margins I feel compelled to join a chorus of voices sceptical of the so-called EEA: Environment of Evolutionary Adaptiveness. Even as a loose heuristic, the concept is ill conceived and at odds with the facts; as a serious theory it is almost certainly false and thus injurious to the development of evolutionary psychology.

37 Bettelheim (1976: 4).

38 See Barkow (1989).

39 Bowlby (1982: 80).

40 Goldberg (1982).

41 Lodge (2001: 62).
42 Plotkin (1997: 220).
43 Borges and Bioy-Casares (1976: 39).
44 Davenport (1981: 43).
45 Davenport (1981: 48).
46 Davenport (1981: 48, 49).
47 Davenport (1981: 50).
48 John (1994: 11).
49 John (1994: 122).
50 John (1994: 45).
51 This in turn directs her attention exclusively to the realistic novel, axing off the entire gamut of fiction represented by modeling classes 2 and 3 discussed in the Chapter 2. By her own admission, John has no account of truth in fiction to cope with what she calls "recalcitrant" examples of non-realistic fiction.
52 John (1994: 44).
53 Carroll, personal communication, June 15, 2005. See also Carroll (forthcoming).

Chapter 4

1 Percy (1983: 71–2).
2 J. R. Brown (1991a: 1). Brown's book provides lucid descriptions and illustrations of thought experiments pertinent to this section; so does Sorensen (1992a).
3 Bokulich's (2001) opening sentence is an almost perfect match.
4 See, for example, Sorensen (1992a: 6); next definition by Szabó Gendler (2000: x).
5 La Caze (2002: 17). Next definition by Rescher (1991: 31).
6 Janis (1991: 113). Second definition by Kujundzic (1993: 574).
7 Irvine (1991: 150). Duhem expounded on the centrality of theory in interpreting experimental results in *The Aim and Structure of Scientific Theory* (Duhem 1991, pt 2: ch. 4).
8 J. R. Brown (1991a: 15).
9 J. R. Brown states as much (1991a: 17). Cf. also Szabó Gendler: "we test various hypotheses by considering cases in which we systematically vary the contributing factors" (Szabó Gendler 2000: 27).
10 Mach (1976: 28); following quotation, 29.
11 See, for example, Duhem (1991: 202). J. R. Brown quotation (1986: 3).
12 Norton (1991: 129). The same frown is evident in Ryle (1993: 106).
13 This elegant argument is developed by Bishop (1999); see also Bokulich (2001: 290–8). J. R. Brown's rebuttal (1991a: 78) of Norton's Elimination Thesis takes a form akin to mine, though it is grounded not in evolution but Platonism. Szabó Gendler (2000) provides another critique of Norton's approach; the latter is shared (though perhaps less intensely) by three other contributors to the Horowitz and Massey (1991) collection: Rescher (1991), Irvine (1991), and Forge (1991).
14 The quotation and example are Pinker's (1994: 66).
15 See, for example, the work of Terry Au (1984) and Lisa Liu (1985).
16 J. R. Brown (1991a: 91). Therein Brown also notes that while, for Kuhn, "there is no new paradigm that is *uniquely* and *determinately* the one that must be adopted," Galileo's thought experiment with falling bodies provides a compelling case to the contrary.
17 Bealer (1998: 207).

18 Dennett (1984: 12). See also Dennett (1980) and Hofstadter and Dennett (1981). The same point is made by Jackson (1992), who articulates a pragmatist indictment of thought experiments in moral philosophy (see point 3 on pp. 000). I am sympathetic to the pragmatic turn, cogently argued by McAllister (1996), and only wish to note that the difference between his and Brown–Sorensen's "logicist" approach evaporates *within* any theoretical system that accepts the same criteria for evidential significance.
19 Dennett (1984: 18).
20 For a recent review of this issue, see J. J. Koehler (1996).
21 Hempel (1965: 165).
22 Barry (1979: 3). Also predating Wilkes, Kuhn (1981: 16) offers pertinent remarks on the effectiveness of thought experiments.
23 Dancy (1985a: 13–14). Next quotation from Sen (1982: 14).
24 Reported in J. Bell (1993: 68). See also Barrow (1999: 9).
25 My usage departs from the standard singular form of EEA for the simple reason that I do not accept its proponent's premises. The EEA proposed by Cosmides and Tooby (1987) is not any biological environment but a statistical aggregate, an idea fraught with problems, beginning with the objection that there cannot be an adaptation to a composite average. Adaptations are to specific real circumstances, which varied greatly throughout the 2–4 million years of Pleistocene in geographic, climatic, foraging, and other terms.
26 For an intense critique in the context of linguistic thought experiments, see Labov (1975). Lyons (1986) also provides a useful analysis.
27 Thomason (1991: 247). In "Thought Experiments Since the Scientific Revolution," J. R. Brown (1986) questions the legitimacy of psycholinguistic thought experiments, arguing that they are not *thought* experiments as such. I'm dubious about his contention that thinking in such cases is the *object* and not the *method* of inquiry. *Prima facie* a contemplation of a grammatical structure with a view to its correctness is a species of thinking where the latter is both the object and the method.
28 Thomason (1991: 247).
29 Adapted from Tetlock and Belkin (1996).
30 See my discussion of time-travel paradoxes in Swirski (2000a: ch. 1).
31 For more on Galton and corrupt interpretations of Darwin, see Boakes (1984).
32 On machine intelligence and creative independence, see Swirski (2000a: ch. 5).
33 Galileo (1953: 145).
34 Lévi-Strauss (1962: 41).
35 Nersessian (1993: 293). Turner quotation (1996: 168). See Nersessian (1993), Turner (1996), Lakoff and Turner (1989), and Bruner (1973) for bibliography.
36 *Nota bene*, Sorensen's five models refute Reiss (2002) and his characterization of what he calls Myth 4 (Reiss 2002: 18–21). Critiquing Reiss lies beyond the scope of this chapter, but I must record my dissent from his rhetorical and occasionally self-refuting salvos aimed at strawmen of his own design rather than at the substance of the polemics about thought experiments.
37 In *The Analytic Imaginary* La Caze also develops a proposition that very broadly construed "images" are central to analytic philosophy and thus to cognitive processing (La Caze 2002: 6). See also Fricker (1991) and Solomon (1993). An early example of research which strongly suggests that animals as well as humans are channelled by evolution to learn and remember some things more quickly and better, see Garcia and Koelling (1966).

38 Such are the results of informal experiments on friends and colleagues. In *Elbow Room*, Dennett devotes a whole page to autostimulation (Dennett 1984: 40).

39 See the classic experimental results by Lyon (1914).

40 Mach (1976: 137).

41 Sorensen (1992a: 88).

42 Alcock (1996: 73). Alongside Alcock, in the same collection see, for example, Rothman and Lichter (1996: 243) and Levitt (1996: 46).

43 This point was brought to wider attention by the statistician I. J. Good in *Nature* (1995).

44 Gigerenzer (1998: 26).

45 For a socio-technological analysis of such a narrative thought experiment, see Swirski (2006c).

46 Simon (1974).

47 See Swirski (forthcoming).

48 Sorensen (1992a: 103).

49 The fact that a work of *fiction* can change readers' real emotional dispositions underlies the so-called paradox of fiction, a hotly debated topic in analytic aesthetics. The cognitive model of identification offered by "thought theorists" in psychology points to a cogent solution.

50 Lakoff and Johnson (2003: 256).

51 I develop a comprehensive pragmatic and game-theoretic model of this process in Swirski (2000a: ch. 1).

52 Mach (1976: 84).

53 Kuhn (1981: 7).

54 Samuels (2000: 37). For other arguments against Massive Modularity, see Wynn (2000); Papineau (2000); and Sterelny (2003).

Chapter 5

1 In the context of game theory, de Ley makes a similar point in "The Name of the Game" (de Ley 1988: 33). Revised here, parts of this chapter appeared previously in "The Role of Game Theory in Literary Studies" (Swirski 1995); "Game Theory In the Third Pentagon" (Swirski 1996a); and "In the Blink of an Eye" (Swirski 2000b).

2 Lanham (1973: 584, 585).

3 Rapoport (1960: ix).

4 Lanham (1973: 585, 588).

5 Schelling (1960: 3).

6 Harsanyi (1961: 179). In *Rational Behavior* (1977) Harsanyi attempts to provide solutions for all games – even two-person non-zero-sum and *n*-person games outside Von Neumann's minimax theorem – by strengthening traditional rationality postulates. On the other hand, Harsanyi and Selten (1988) introduce a heuristic of a rational decision maker composed of a number of sub-players whose preferences may differ to the point of total incompatibility.

7 M. D. Davis (1983: 116–18). Although *Fights, Games, and Debates* (Rapoport 1960) is rightly commended in the field, for instance in the annotated bibliography to Shubik's *Game Theory and Related Approaches to Social Behavior* (1964), as M. D. Davis shows (1983: 43–4), even Rapoport can commit himself to positions not supported by other researchers.

8 Lanham (1973: 589, 590).

9 Rapoport (1960: 10).
10 I flesh out this research program in *Between Literature and Science* (Swirski 2000a: ch. 1). From primers on game theory that ought to be open to literature scholars, one must single out M. D. Davis (1983); Poundstone (1993); and Brams (1994). Penetrable expositions can also be found in Luce and Raiffa (1957); Shubik (1964, 1982); Williams (1966); M. D. Davis (1986); de Ley (1988); and Heap *et al.* (1992).
11 In Brams (1994: 27); next quotation on 27–8.
12 Wright (1994: 146). See also Alexander (1987).
13 Nuclear Posture Review (p. 7). An easily accessible transcript can be found in Nuclear Posture Review (2002).
14 Krieger (1998). El Baradei cited in Delong (2003: 2).
15 Kerry (2003: S6924); Kennedy (2003: S6803); Gore (2003); Gottemoeller, former deputy undersecretary, cited in I. Hoffman (1993).
16 From a plethora of background material on the Cuban crisis, for self-evident reasons I want to single out Lebow and Stein (1995), especially in the context of the 2003 Oscar-winning *The Fog of War* and Robert McNamara's reappraisal.
17 One conspicuous reason for a game-theoretic approach to Lem's works is its absence. The author eloquently argues on its behalf in his compendium on literary theory, *Filozofia Przypadku* (Lem 1968, vol. I: 136–41; vol. II: 208–18; and 233–41). In "Markiz w grafie" (1979) Lem himself used elements of game theory to discuss the writings of the Marquis de Sade. J. M. Davis (1990) sees it only as a black-humour satire; even Rothfork's (1984) ingenious reading as a critique of cybernetics falls short of doing justice to this complex work.
18 See Howard (1971: 146).
19 Stoff (1983: 105).
20 Commander-in-chief in the English translation. In view of consistent inaccuracies, I sometimes depart from the English translation published by Harcourt.
21 Lem (1976: 27).
22 Borges (1962: 32).
23 Lem (1970: II, 289).
24 Stoff (1983: 125). Stoff partially contradicts himself in *Lem i inni* when he refers to Agent being "outside the Building's structure" (Stoff 1990: 66).
25 Schelling (1960: 16). (Schelling is a 2005 Nobel Prize winner).
26 Lem (1976: 15).
27 Lem (1970: 268).
28 See Taylor (1995: ch. 5).
29 Shubik (1975: 24).
30 Lem (1976: 34).
31 The Gate is again more symbolic than realistic. Stoff makes a similar point (Stoff 1983: 125). For further analysis of this obvious allusion to Kafka, see Rothfork (1984) and J. M. Davis (1990).
32 Lem (1976: 190).
33 Lem (1976: 127).
34 Lem (1976: 169).
35 For more on metagames, see Rapoport *et al.* (1976: esp. 62 ff.).
36 Lem (1976: 70).
37 Utility payoffs describe a situation *as is*, without inquiring into players' motivations, subject of the game-theoretic analysis proper.
38 Lem (1976: 175).

39 Lem (1976: 176).
40 See also the suggestions made by Luce and Raiffa (1957: 105). The key assumption behind these postulates is that there exists a solution to the game in which the Building's employees participate (William F. Lucas (1968) showed that there may be *n*-person games without a solution). In our context, the solution means that the Building's tacit rules of behaviour generate a social equilibrium – an "equilibrium solution" to the game of its social organization.
41 Lem (1976: 192).
42 Balcerzak (1973: 137).
43 Lem (1976: 63, 67).
44 Lem (1976: 99).
45 The knitting secretary in the next scene echoes Conrad's *Heart of Darkness*, in which knitting secretaries symbolize Parkas, which in the ancient pantheon were said to knit people's lives.
46 Kuhn (1981: 36, 37).
47 Chadwick (1958: 67).
48 Barrow (1988: 18–19).
49 Chadwick (1958: 40).
50 Kuhn (1992: 8–9). On this topic, see Field (1982); Boyd (1983, 1990); Miller (1988); Davenport (1989, 1990); Haack (1993); Laudan (1996); and Sayer (2000).

Conclusion

1 Backed by anonymity, iteration, and intermediaries who control the feedback in the successive rounds. None of these conditions are relevant to the point I'm making.
2 Falke (1974: 59).
3 For an update on intelligent design, see Scott (1996) and Barrow (2000).
4 Updike (1996: 216).
5 Weiss (1987: 47).
6 For in-depth analysis, see Swirski (2005).
7 Psychoanalysis, these days transmuted into the many strands of neo-Freudian or Lacanian dogma, is only a convenient synecdoche. The case can be made with equal forcefulness with regard to many other attempts at what passes for "interdisciplinarity" in literary studies. For an overview and trenchant critique of those attempts, see Levin (1993, 1995).
8 Grey (1984: 47). The list of conclusive refutations of psychoanalysis' claims to the status of science may begin with biographical studies by Cioffi (1974, 1985) and Macmillan (1991) and end with more clinical but no less devastating studies by Scharnberg (1993) and Grünbaum (1993).
9 Casti (1989: 59).
10 Fox (1996: 343).
11 This short list is culled from scores of books whose titles are variations on the theme. See Rajab and O'Driscoll (2002); C. Davis (2004); Simons and Billig (1994); Lópes and Potter (2001); Smith and Wexler (1995); Easterlin and Riebling (1993).
12 Coincidentally, the consensus today is that Sidney's actual views are not necessarily reflected by this much cited dictum. See Graff (1980).
13 Swirski (2000a: 139).

Bibliography

Abbott, Edwin Abbott. *The Annotated Flatland*. Introduction and Notes by Ian Stewart. Cambridge, MA: Perseus, 2002.

Adams, Jeff. *The Conspiracy of the Text: the Place of Narrative in the Development of Thought*. New York: Routledge, 1986.

Alcock, James E. "The Propensity to Believe." In Gross, Paul R., Norman Levitt, and Martin W. Lewis, eds. *The Flight from Science and Reason*. New York: The New York Academy of Sciences, 1996: 64–78.

Alexander, Richard D. "The Biology of Moral Systems." Hawthorne, NY: A. de Gruyter, 1987.

Anderson, Barry F. *Cognitive Psychology: the Study of Knowing, Learning, and Thinking*. New York: Academic Press, 1975.

Applebaum, Anne. "When Kicking a Dead Dog Can Upset the Applecart." *Literary Review (London)*, July (1998): 43.

Argyros, Alex. *A Blessed Rage for Order: Deconstruction, Evolution, and Chaos*. Ann Arbor: University of Michigan Press, 1991.

———. "Narrative and Chaos." *New Literary History* 23 (1992): 659–73.

Arnold, Matthew. "Literature and Science." In *Discourses in America*. London: Macmillan, 1885. Reprinted in Fiedler, Leslie A., and Jacob Vinocur. *The Continuing Debate: Essays on Education*. New York: St. Martin's, 1964.

Au, Terry. "Counterfactuals: In Reply to Alfred Bloom." *Cognition* 17 (1984): 155–87.

Bach, Kent, and Robert M. Harnish. *Linguistic Communication and Speech Acts*. Cambridge, MA: MIT Press, 1979.

Bachmann, Thomas. "Creating Analogies: On Aspects of the Mapping Process between Knowledge Domains." In Brzezinski, Jerzy, ed. *Idealization VIII: Modelling in Psychology*. Amsterdam: Rodopi, 1997.

Baillie, James. "Identify, Survival and Sortal Concepts." *Philosophical Quarterly* 40 (1990): 183–94.

Balcerzak, Ewa. *Lem*. Trans. Krystyna Cekalska. Warsaw: Author's Agency, 1973.

Barkow, Jerome H. *Darwin, Sex, and Status: Biological Approaches to Mind and Culture*. Toronto: University of Toronto Press, 1989.

Barrow, John. *The World within the World*. Oxford: Clarendon, 1988.

———. *Theories of Everything: The Quest for Ultimate Explanation*. New York: Oxford University Press, 1991.

———. "Survival of the Artiest." *Daily Telegraph*, 9 December (1995): A1.

———. *Impossibility: The Limits of Science and the Science of Limits.* Oxford: Oxford University Press, 1998.

———. *Inner Space and Outer Space. Essays on Science, Art, and Philosophy.* Oxford: Oxford University Press, 1999.

———. *The Book of Nothing: Vacuums, Voids, and the Latest Ideas about the Origins of the Universe.* New York: Vintage, 2000.

Barrow, John, and Frank Tipler. *The Anthropic Cosmological Principle.* Oxford: Clarendon, 1986.

Barry, Brian. "On Editing Ethics." *Ethics* 90: 1 (1979): 1–6.

Bartlett, Frederic C. *Remembering: A Study in Experimental and Social Psychology.* Cambridge: Cambridge University Press, 1995 (orig. 1932).

Bealer, George. "The Autonomy of Philosophy." In DePaul, Michael R., and William Ramsey, eds. *Rethinking Intuition.* Lanham, MD: Rowman & Littlefield, 1998: 201–40.

Beardsley, Monroe C. *Aesthetics: Problems in the Philosophy of Criticism.* New York: Harcourt, 1958.

Beck, Simon. "Parfit and Russians." *Analysis* 49 (1989): 205–9.

———. "Should We Tolerate People Who Split?" *Southern Journal of Philosophy* 30: 1 (1992): 1–17.

Bell, David F. *Models of Power: Politics and Economics in Zola's Rougon-Macquart.* Lincoln, NE: University of Nebraska Press, 1988.

Bell, John. "How to Teach Special Relativity." *Speakable and Unnspeakable in Quantum Mechanics.* Cambridge: Cambridge University Press, 1993: 67–80.

Bereś, Stanislaw, and Stanislaw Lem. *Tako rzecze Lem . . . .* 2nd edn. Cracow: Wydawnictwo Literackie, 2002.

Bernstein, Michael A. *Foregone Conclusions: Against Apocalyptic History.* Berkeley: University of California Press, 1994.

Bettelheim, Bruno. *The Uses of Enchantment.* New York: Knopf, 1976.

Bishop, Michael A. "Why Thought Experiments Are Not Arguments." *Philosophy of Science* 66 (December 1999): 534–41.

Black, John B, and Gordon H. Bower. "Story Understanding as Problem Solving." *Poetics* 9 (1980): 223–50.

Blackburn, Simon. *"Thought Experiments." Times Literary Supplement* 4707 (June 18, 1993): 10–11.

Blackmore, John T. *Ernst Mach: His Life, Work, and Influence.* Berkeley: University of California Press, 1972.

Bloom, Alfred H. *The Linguistic Shaping of Thought: A Study in the Impact of Language on Thinking in China and in the West.* Hillsdale, NJ: Erlbaum, 1981.

Boakes, Robert. *From Darwin to Behaviourism: Psychology and the Minds of Animals.* Cambridge: Cambridge University Press, 1984.

Bojko, Piotr. *"Pamietnik znaleziony w wannie* Stanisława Lema – powieść o poznaniu uwikłanym w język." In Cyzman, Marzena, and Katarzyna Szostakowska, eds. *Z filozoficznych inspiracji literatury.* Torun: Interdyscyplinarne Koło Doktorantów, 2005.

Bokulich, Alisa. "Rethinking Thought Experiments." *Perspectives on Science* 9:3 (2001): 285–307.

Bono, Edward de. *The Mechanism of Mind.* Hammondsworth: Penguin, 1971.

Borges, Jorge L. "The Lottery in Babylon." *Labyrinths.* New York: New Directions, 1962.

———. "Of Exactitude in Science." *A Universal History of Infamy*. Trans. Thomas di Giovanni. New York: Dutton, 1972.

Borges, Jorge L., and Adolfo Bioy-Casares. *Chronicles of Bustos Domecq*. Trans. Norman Thomas de Giovanni. New York: E. P. Dutton, 1976 (orig. 1967).

Booth, William. "Sultan of Science Fiction." *Edmonton Journal* (January 14, 2001): E13.

Bornstein, M., and J. Stiles-Davis. "Discrimination and Memory for Symmetry in Young Children." *Developmental Psychology* 20 (1984): 637–49.

Bowlby, John. *Attachment and Loss*. Vol 1. *Attachment*. 2nd edn. New York: Basic Books, 1982.

Boyd, Richard. "On the Current Status of the Issue of Scientific Realism." *Erkenntnis* 19 (1983): 45–90.

———. "Realism, Approximate Truth and Philosophical Method." In Savage, Wade, ed. *Scientific Theories*. Minnesota Studies in the Philosophy of Science vol. 14. Minneapolis: University of Minnesota Press, 1990.

Brams, Steven J. *Biblical Games*. Cambridge, MA: MIT Press, 1980.

———. "Theory of Moves." *American Scientist* 81 (1993): 562–70.

———. "Game Theory and Literature." *Games and Economic Behavior* 6 (1994): 32–54.

Brewer, Laura. "When Characters Develop Minds of Their Own." 2003. Available at http://fmwriters.com/Visionback/issue13/Issue13/whencharacters.htm (May 3, 2005).

Brook, Donald. "A Transinstitutional Nonvoluntary Modelling Theory of Art." *Educational Philosophy and Theory* 11 (1979): 37–54.

Brown, Donald E. *Human Universals*. New York: McGraw-Hill, 1991.

Brown, James R. "Thought Experiments Since the Scientific Revolution." *International Studies in the Philosophy of Science* (1986): 1–15.

———. *The Laboratory of the Mind: Thought Experiments in the Natural Sciences*. New York: Routledge, 1991a.

———. "Thought Experiments: A Platonic Account." In Horowitz, Tamara, and Gerald J. Massey, eds. *Thought Experiments in Science and Philosophy*. Savage, MD: Rowman and Littlefield, 1991b: 119–28.

———. "Why Empiricism Won't Work?" In Hull, David, Micky Forbes, and Kathleen Okruhlik, eds. *Proceedings of the Biennial Meeting of the Philosophy of Science Association*: 2. East Lansing: Philosophy of Science Association, 1993: 271–79.

———. "Thought Experiments." *Canadian Journal of Philosophy* 25 (1995): 135–42.

Bruce, Donald, and Anthony Purdy. *Literature and Science*. Atlanta: Rodopi, 1994.

Bruner, Jerome S. *Beyond the Information Given: Studies in the Psychology of Knowing*. New York: Norton, 1973.

Bunge, Mario. *Causality and Modern Science*. Cambridge, MA: Harvard University Press, 1959.

Buss, David M. *The Evolution of Desire*. New York: Basic Books, 1994.

———. *Evolutionary Psychology: The New Science of the Mind*. Boston: Allyn and Bacon, 1999.

Calvin, William H. *The Cerebral Code: Thinking a Thought in the Mosaics of the Mind*. Cambridge, MA: MIT Press, 1996.

Calvino, Italo. "Two Interviews on Science and Literature." *L'approdo letterario* (1968). Available at http://www.brown.edu/Departments/Italian_Studies/people/riva/n2k/twointer.html (May 3, 2005).

Cameron, Sharon. *Thinking in Henry James*. Chicago: University of Chicago Press, 1989.

Camus, Albert. "Albert Camus – Acceptance Speech." In Frenz, Horst, ed. *From Nobel Lectures, Literature 1901–1967*. Elsevier: Amsterdam, 1969. 524–27.

Cantor, Georg. "Ueber unendliche, lineare Punktmannischfaltigkeiten." *Mathematische Annalen* 21 (1883).

Carden, Guy, and Thomas G. Dieterich. "Introspection, Observation, and Experiment: An Example Where Experiment Pays Off." *PSA* 2 (1980): 583–97.

Carroll, Joseph. *Evolution and Literary Theory*. Columbia: University of Missouri Press, 1995.

——. *Literary Darwinism: Evolution, Human Nature, and Literature*. New York: Routledge, 2004.

——. "The Adaptive Function of Literature." In Locher, Paul, Colin Martindale, Leonid Dorfman, Vladimir Petrov, and Dimitry Leontiev, eds. *Evolutionary Approaches to the Arts*. Amityville, NY: Baywood Publishing, forthcoming.

Carruthers, Peter, and Jill Boucher, eds. *Language and Thought: Interdisciplinary Themes*. New York: Cambridge University Press, 1998.

Carruthers, Peter, and Andrew Chamberlain, eds. *Evolution and the Human Mind: Modularity, Language and Meta-cognition*. Cambridge: Cambridge University Press, 2000.

Cartwright, Nancy. "False Idealisation: A Philosophical Threat to Scientific Method." *Philosophical Studies* 77 (March 1995): 339–52.

Casti, John L. *Paradigms Lost: Tackling the Unanswered Mysteries of Modern Science*. New York: Avon, 1989.

Chadwick, John. *The Decipherment of Linear B*. Cambridge: Cambridge University Press, 1958.

Chandrasekhar, Subrahmanyan. *Truth and Beauty: Aesthetics and Motivation in Science*. Chicago: University of Chicago Press, 1987.

Chen, Zhengxin. "Metaphor and Problem Solving Paradigms." *Communication and Cognition* 28: 4 (1995): 353–66.

Chomsky, Noam. *Modular Approaches to the Study of Mind*. San Diego: San Diego State University Press, 1984.

——. *Language and Problems of Knowledge: The Managua Lectures*. Cambridge, MA: MIT Press, 1988.

Cioffi, Frank. "Was Freud a Liar?" *The Listener* 91 (1974): 172–74.

——. "Psychoanalysis, Pseudo-science and Testability." In Curie, Gregory, and Alan Musgrave. *Popper and the Human Sciences*. Dordrecht: Nijhoff, 1985.

Cole, David. "Thought and Thought Experiments." *Philosophical Studies* 45 (1984): 431–44.

Cole, Stephen. *Making Science: Between Nature and Society*. Cambridge, MA: Harvard University Press, 1992.

Constable, John. "Verse Forms: A Pilot Study in the Epidemiology of Representations." *Human Nature* 8 (1997): 171–203.

Cooke, Brett B. "The Promise of a Biomathematics." In Bedaux, Jan Baptist, and Brett B. Cooke. *Sociobiology and the Arts*. Amsterdam: Editions Rodopi, 1999: 43–62.

Cooke, Brett B., and Frederick Turner. *Biopoetics: Evolutionary Explorations in the Arts*. Lexington, KY: ICUS, 1999.

Cooper, Gregory. "Theoretical Modeling and Biological Laws." *Proceedings of the Philosophy of Biology* 63 (1996): S28–S35.

Cosmides, Leda. "The Logic of Social Exchange: Has Natural Selection Shaped How Humans Reason? Studies with the Wason Selection Task." *Cognition* 31 (1989): 187–276.

Cosmides, Leda, and Tooby John. "From Evolution to Behavior: Evolutionary Psychology as the Missing Link." In Dupré, John, ed. *The Latest on the Best: Essays on Evolution and Optimality*. Cambridge, MA: MIT Press, 1987.

Craik, Kenneth. *The Nature of Explanation*. Cambridge: Cambridge University Press, 1943.

Crews, Frederick. *Postmodern Pooh*. New York: North Point Press, 2001.

———. *Skeptical Engagements*. Cybereditions, 2002.

———. *Follies of the Wise: Dissenting Essays*. Emeryville, CA: Shoemaker and Hoard, 2006.

Csicsery-Ronay, Istvan, Jr. "How Not to Write a Book about Lem." *Science-Fiction Studies* 40 (1986): 387–91.

Cummins, Denise Dellarosa, and Colin Allen. *The Evolution of Mind*. New York: Oxford University Press, 1998.

Currie, Gregory. *The Nature of Fiction*. Cambridge: Cambridge University Press, 1990.

Curtin, Deane W., ed. *The Aesthetic Dimension of Science*. New York: Philosophical Library, 1982.

Damasio, Antonio R. *Descartes' Error: Emotion, Reason, and the Human Brain*. New York: G. P. Putnam, 1994.

———. *The Feeling of What Happens: Body and Emotion in the Making of Consciousness*. New York: Harcourt Brace, 1999.

Dancy, Jonathan. *An Introduction to Contemporary Epistemology*. Oxford: Blackwell, 1985a.

———. "The Role of Imaginary Cases in Ethics." *Pacific Philosophical Quarterly* 66 (1985b): 141–53.

Danielson, Peter. "How Computers Extend Artificial Morality." In Bynum, Terrell W., ed. *The Digital Phoenix*. Cambridge: Blackwell, 1998.

Danly, John R. "An Examination of the Fundamental Assumptions of Hypothetical Process Arguments." *Philosophical Studies* 48 (1985): 83–89.

Darwin, Charles. *The Descent of Man and Selection in Relation to Sex*. Princeton, NJ: Princeton University Press, 1981 (orig. 1871).

———. *The Origin of Species*. New York: Penguin, 1985 (orig. 1859).

Dauben, Joseph. *Georg Cantor*. Cambridge, MA: Harvard University Press, 1979.

Davenport, Edward. "Literature as Thought Experiment." *Literary Criterion* 16: 2 (1981): 43–55.

———. "The Scientific Spirit." *Literary Theory's Future(s)*. In Natoli, Joseph, ed. Urbana, IL: University of Illinois Press, 1989.

———. "The Devils of Positivism." In Peterfreund, Stewart, ed. *Literature and Science: Theory and Practice*. Boston: Northeastern University Press, 1990.

Davis, Colin. *After Poststructuralism: Reading Stories and Theory*. London: Routledge, 2004.

Davis, J. Madison. *Stanislaw Lem*. Mercer Island, WA: Starmont, 1990.

Davis, Morton D. *Game Theory: A Nontechnical Introduction: Revised Edition*. New York: Basic Books, 1983.

———. *The Art of Decision-Making*. New York: Springer-Verlag, 1986.

Davitz, Joel R. *The Language of Emotion*. New York: McGraw-Hill, 1969.

de Ley, Herbert. "The Name of the Game: Applying Game Theory in Literature." *SubStance* 55 (1988): 33–46.

Deacon, Terrence. *The Symbolic Species: The Co-evolution of Language and the Brain*. New York: W. W. Norton, 1997.

Delong, Bev. "Dr. El Baradei Speaks Out!" *Lawyers for Social Responsibility Newsletter* 15: 2 (Fall 2003): 2.

Dennett, Daniel. "The Milk of Human Intentionality." *Behavioral and Brain Sciences* 3 (1980): 428–30.

——. "Intentional Systems in Cognitive Ethology: The 'Panglossian Paradigm' Defended." *Behavioral and Brain Sciences* 6 (1983): 343–90.

——. *Elbow Room.* Cambridge, MA: MIT Press, 1984.

Dewdney, Alexander K. *The Planiverse: Computer Contact with a Two-dimensional World.* New York: Copernicus, 2001.

Dissanayake, Ellen. *Homo Aestheticus: Where Art Comes From and Why.* New York: Free Press, 1992.

Donaldson, Margaret. *Human Minds: An Exploration.* New York: Penguin, 1993.

Duhem, Pierre. *The Aim and Structure of Scientific Theory.* Trans. Philip P. Wiener. Princeton, NJ: Princeton University Press, 1991 [1914].

Eagleton, Terry. *The Illusions of Postmodernism.* Oxford: Blackwell, 1996.

Easterlin, Nancy, and Barbara Riebling, eds. *After Poststructuralism: Interdisciplinarity and Literary Theory.* Evanston, IL: Northwestern University Press, 1993.

Eco, Umberto. *The Name of the Rose.* San Diego: Harcourt Brace Jovanovich, 1983.

——. Postscript to *The Name of the Rose.* San Diego: Harcourt Brace Jovanovich, 1984.

Editors of *Lingua Franca. The Sokal Hoax: The Sham that Shook the Academy.* Lincoln, NE: University of Nebraska Press, 2000.

Ellis, John M. *Literature Lost: Social Agendas and the Corruption of the Humanities.* New Haven, CT: Yale University Press, 1999.

Elster, Jon. *Sour Grapes: Studies in the Subversion of Rationality.* Cambridge: Cambridge University Press, 1983.

Evans, Jonathan St. B. T. *Thinking and Reasoning.* London: Routledge, 1983.

Evans, Jonathan St. B. T., and David E. Over. *Rationality and Reasoning.* Hove, East Sussex, UK: Psychology Press, 1996.

Falke, Wayne. "American Strikes Out: Updike's *Rabbit Redux.*" *American Examiner* 3: 3 (1974): 18–21.

Field, Hartry. "Realism and Relativism." *Journal of Philosophy* 79 (1982): 553–57.

Finke, Ronald A., and Jonathan Bettle. *Chaotic Cognition: Principles and Applications.* Mahwah, NJ: Lawrence Erlbaum, 1996.

Flesch, Rudolf F. *The Art of Clear Thinking.* New York: Harper, 1951.

Fodor, Jerry A. *The Modularity of Mind.* Cambridge, MA: MIT Press, 1983.

Fogel, Robert. *Railoards and American Economic Growth: Essays in Econometric History.* Baltimore: Johns Hopkins University Press, 1964.

Forge, John. "Thought Experiments in the Philosophy of Physical Science." In Horowitz, Tamara, and Gerald J. Massey, eds. *Thought Experiments in Science and Philosophy.* Savage, MD: Rowman and Littlefield, 1991.

Fox, Robin. "Anthropology and the 'Teddy-Bear' Picnic." *Society* (November/ December 1992): 47–55.

——. "State of the Art/Science in Anthropology." In Gross, Paul R., Norman Levitt, and Martin W. Lewis, eds. *The Flight from Science and Reason.* New York: The New York Academy of Sciences, 1996: 327–45.

Franklin, Allan. *The Neglect of Experiment.* New York: Cambridge University Press, 1986.

Fricker, Miranda. "Reason and Emotion." *Radical Philosophy* 57 (1991): 14–19.

Frye, Northrop. *Anatomy of Criticism.* Princeton, NJ: Princeton University Press, 1957.

Fuger, Wilhelm. "Literatur und Spieltheorie: Erprobung eines ungenutzten Inter-pretationsmodells." In Hasler, Jorg, ed. *Anglistentag 1981: Vortrage.* Frankfurt am Main: Lang, 1983.

Galileo. *Dialogue Concerning Two World Systems, Ptolemaic and Copernican.* Trans. Stillman Drake. Berkeley: University of California Press, 1953.

Garcia, John and Koelling, R. A. "Prolonged Relation of Cue to Consequence in Avoidance Learning." *Psychonomic Science* 4 (1966): 123–24.

Gardner, Howard. *The Quest for Mind: Piaget, Levi-Strauss, and the Structuralist Movement.* 2nd edn. Chicago: University of Chicago Press, 1981.

Gardner, Martin. *The Ambidextrous Universe: Mirror Asymmetry and Time-reversed Worlds.* New York: Charles Scribner's Sons, 1979.

——. *Whys and Wherefores.* Oxford: Oxford University Press, 1990.

——. "Alan Sokal's Hilarious Hoax." *Did Adam and Eve Have Navels?* New York: Norton, 2000.

Geanakoplos, John, David Pearce, and Ennio Stacchetti. "Psychological Games and Sequential Reality." *Games and Economic Behavior* 1 (1989): 60–79.

Gentner, Derdre, and Albert L. Stevens. *Mental Models.* Hillsdale, NJ: Lawrence Erlbaum, 1983.

Gigerenzer, Gerd. "Ecological Intelligence: An Adaptation for Frequencies." In Cummins, Denise Dellarosa, and Colin Allen. *The Evolution of Mind.* New York: Oxford University Press, 1998.

Gilboa, Ishak, and David Schmeidler. "Information Dependent Games: Can Common Sense Be Common Knowledge?" *Economics Letters* 4 (1988): 215–22.

Gilhooly, K. J., M. T. G. Keane, R. H. Logie, and G. Erdos, eds. *Lines of Thinking: Reflections on the Psychology of Thought.* New York: Wiley, 1990.

Girard, René. *Deceit, Desire, and the Novel: Self and Other in Literary Structure.* Baltimore: Johns Hopkins University Press, 1965.

Glouberman, Mark. "Error Theory: Logic, Rhetoric, and Philosophy." *Journal of Speculative Philosophy* 4: 1 (1990): 37–65.

Goldberg, Lewis R. "From Ace to Zombie: Some Explorations in the Language of Personality." In Spielberger, Charles, and J. Butcher, eds. *Advances in Personality Assessment.* Hillsdale, NJ: Lawrence Erlbaum, 1982: 203–34.

Goldstrom, Jean. "James Morrow." 2000. Available at http://www.anotherealm.com/interview/marrow.html (May 3, 2005).

Gomila, Antoni. "What Is a Thought Experiment?" *Metaphilosophy* (January–April 1992): 84–92.

Good, Graham. *Humanism Betrayed: Theory, Ideology, and Culture in Contemporary University.* Montreal: McGill-Queen's University Press, 2001.

Good, Irving John. "When Batterer Turns Murderer." *Nature* 375 (1995): 541.

Gooding, David C. "Thought Experiments." *British Journal for the Philosophy of Science* 45 (1994): 1029–45.

Gooding, David C., Trevor Pinch, and Simon Schaffer, eds. *The Uses of Experiment.* Cambridge: Cambridge University Press, 1989.

——. "What Is Experimental about Thought Experiments?" In Hull, David, Micky Forbes, and Kathleen Okruhlik, eds. *Proceedings of the Biennial Meeting of the Philosophy of Science Association: 2.* East Lansing: Philosophy of Science Association, 1993: 280–90.

Goodman, Nelson. "Seven Strictures on Similarity." *Problems and Projects.* Indianapolis: Bobbs-Merrill, 1972.

Goodman, Nelson, and Catherine Z. Elgin. "Interpretations and Identity: Can the Work Survive the World?" *Reconceptions in Philosophy*. Indianapolis: Hackett, 1988.

Gore, Al. "Remarks to MoveOn.org." *MoveOn.org Political Action, New York University*, August 7 (2003). Available at http://www.moveon.org/gore-speech.html (May 3, 2005).

Gottschall, Jonathan, Rachel Berkey, Mitch Cawson, Carly Drown, Matthew Fleischner, Melissa Glotzbecker, Kimberly Kernan, Tyler Magnan, Kate Muse, Celeste Ogburn, Stephen Patterson, Christopher Skeels, Stephanie St. Joseph, Shawna Weeks, Alison Welsh, Erin Welch, eds. "Patterns of Characterization in Folk Tales across Geographic Regions and Levels of Cultural Complexity: Literature as a Neglected Source of Quantitative Data." *Human Nature* 14 (2003): 365–82.

———. "Sex Differences in Mate Choice Criteria Are Reflected in Folktales from around the World and in Historical European Literature." *Evolution and Human Behavior* 25 (2004): 102–12.

Gould, Stephen, and E. Vrba. "Exaptation: A Missing Term in the Science of Form." *Paleobiology* 8 (1982): 4–15.

GPO. "National Defense Authorization Act for Fiscal Year 2004." Congressional Record 149 (Senate) (May 21, 2003a): s6800–801, s6803. U.S. Government Printing Office. Available at http://frwebgate5.access.gpo.gov/cgi-bin/waisgate.cgi?WAISdocID = 274897320415+0+0+0&WAISaction = retrieve (December 6, 2004).

———. "National Defense Authorization Act for Fiscal Year 2004 – Continued." Congressional Record 149 (Senate) (May 22, 2003b): s6924. U.S. Government Printing Office. Available at http://frwebgate5.access.gpo.gov/cgi-bin/waisgate.cgi?WAISdocID = 274343319929+0+0+0&WAISaction = retrieve (December 6, 2004).

Graesser, Arthur C. *Prose Comprehension beyond the Word*. New York: Springer, 1981.

Graff, Gerald. *Poetic Statement and Critical Dogma*. Chicago: University of Chicago Press, 1980.

Graves, Barbara, and Carl H. Frederiksen. "Literary Expertise in the Description of a Fictional Narrative." *Poetics* 20 (1991): 1–26.

Gray, Russell, Megan Heaney, and S. Fairhill. "Evolutionary Psychology and the Challene of the Adaptive Explanation." In Kim Sterelny, and Julie Fitness, eds. *From Mating to Mentality: Evaluating Evolutionary Psychology*. Hove, East Sussex, UK: Psychological Press, 2003.

Grey, Paul. "Sci-Phi." *Time* (September 17, 1984): 87–90.

Grice, Herbert. P. "Intention and Uncertainty." *Proceedings of the British Academy* 57 (1971): 263–79.

Gross, Barry R. "What Could a Feminist Scientist Be?" *The Monist* 77: 4 (1994): 434–44.

Gross, Paul R., and Norman Levitt. *Higher Superstition: The Academic Left and Its Quarrels with Science*. Baltimore: Johns Hopkins University Press, 1994.

Gross, Paul R., Norman Levitt, and Martin W. Lewis, eds. *The Flight from Science and Reason*. New York: The New York Academy of Sciences, 1996.

Grosz, Elizabeth. "Bodies and Knowledges: Feminism and the Crisis of Reason." In Alcoff, Linda, and Elizabeth Potter, eds. *Feminist Epistemologies*. London: Routledge, 1993.

Grünbaum, Adolf. *Validation in the Clinical Theory of Psychoanalysis: A Study in the Philosophy of Psychoanalysis*. Madison, CT: International Universities Press, 1993.

Haack, Susan. *Evidence and Inquiry: Towards Reconstruction in Epistemology.* Oxford: Blackwell, 1993.

Hacking, Ian. "Do Thought Experiments Have a Life of Their Own? Comments on James Brown, Nancy Nersessian and David Gooding." In Hull, David, Micky Forbes, and Kathleen Okruhlik, eds. *Proceedings of the Biennial Meeting of the Philosophy of Science Association:* 2. East Lansing: Philosophy of Science Association, 1993: 302–8.

———. *The Social Construction of What?* Cambridge, MA: Harvard University Press, 2000.

Hadamard, Jacques. *The Psychology of Invention in the Mathematical Field.* Princeton, NJ: Princeton University Press, 1949.

Hagendorf, H., and B. Sá. "The Function of Working Memory in Coordination of Mental Transformation." In Brzezinski, Jerzy, ed. *Idealization VIII: Modelling in Psychology.* Amsterdam: Rodopi, 1997.

Hahn, Hans. "Logic, Mathematics, and Knowledge of Nature." In Weitz, Morris, ed. *Twentieth-Century Philosophy.* New York: Macmillan, 1966.

Haraway, Donna. *Simians, Cyborgs and Women: The Reinvention of Nature.* New York: Routledge, 1991.

Harding, Sandra. *The Science Question in Feminism.* Ithaca, NY: Cornell University Press, 1986.

Hare, Richard M. *Moral Thinking: Its Levels, Method, and Point.* Oxford: Oxford University Press, 1981.

Harman, Gilbert. "Moral Explanations of Natural Facts – Can Moral Claims Be Tested against Moral Reality?" *Southern Journal of Philosophy* 24 (suppl.) (1986): 57–68.

Harsanyi, John C. "On the Rationality Postulates Underlying the Theory of Cooperative Games." *Journal of Conflict Resolution* 5 (1961): 179–96.

———. *Rational Behaviour and Bargaining Equilibrium in Games and Social Situations.* Cambridge: Cambridge University Press, 1977.

Harsanyi, John C., and Reinhard Selten. *A General Theory of Equilibrium Selection in Games.* Cambridge, MA: MIT Press, 1988.

Hayles, N. Katherine. "Chaos and Dialectic: Stanislaw Lem and the Space of Writing." *Chaos Bound: Orderly Disorder in Contemporary Literature and Science.* Ithaca, NY: Cornell, 1990.

Hays, Janice N., Robert D. Foulke, Jon A. Ramsey, and Phyllis A. Roth, eds. *The Writer's Mind: Writing as a Mode of Thinking.* Urbana, IL: National Council of Teachers of English, 1983.

Heap, Shaun Hargreaves, Martin Hollis, Bruce Lyons, Robert Sugden, and Albert Weale. *The Theory of Choice: A Critical Guide.* Cambridge, MA: Blackwell, 1992.

Heil, John. *The Cambridge Dictionary of Philosophy.* Ed. Audi, Robert. Cambridge: Cambridge University Press, 1995.

Held, Barbara S. "Constructivism in Psychotherapy." In Gross, Paul R., Norman Levitt, and Martin W. Lewis, eds. *The Flight from Science and Reason.* New York: The New York Academy of Sciences, 1996: 198–206.

Hempel, Karl. "The Theoretician's Dilemma." In Feigl, Herbert, Michael Scriven, and Grover Maxwell, eds. *Minnesota Studies in the Philosophy of Science II.* Minneapolis: University of Minnesota Press, 1958.

———. *Aspects of Scientific Explanation.* New York: Free Press, 1965.

Hersh, Reuben. *What Is Mathematics, Really?* London: Jonathan Cape, 1997.

Hershbach, Dudley R. "Imaginary Gardens with Real Toads." In Gross, Paul R., Norman Levitt, and Martin W. Lewis, eds. *The Flight from Science and Reason*. New York: The New York Academy of Sciences, 1996: 11–30.

Hess, Peter Hans. *Thought and Experience*. Toronto: University of Toronto Press, 1988.

Hicks, Stephen R. C. *Explaining Postmodernism: Skepticism and Socialism from Rousseau to Foucault*. Phoenix, AZ: Scholargy Publishing, 2004.

Hiebert, Erwin. "Mach's Conception of Thought Experiments in the Natural Sciences." In Elkana, Yehuda, ed. *The Interaction Between Science and Philosophy*. Atlantic Highlands, NJ: Humanities Press, 1974.

Hirsch, E. D., Jr. "Value and Knowledge in the Humanities." In Bloomfield, Morton W., ed. *In Search of Literary Theory*. Ithaca, NY: Cornell University Press, 1972: 55–72.

———. *The Aims of Interpretation*. Chicago: University of Chicago Press, 1976.

Hoffman, Ian. "Debate Over New Nukes Begins." *Oakland Tribune* (March 7, 2003): 1 (headline news).

Hoffman, Roald. *The Same and Not the Same*. New York: Columbia University Press, 1995.

Hofstadter, Douglas, and Daniel Dennett. *The Mind's I: Fantasies and Reflections on Mind and Soul*. New York: Basic Books, 1981.

Hollis, Martin. *The Philosophy of Social Science*. Cambridge: Cambridge University Press, 1994.

Horowitz, Tamara, and Gerald J. Massey, eds. *Thought Experiments in Science and Philosophy*. Savage, MD: Rowman and Littlefield, 1991.

Horton, Marc. "Fantasy Life." *Edmonton Journal*, May 19 (2002): D10.

Howard, Nigel. *Paradoxes of Rationality: Theory of Metagames and Political Behaviour*. Cambridge, MA: MIT Press, 1971.

Hrdy, Sarah B. *Mother Nature: Natural Selection and the Female of the Species*. London: Chatto & Windus, 1999.

Hull, David L. "A Function for Actual Examples in Philosophy of Science." *What the Philosophy of Biology Is*. Dordrecht: Kluwer, 1989.

Husserl, Edmund. *Ideas: General Introduction to Pure Phenomenology*. Trans. William Ralph Boyce Gibson. London: Collier, 1975.

Ingarden, Roman. *The Cognition of the Literary Work of Art*. Trans. Ruth A. Crowley and Kenneth R. Olson. Evanston, IL: Northwestern University Press, 1973.

Irvine, Andrew D. "On the Nature of Thought Experiments in Scientific Reasoning." In Horowitz, Tamara, and Gerald J. Massey, eds. *Thought Experiments in Science and Philosophy*. Savage, MD: Rowman and Littlefield, 1991: 149–66.

Jackson, Michael W. "The 'Gedankenexperiment' Method of Ethics." *Journal of Value Inquiry* 26: 4 (1992): 525–35.

Jaki, Stanley. *The Relevance of Physics*. Chicago: University of Chicago Press, 1966.

Jameson, Frederic. *Postmodernism, or, the Cultural Logic of Late Capitalism*. Durham: Duke University Press, 1991.

Janis, Allen I. "Can Thought Experiments Fail?" In Horowitz, Tamara, and Gerald J. Massey, eds. *Thought Experiments in Science and Philosophy*. Savage, MD: Rowman and Littlefield, 1991: 113–18.

Jarzębski, Jerzy. "The World as Code and Labyrinth: Stanisław Lem's *Memoirs Found in a Bathtub*." Trans. Franz Rottensteiner. In Garnett, Rhys, and Richard J. Ellis, eds. *Science Fiction Roots and Branches: Contemporary Critical Approaches*. New York: St. Martin's, 1990: 79–87.

John, Alice E. "Fiction as Conceptual Thought Experiment." *Dissertation Abstracts International* 54: 11 (May 1994): 4124A.

Johnson, Donald McEwen. *A Systematic Introduction to the Psychology of Thinking.* New York: Harper, 1972.

Johnston, Mark. "Human Beings." *Journal of Philosophy* 84 (1987): 59–83.

Kahneman, Daniel. "Varieties of Counterfactual Thinking." In Roese, Neil. J., and James. M. Olson, eds. *What Might Have Been: The Social Psychology of Counterfactual Thinking.* Mahwah, NJ: Erlbaum, 1995: 375–96.

Kahneman, Daniel, and Amos Tversky, eds. *Choices, Values, and Frames.* New York: Russell Sage Foundation; Cambridge: Cambridge University Press, 2000.

Kahneman, Daniel, Paul Slovic, and Amos Tversky, eds. *Judgment Under Uncertainty: Heuristics and Biases.* Cambridge: Cambridge University Press, 1982.

Kemeny, John G. *A Philosopher Looks at Science.* New York: Van Nostrand Reinhold, 1959.

Kennedy, Edward. In "National Defence Authorization Act for Fiscal year 2004." *Congressional Record 108th Congress (2003–2003).* May 21 (2003): S6803.

Kernan, Alvin. "Henry Rosovsky. The University: An Owner's Manual." *ADE Bulletin* 100 (Winter 1991): 49–53.

Kerry, John. In "National Defence Authorization Act for Fiscal year 2004." *Congressional Record 108th Congress (2003–2003).* May 22 (2003): S6924.

Kitcher, Patricia. "Natural Kinds and Unnatural Persons." *Philosophy* 54 (1979): 541–7.

Kluwe, Rainer H., and Hans Spada, eds. *Developmental Models of Thinking.* New York: Academic, 1980.

Koch, Walter A., ed. *The Biology of Literature.* Bochum: N. Brockmeyer, 1993.

Koehler, Jonathan Jay. "The Base Rate Fallacy Reconsidered: Descriptive, Normative, and Methodological Challenges." *Behavioral and Brain Sciences* 19 (1996): 1–53.

Koehler, Otto. "The Ability of Birds to Count." *Bulletin of Animal Behaviour* 9 (March 1951): 41–45.

Korner, Stephan. *Experience and Conduct: A Philosophical Enquiry into Practical Thinking.* New York: Cambridge University Press, 1976.

Koyré, Alexander. *Metaphysics and Measurements.* Cambridge, MA: Harvard University Press, 1968.

———. *Galileo Studies.* Atlantic Highlands, NJ: Humanities Press, 1979 (orig. 1939).

Krieger, David. "US Policy and the Quest for Nuclear Disarmament." *Nuclear Age Peace Foundation* (1998). Available at http://www.wagingpeace.org/articles/2004/07/00_krieger_us-policy-quest.htm (December 4, 2004).

Kuhn, Thomas. "A Function for Thought Experiments." In Hacking, Ian, ed. *Scientific Revolutions.* Oxford: Oxford University Press, 1981 (orig. 1964): 6–27.

———. *The Trouble With the Historical Philosophy of Science (Robert and Maurine Rothschild Lecture).* Cambridge, MA: Harvard University/Derek Bok Center, 1992.

Kujundzic, Nebojsa. "How Does the Laboratory of the Mind Work?" *Dialogue* 32 (Summer 1993): 573–77.

La Caze, Marguerite. *The Analytic Imaginary.* Ithaca, NY: Cornell University Press, 2002.

Labov, William. "Empirical Foundations of Linguistic Theory." In Austerlitz, Robert, ed. *The Scope of American Linguistics.* Lisse: Peter de Ridder Press, 1975: 77–133.

Lakoff, George, and Mark Johnson. *Metaphors We Live By.* Chicago: University of Chicago Press, 2003 (orig. 1980).

Lakoff, George, and Rafael Nuñez. *Where Mathematics Comes From: How the Embodied Mind Brings Mathematics into Being.* New York: Basic, 2000.

Lakoff, George, and Mark Turner. *More than Cool Reason: A Field Guide to Poetic Metaphor.* Chicago: University of Chicago Press, 1989.

Laland, Kevin N., and Gillian R. Brown. *Sense and Nonsense: Evolutionary Perspectives on Human Behaviour.* Oxford: Oxford University Press, 2002.

Langer, Jonas, and Melanie Killen, eds. *Piaget, Evolution, and Development.* London: Lawrence Erlbaum, 1998.

Lanham, Richard A. "Games, Play, Seriousness." *Tristram Shandy and the Games of Pleasure.* Berkeley and Los Angeles: University of California Press, 1973.

Latour, Bruno. "Who Speaks for Science?" *The Sciences* 35 (1995): 6–7.

Latour, Bruno, and Steve Woolgar. *Laboratory Life: The Construction of Scientific Facts.* 2nd edn. Princeton, NJ: Princeton University Press, 1986.

Laudan, Larry. *Science and Relativism: Some Key Controversies in the Philosophy of Science.* Chicago: University of Chicago Press, 1990.

——. *Beyond Positivism and Relativism: Theory, Method and Evidence.* Boulder, CO: Westview, 1996.

Lawden, Derek F. "Modelling Physical Reality." *Journal of Philosophy* 5 (February 1968): 87–104.

Lawson, Lewis A., and Victor A. Kramer. *Conversations with Walker Percy.* Jackson: University Press of Mississippi, 1985.

Lebow, Richard Ned, and Janice Gross Stein. *We All Lost the Cold War.* Princeton, NJ: Princeton University Press, 1995.

Lem, Stanislaw. *Filozofia przypadku: literatura w świetle empirii.* Kraków: Wydawnictwo Literackie, 1968.

——. *Fantastyka i futurologia.* Kraków: Wydawnictwo Literackie, 1970.

——. *Memoirs Found in a Bathtub.* Trans. Michael Kandel and Christine Rose. New York: Avon, 1976 (orig. 1961).

——. "Markiz w Grafie." *Teksty* 43 (1979): 7–43.

——. *His Master's Voice.* Trans. Michael Kandel. San Diego: Harcourt, Brace, Jovanovich, 1983a (orig. 1968).

——. *"De Impossibilitate Vitae* and *De Impossibilitate Prognoscendi." A Perfect Vacuum.* Trans. Michael Kandel. Orlando, FL: Harvest/HBJ, 1983b (orig. 1971).

——. *Prowokacja* [*Provocation*]. Kraków: Wydawnictwo Literackie, 1984.

——. *Okamgnienie* [*The Blink of an Eye*]. Kraków: Wydawnictwo Literackie, 2000.

Lévi-Strauss, Claude. "Les Limites de la notion de structure en ethnologie." In Bastide, R., ed. *Sens et usages du terme structure dans les sciences humaines et sociales.* The Hague: Mouton, 1962.

Levin, Richard. "The New Interdisciplinarity in Literary Criticism." In Easterlin, Nancy, and Barbara Riebling, eds. *After Poststructuralism: Interdisciplinarity and Literary Theory.* Evanston, IL: Northwestern University Press, 1993.

——. "Negative Evidence." *Studies in Philology* 42 (Fall 1995): 383–410.

Levitt, Norman. "Mathematics as the Stepchild of Contemporary Culture." In Gross, Paul R., Norman Levitt, and Martin W. Lewis, eds. *The Flight from Science and Reason.* New York: The New York Academy of Sciences, 1996: 39–53.

Lewis, David. *On the Plurality of Worlds.* New York: Blackwell, 1986.

Liu, Lisa. "Reasoning Counterfactually in Chinese: Are There Any Obstacles?" *Cognition* 21 (1985): 239–70.

Livingston, Paisley. *Literary Knowledge: Humanistic Inquiry and the Philosophy of Science.* Ithaca, NY: Cornell University Press, 1988.

——. "Literary Studies and the Sciences." *Modern Language Studies* 20 (1990): 15–31.

——. *Models of Desire: René Girard and the Psychology of Mimesis*. Baltimore: Johns Hopkins University Press, 1992a.

——. "Literature and Knowledge." In Dancy, Jonathan, and Ernest Sosa, eds.. *A Companion to Epistemology*. Oxford: Blackwell, 1992b.

——. "What's the Story?" *SubStance* 71/71 (1993): 98–112.

——. *Art and Intention*. Oxford: Clarendon, 2005.

Lodge, David. *Thinks*. London: Secker & Warburg, 2001.

Logie, Robert H., and Kenneth J. Gilhooly, eds. *Working Memory and Thinking*. Hove, East Sussex, UK: Psychology Press, 1998.

Lópes, José, and Gary Potter, eds. *After Postmodernism: An Introduction to Critical Realism*. London: Athlone Press, 2001.

Lorenz, Konrad. "Kant's Doctrine of the a Priori in the Light of Contemporary Biology." In Evans, Richard I., ed. *Konrad Lorenz: The Man and His Ideas*. New York, London: Harcourt, Brace, Jovanovich, 1975: 181–217.

——. "Konrad Lorenz (Autobiographical Sketch)." *Les Prix Nobel en 1973*. Stockholm: Nobel Foundation. Available at http://nobelprize.org/medicine/laureates/1973/lorenz-autobio.html (May 3, 2005).

Lowe, E. Jonathan. "Review of *Personal Identity*, by H. Noonan." *Mind* 99 (1990): 477–79.

Lucas, William F. "A Game with No Solution." *Bulletin of the American Mathematical Society* 74 (1968): 237–39.

Luce, R. Duncan, and Howard Raiffa. *Games and Decisions: Introduction and Critical Survey*. New York: Wiley, 1957.

Luhmann, Niklas. *Art as a Social System*. Stanford: Stanford University Press, 2000.

Lyon, Darwin Oliver. "The Relative of Length of Material to Time Taken for Learning, and the Optimum Distribution of Time. Part I." *Journal of Educational Psychology* 5: 1 (1914a): 1–9.

——. "The Relative of Length of Material to Time Taken for Learning, and the Optimum Distribution of Time. Part II." *Journal of Educational Psychology* 5: 2 (1914b): 85–91.

——. "The Relative of Length of Material to Time Taken for Learning, and the Optimum Distribution of Time. Part III." *Journal of Educational Psychology* 5: 3 (1914c): 155–63.

Lyons, William. *The Disappearance of Introspection*. Cambridge, MA: MIT Press, 1986.

Lyotard, Jean François. *La Condition postmoderne*. Paris: Minuit, 1979.

McAllister, James W. "*Thought Experiments*." *Mind* 102 (October, 1993): 686–89.

——. "The Evidential Significance of Thought Experiments in Science." *Studies in History and Philosophy of Science* 27: 2 (1996): 233–50

MacDonald, Heather. "The Ascendancy of Theor-ese." *Hudson Review* 45 (1992): 358–65.

Mach, Ernst. *Popular Scientific Lectures*. 5th edn. Trans. Thomas J. McCormack. London: Open Court, 1948.

——. *The Science of Mechanics: A Critical and Historical Account of Its Development*. La Salle, IL: Open Court, 1960 (orig. 1883).

——. *Knowledge and Error: Sketches on the Psychology of Enquiry*. Trans. Thomas J. McCormack and Paul Foulkes. Boston: D. Reidel, 1976.

——. *Contributions to the Analysis of the Sensations*. Trans. C. M. Williams. La Salle, IL: Open Court, 1984.

Macmillan, Malcolm. *Freud Evaluated: The Complete Arc.* Amsterdam: North-Holland, 1991.

Magliano, Joseph, and Arthur C. Graesser. "A Three-pronged Method for Studying Inference Generation in Literary Text." *Poetics* 20 (1991): 193–232.

Malamud, Bernard. *The Tenants.* Harmondsworth: Penguin, 1972.

——. "God, Bernard Malamud, and the Rebirth of Man." In Lasher, Lawrence M., ed. *Conversations with Bernard Malamud.* Jackson: University Press of Mississippi, 1991.

——. *Talking Horse.* Ed. Cheuse, Alan, and Nicholas Delbanco. New York: Columbia University Press, 1997.

Massey, Gerald J. "Thought Experiments." *Philosophical Quarterly* 44 (1994): 530–34.

Matuška, Alexander. *Karel Čapek: An Essay.* Trans. Cathryn Allan. Prague: Artia, 1964.

Maupin, Armistead. "A Tale of the Seventies." 1994–2001. Available at http://www.literarybent.com/am_04_also_by_taleofthe70s.html (May 3, 2005).

Mayer, Richard E. *Thinking and Problem Solving: an Introduction to Human Cognition and Learning.* Glenview, IL: Scott, Foresman, 1977.

——. *Thinking, Problem Solving, Cognition.* New York: W. H. Freeman, 1983.

Mayhill, John. "Some Philosophical Implications for Mathematical Logic." *Review of Metaphysics* 165 (1952): 165–98.

Mendola, Joseph. *Human Thought.* Boston: Kluwer, 1997.

Milgram, Stanley. "Behavioral Study of Obedience." *Journal of Abnormal and Social Psychology* 67 (1963): 371–78.

Miller, Richard W. *Fact and Method: Explanation, Confirmation and Reality in the Natural and the Social Sciences.* Princeton, NJ: Princeton University Press, 1988.

Minsky, Marvin. *The Society of Mind.* New York: Simon and Schuster, 1986.

Miščević, Nenad. "Mental Models and Thought Experiments." *International Studies in the Philosophy of Science* 6 (1992): 215–26.

Mithen, Steven. *The Prehistory of the Mind: The Cognitive Origins of Art, Religion and Science.* London: Thames and Hudson, 1996.

Montague, Richard. "Universal Grammar." In Thomason, Richard H., ed. *Formal Philosophy: Selected Papers of R. Montague.* New Haven, CT: Yale University Press, 1974: 222–46.

Moser, Paul. *Knowledge and Evidence.* Cambridge: Cambridge University Press, 1989.

Moskvitin, Jurij. *Essay on the Origin of Thought.* Athens: Ohio University Press, 1974.

Munz, Peter. *Philosophical Darwinism: On the Origin of Knowledge by Means of Natural Selection.* London: Routledge, 1993.

Myers, C. Mason. "Analytical Thought Experiments." *Metaphilosophy* 17 (1986): 109–18.

Nersessian, Nancy. "In the Theoretician's Laboratory: Thought Experimenting as Mental Modelling." In Hull, David, Micky Forbes, and Kathleen Okruhlik, eds. *Proceedings of the Biennual Meeting of the Philosophy of Science Association.* East Lansing: Philosophy of Science Association, 1993.

Nietzsche, Friedrich. *Human, All too Human.* Trans R. J. Hollingdale. Cambridge: Cambridge University Press, 1996.

Nigel, Howard. *Paradoxes of Rationality: Theory of Metagames and Political Behaviour.* Cambridge, MA: MIT Press, 1971.

Nobel Foundation. "Albert Camus – Banquet Speech." *The Nobel Prize in Literature.* The Nobel Foundation, 2004. Available at http://nobelprize.org/literature/laureates/1957/camus-speech-e.html (December 4, 2004).

Norton, John. "Thought Experiments in Einstein's Work." In Horowitz, Tamara, and Gerald J. Massey, eds. *Thought Experiments in Science and Philosophy*. Savage, MD: Rowman and Littlefield, 1991: 129–48.

———. "Are Thought Experiments Just What You Thought?" *Canadian Journal of Philosophy* 26: 3 (1996): 333–66.

Nowak, Leszek. "On Common-Sense and (Para-)Idealization." In Brzezinski, Jerzy, ed. *Idealization VIII: Modelling in Psychology*. Amsterdam: Rodopi, 1997.

"Nuclear Posture Review [Excerpts]. 8 January 2002. Nuclear Posture Review Report." (2002). Available at http://www.globalsecurity.org/wmd/library/policy/dod/npr.htm (May 3, 2005).

O'Connor, Daniel J., ed. *A Critical History of Western Philosophy*. New York: Free Press, 1964.

O'Hear, Anthony. "Science and Art." In Cooper, David, ed. *A Companion to Aesthetics*. Oxford: Blackwell, 1992.

O'Neill, Barry. "The Strategy of Challenges: Two Beheading Games in Medieval Literature." In Selten, Reinhard, ed. *Game Equilibrium Models*. Berlin: Springer-Verlag, 1991.

Oldershaw, Robert. "Hierarchical Modelling in the Sciences." *Nature and System* 2 (1980): 189–98.

Ortiz de Montellano, Bernard. "Multicultural Pseudoscience: Spreading Scientific Illiteracy among Minorities: Part I." *Skeptical Inquirer* 16 (1991): 46–50.

———. "Magic Melanin: Spreading Scientific Illiteracy among Minorities: Part II." *Skeptical Inquirer* 16 (1992): 163–66.

Ortony, Andrew, ed. *Metaphor and Thought*. New York: Cambridge University Press, 1979.

Papineau, David. "The Evolution of Knowledge." In Carruthers, Peter, and Andrew Chamberlain, eds. *Evolution and the Human Mind: Modularity, Language and Meta-cognition*. Cambridge: Cambridge University Press, 2000: 170–206.

Parfit, Derek. *Reasons and Persons*. Oxford: Oxford University Press, 1984.

Paris, Bernard J. "The Uses of Psychology." In Keesey, Donald, ed. *Contexts for Criticism*. 3rd edn. Mountain View, CA: Mayfield, 1998: 226–34.

Patai, Daphne, and Noretta Koertge. *Professing Feminism. Cautionary Tales from the Strange World of Women's Studies*. New York: Basic, 1994.

Peacocke, Christopher. *Thoughts: An Essay on Content*. Oxford: Blackwell, 1986.

Percy, Walker. "The State of the Novel: Dying Art or New Science?" *Michigan Quarterly Review* 16: 4 (Fall 1977): 359–73.

———. *Lost in the Cosmos: The Last Self-Help Book*. New York: Farrar, Straus & Giroux, 1983.

Piaget, Jean. *Genetic Epistemology*. Trans. Eleanor Duckworth. New York: Norton, 1971.

Pinker, Steven. *The Language Instinct*. New York: Morrow, 1994.

———. *How the Mind Works*. New York: Norton, 1997.

Plato. *Republic. Collected Dialogues*. Ed. Hamilton, Edith, and Huntington Cairns. Princeton, NJ: Bolligen, 1999.

Plotkin, Henry. *Darwin Machines and the Nature of Knowledge*. Cambridge, MA: Harvard University Press, 1997.

Plotnitsky, Arkady. *The Knowable and the Unknowable: Modern Science, Nonclassical Thought, and the "Two Cultures."* Ann Arbor: University of Michigan Press, 2002.

Podhoretz, Norman. *Doings and Undoing: The Fifties and after in American Writing*. New York: Farrar, Straus and Giroux, 1966.

Poe, Edgar Allan. "Eureka." *The Science Fiction of Edgar Allan Poe*. Ed. Beaver, Harold. London: Penguin, 1987.

Poincaré, Henri. "Non-Euclidian Geometries." *Science and Hypothesis*. New York: Dover, 1952.

Polkinghorne, Donald E. "Postmodern Epistemology in Practice." In Kvale, Steinar, ed. *Psychology and Postmodernism*. Newbury Park, CA: Sage, 1992: 146–65.

Pope, Rob. *Creativity: Theory, History, Practice*. London: Routledge, 2005.

Popper, Karl. "On the Use and Misuse of Imaginary Experiments, Especially in Quantum Theory." *The Logic of Scientific Discovery*. New York: Basic Books, 1959.

——. *Objective Knowledge: An Evolutionary Approach*. Oxford: Clarendon Press, 1972.

Potts, Richard. *Humanity's Descent: The Consequences of Ecological Instability*. New York: Avon, 1996.

Poundstone, William. *The Recursive Universe. Cosmic Complexity and the Limits of Scientific Knowledge*. Oxford: Oxford University Press, 1987.

——. *Labyrinths of Reason. Paradox, Puzzles, and the Frailty of Knowledge*. New York: Anchor, 1988.

——. *Prisoner's Dilemma*. New York: Anchor, 1993.

Prudowsky, Gad. "The Confirmation of the Superposition Principle: The Role of a Constructive Thought Experiment in Galileo's *Discorsi*." *Studies in the History of the Philosophy of Science* 20: 4 (1989): 453–68.

Quine, Willard V. O. "Natural Kinds." *Ontological Relativity and Other Essays*. New York: Columbia University Press, 1969.

——. *Quiddities: An Intermittently Philosophical Dictionary*. Cambridge, MA: Harvard University Press, 1987.

Rabaté, Jean-Michel. *The Future of Theory*. Oxford: Blackwell, 2002.

Rajab, Tilottama, and Michael J. O'Driscoll, eds. *After Poststructuralism: Writing the Intellectual History of Theory*. Toronto: University of Toronto Press, 2002.

Ramsey, A. Ogden. "The Mentality of Birds." *North American Bird Bander* 3: 1 (1978): 6–10.

Rapoport, Anatol. *Fights, Games, and Debates*. Ann Arbor: University of Michigan Press, 1960.

——. "The Use and Misuse of Game Theory." *Scientific American* 207 (1962): 108–18.

——. *Two Person Game Theory: The Essential Idea*. Ann Arbor: University of Michigan Press, 1964.

Rapoport, Anatol, David Gordon, and Melvin J. Guyer. *The 2x2 Game*. Ann Arbor: University of Michigan Press, 1976.

Rasmusen, Eric. *Games and Information: An Introduction to Game Theory*. Oxford: Blackwell, 1989.

Reinhard, Selten. *Arms and Influence*. New Haven, CT: Yale University Press, 1966.

——. *Models of Strategic Rationality*. Boson: Kluwer, 1987.

Reiss, Julian. "Causal Inference in the Abstract or Seven Myths about Thought Experiments." 2002. Available at http://www.lse.ac.uk/collections/CPNSS/pdf/pdfcaus/CTR03–02.pdf (May 3, 2005).

Rescher, Nicolas. *Hypothetical Reasoning*. Amsterdam: North-Holland, 1964.

——. "Thought Experimentation in Presocratic Philosophy." In Horowitz, Tamara, and Gerald J. Massey, eds. *Thought Experiments in Science and Philosophy*. Savage, MD: Rowman and Littlefield, 1991: 31–42.

——. "Counterfactuals in Pragmatic Perspective." *Review of Metaphysics* 50 (1996): 35–61.

Rickert, Heinrich. *Kulturwissenschaft und Naturwissenschaft*. Freiburg: J. C. B. Mohr, 1899.

Roese, Neal J., and James Olson. *What Might Have Been: the Social Psychology of Counterfactual Thinking*. Hillsdale, NJ: Lawrence Erlbaum, 1995.

Rorty, Richard. "Trotsky and the Wild Orchids." *Common Knowledge* 1: 3 (1992): 140–53.

Rosovsky, Henry. *The University: An Owner's Manual*. New York: Norton, 1991.

Ross, Andrew. *Strange Weather: Culture, Science and Technology in the Age of Limits*. London: Verso, 1991.

——. "New Age Technologies." In Grossberg, Lawrence, C. Nelson, and P. Treichler, eds. *Cultural Studies*. New York: Routledge, 1992.

——, ed. *Science Wars*. Durham: Duke University Press, 1996.

Ross, Charles. *Richard III*. Berkeley: University of California Press, 1981.

Rothfork, John. "*Memoirs Found in a Bathtub*: Stanislaw Lem's Critique of Cybernetics." *Mosaic* 17 (1984): 53–71.

Rothman, Stanley, and S. Robert Lichter. "Is Environmental Cancer a Political Disease?" In Gross, Paul R., Norman Levitt, and Martin W. Lewis, eds. *The Flight from Science and Reason*. New York: The New York Academy of Sciences, 1996: 231–45.

Rudner, Richard. "On Seeing What We Shall See." In Rudner, Richard, and Israel Scheffler, eds. *Logic and Art: Essays in Honor of Nelson Goodman*. Indianapolis and New York: Bobbs-Merrill, 1972.

Ryle, Gilbert. *Aspects of Mind*. Ed. Meyer, René. Oxford: Blackwell, 1993.

Sagan, Carl. "An Analysis of *Worlds in Collision*." In Goldsmith, Donald, ed. *Scientists Confront Velikovsky*. Ithaca, NY: Cornell University Press, 1977: 41–104.

Samuels, Richard. "Massively Modular Minds: Evolutionary Psychology and Cognitive Architecture." In Carruthers, Peter, and Andrew Chamberlain, eds. *Evolution and the Human Mind: Modularity, Language and Meta-cognition*. Cambridge: Cambridge University Press, 2000: 13–46.

Sayer, Andrew. *Realism and Social Science*. Newbury Park, CA: Sage, 2000.

Scharnberg, Max. *The Non-authentic Nature of Freud's Observations*. Upsala: Textgruppen i Upsala, 1993.

Schell, Jonathan. *The Fate of the Earth*. New York: Knopf, 1982.

——. "The Unfinished Twentieth Century: What We Have Forgotten about Nuclear Weapons." *Harper's Magazine* (January 2000): 41–56.

Schellenberg, James A. *Primitive Games*. Boulder, CO: Westview, 1990.

Schelling, Thomas C. *The Strategy of Conflict*. Cambridge, MA: Harvard University Press, 1960.

Schmidt, Siegfried J. "Conventions and Literary Systems." In Hjort, Mette, ed. *Rules and Conventions: Literature, Philosophy, Social Theory*. Baltimore: John Hopkins University, 1992.

Schnädelbach, Herbert. *Philosophy in Germany, 1831–1933*. Trans. Eric Matthews. Cambridge: Cambridge University Press, 1984.

Scott, Eugenie C. "Creationism, Ideology, and Science." In Gross, Paul R., Norman Levitt, and Martin W. Lewis, eds. *The Flight from Science and Reason*. New York: The New York Academy of Sciences, 1996: 505–22.

Seddon, George. "Logical Possibility." *Mind* 82 (1972): 481–94.

Sen, Amartya. "Rights and Agency." *Philosophy and Public Affairs* 11 (1982): 3–39.

Serafini, Luigi. *Codex Seraphinianus*. Milan: Franco Maria Ricci, 1981.

Shackle, George Lennox Sharman. *Imagination and the Nature of Choice*. Edinburgh: Edinburgh University Press, 1979.

Shapin, Steven. "Pump and Circumstance: Robert Boyle's Literary Technology." *Social Studies of Science* 14 (1984): 481–520.

Shattuck, Roger. "Does It All Fit Together: Evolution, the Arts and Consilience." *Academic Questions* 11 (1998): 56–61.

Sheets-Johnstone, Maxine. *The Roots of Thinking.* Philadelphia: Temple University Press, 1990.

Shelling, Thomas C. *The Strategy of Conflict.* Cambridge, MA: Harvard University Press, 1960.

——. *Arms and Influence.* New Haven, CT: Yale University Press, 1966.

Shettleworth, Sara J. "Modularity and the Evolution of Cognition." In Heyes, Cecilia, and Ludwig Huber, eds. *The Evolution of Cognition.* Cambridge, MA: MIT Press, 2000.

Shreeve, James. "Beyond the Brain." *National Geographic* (March 2005): 2–31.

Shubik, Martin. *Game Theory and Related Approaches to Social Behaviour: Selections.* New York: Wiley, 1964.

——. *The Uses and Methods of Gaming.* New York: Elsevier, 1975.

——. *Game Theory in the Social Sciences: Concepts and Solutions.* Cambridge, MA: MIT Press, 1982.

Siegel, Harvey. *Relativism Refuted: A Critique of Contemporary Epistemological Relativism.* Dordrecht: Reidel, 1987.

Simon, Herbert. "How Big Is a Chunk?" *Science* 183 (1974): 482–88.

——. *Reason in Human Affairs.* Stanford: Stanford University Press, 1983.

Simons, Herbert W., and Michael Billig, eds. *After Postmodernism: Reconstructing Ideology Critique.* London: Sage, 1994.

Simpson, Jeffry, and Minda Oriña. "Strategic Pluralism and Context-Specific Mate Preferences in Humans." In Sterelny, Kim, and Julie Fitness, eds. *From Mating to Mentality: Evaluating Evolutionary Psychology.* Hove, East Sussex, UK: Psychological Press, 2003.

Smets, Gerda. *Aesthetic Judgment and Arousal: An Experimental Contribution to Psychoaesthetics.* Leuven: Leuven University Press, 1973.

Smith, Richard, and Philip Wexler, eds. *After Postmodernism: Education, Politics, and Identity.* London: Falmer Press, 1995.

Sokal, Alan. "A Physicist Experiments with Cultural Studies." *Lingua Franca* (May/June 1996a): 62–64.

——, Alan. "Transgressing the Boundaries: Toward a Transformative Hermeneutics of Quantum Gravity." *Social Text* 46/47 (Spring/Summer 1996b): 217–52.

Sokal, Alan, and Jean Bricmont. *Intellectual Impostures: Postmodern Philosophers' Abuse of Science.* London: Profile, 2003 (orig. 1997).

Solomon, Robert. *The Passions: Emotions and the Meaning of Life.* Indianapolis: Hackett, 1993.

Sorensen, Roy A. "Moral Dilemmas, Thought Experiments, and Conflict Vagueness." *Philosophical Studies* (1991): 291–308.

——. *Thought Experiments.* New York: Oxford University Press, 1992a.

——. "Thought Experiments and the Epistemology of Laws." *Canadian Journal of Philosophy* 22: 1 (1992b): 15–44.

——. "A Thousand Clones." *Mind* 103 (1994): 47–54.

——. "Unknowable Obligations." *Utilitas* 7 (1995): 247–71.

Sorman, Guy. *Les Vrais Penseurs de notre temps.* Paris: Fayard, 1989.

Souder, Lawrence. "What Are We to Think of Thought Experiments." *Argumentation* 17 (2003): 203–17.

Stecker, Robert. "A Definition of Literature." Unpublished manuscript, n.d.

Sterelny, Kim. *Thought in a Hostile World: The Evolution of Human Cognition*. Malden: Blackwell, 2003.

Sterelny, Kim, and Julie Fitness, eds. *From Mating to Mentality: Evaluating Evolutionary Psychology*. Hove, East Sussex, UK: Psychological Press, 2003.

Sternberg, Robert J., and Peter A. Frensch, eds. *Complex Problem Solving: Principles and Mechanisms*. Hillsdale, NJ: Lawrence Erlbaum, 1991.

Sternberg, Robert J., and Edward E. Smith, eds. *The Psychology of Human Thought*. New York: Cambridge University Press, 1988.

Stevenson, Rosemary J. *Language, Thought, and Representation*. New York: Wiley, 1993.

Stewart, Ian. *Concepts of Modern Mathematics*. Harmondsworth: Penguin, 1975.

Stober, Dan. "Nuclear 'Bunker Busters' Sought." *San Jose Mercury News*, April 23 (2003): 1A.

Stockman, Norman. *Anti-Positivist Theories of the Sciences: Critical Rationalism, Critical Theory, and Scientific Realism*. Dordrecht: Reidel, 1983.

Stoff, Andrzej. *Powieści fantastyczno-naukowe Stanisława Lema*. Warszawa: Państwowe Wydawnictwo Naukowe, 1983.

——. "Świat ze słów (o *Pamietniku znalezionym w wannie*) Stanisława Lema." *Acta universitatis Nicolai Copernici* 193 (1989): 123–45.

——. *Lem i inni: szkice o Polskiej science fiction*. Bydgoszcz: Pomorze, 1990.

Storey, Robert. *Mimesis and the Human Animal: On the Biogenetic Foundations of Literary Representation*. Evanston, IL: Northwestern University Press, 1996.

Sugiyama, Michelle S. "Food, Foragers, and Folklore: The Role of Narrative in Human Subsistence." *Evolution and Human Behavior* 22 (2001a): 221–40.

——. "Narrative Theory and Function: Why Evolution Matters." *Philosophy and Literature* 25 (2001b): 233–50.

Swirski, Peter. "The Role of Game Theory in Literary Studies." In Rusch, Gebhard, ed. *Empirical Approaches to Literature. Proceedings of the Fourth Biannual Conference of the International Society for the Empirical Study of Literature–IGEL*. Siegen: LUMIS–Publications, 1995: 37–43.

——. "Game Theory In the Third Pentagon: A Study in Strategy and Rationality." *Criticism – A Quarterly for Literature & the Arts* 38 (1996a): 303–30.

——. "Literary Studies and Literary Pragmatics: The Case of 'The Purloined Letter.'" *SubStance* 81 (1996b): 69–89.

——. *A Stanislaw Lem Reader*. Evanston, IL: Northwestern University Press, 1997.

——. "Bernard Malamud: *God's Grace*." In Beetz, Kirk, ed. *Beacham's Encyclopedia of Popular Fiction*. Osprey, FL: Beacham Publishing, 1998a. Vol. 9. 5: 592–601.

——. "Stanislaw Lem: *Fiasco*." *Beacham's Encyclopedia of Popular Fiction. Vol. 12*. Osprey, FL: Beacham Publishing, 1998b. 5: 491–500.

——. "Literature and Literary Knowledge." *M/MLA: Journal of the Midwest Modern Language Association* 31 (1998c): 6–23.

——. "Stanislaw Lem." *Science Fiction Writers*. New York: Scribner's, 1999: 453–66.

——. *Between Literature and Science. Poe, Lem, and Explorations in Aesthetics, Cognitive Science, and Literary Knowledge*. Montreal: McGill-Queen's University Press, 2000a.

——. "In the Blink of an Eye: Games of Power in Y2K." *Dialogue and Universalism* 7/8 (2000b): 17–38.

——. "The Nature of Literary Fiction: From Carter to Spiegelman." *M/MLA: Journal of the Midwest Modern Language Association* 33 (2000c): 58–73.

——. "Interpreting Art, Interpreting Literature." *Orbis Litterarum: International Review of Literary Studies* 56: 1 (2001): 17–36.

——. *From Lowbrow to Nobrow*. Montreal: McGill-Queen's University Press, 2005.

——. *All Roads Lead to the American City*. Edmonton: M. V. Dimič Research Institute, 2006a.

——, ed. *The Art and Science of Stanislaw Lem*. Montreal: McGill-Queen's University Press, 2006b.

——. "Betrization Is the Worst Solution . . . with the Exception of All Others." In Swirski, Peter, ed. *The Art and Science of Stanislaw Lem*. Montreal: McGill-Queen's University Press, 2006c.

——. "'A' is for American, 'B' is for Bad, 'C' is for City: The ABC of Police and Urban Procedurals." *All Roads Lead to the American City*. Hong Kong, London: Hong Kong University Press, 2007 (forthcoming).

Swirski, Peter, and Faye Wong. "Briefcases for Hire: American Hardboiled to Legal Fiction." *Journal of American Culture* 29: 3 (2006): 307–20.

Sylvester, James J. "A Plea for the Mathematician." *Collected Papers*. Cambridge: Cambridge University Press, 1904: 650–719.

Szabó Gendler, Tamar. *Thought Experiment: On the Powers and Limits of Imaginary Cases*. New York: Garland, 2000.

Taylor, Alan. *Mathematics and Politics: Strategy, Voting, Power and Proof*. New York: Springer, 1995.

Tetlock, Philip E., and Aaron Belkin. *Counterfactual Thought Experiments in World Politics*. Princeton, NJ: Princeton University Press, 1996.

Thackeray, William Makepeace. *The History of Henry Esmond*. Oxford: Oxford University Press, 1991.

Thagard, Paul. *Mind: Introduction to Cognitive Science*. Cambridge, MA: MIT Press, 1996.

——. "Computation and the Philosophy of Science." In Bynum, Terrell Ward, ed. *The Digital Phoenix*. Cambridge: Blackwell, 1998.

Thomason, Sarah. "Thought Experiments in Linguistics." In Horowitz, Tamara, and Gerald J. Massey, eds. *Thought Experiments in Science and Philosophy*. Savage, MD: Rowman and Littlefield, 1991: 247–57.

Thomson, Robert. *The Pelican History of Psychology*. Harmondsworth: Penguin, 1968.

Turner, Mark. *The Literary Mind*. New York: Oxford, 1996.

Tversky, Amos. *Preference, Belief, and Similarity: Selected Writings*. Ed. Shafir, Eldar. Cambridge, MA: MIT Press, 2004.

Unger, Peter. "Toward a Psychology of Common Sense." *American Philosophical Quarterly* 19 (1982): 117–29.

Updike, John. *Roger's Version*. New York: Knopf, 1996.

Uttal, David. "Angles and Distances: Children's and Adults' Reconstruction and Scaling of Spatial Configurations." *Child Development* 67 (1996): 2763–69.

Vaihinger, Hans. *The Philosophy of "As if."* Trans. C. K. Ogden. London: Routledge, 1924.

Von Neumann, John, and Oskar Morgenstern. *Theory of Games and Economic Behavior*. Princeton, NJ: Princeton University Press, 1953.

Voss, Richard, and John Clarke. "$1/f$ (flicker) Noise: A Brief Review." *Proceedings of the 33rd Annual Symposium on Frequency Control*. Atlantic City: Electronic Industries Association, 1975: 40–6.

——. "$1.f$ Noise in Music: Music from $1.f$ Noise." *Journal of the Acoustical Society of America* 63: 1 (1978): 258–63.

Waldrop, Mitchell. "Machinations of Thought." *Science 85* 6: 2 (1985): 38–45.

Walsh, Dorothy. *Literature and Knowledge*. Middletown, CT: Wesleyan University Press, 1969.

Walter, Eugene V. *Placeways: A Theory of the Human Environment*. Chapel Hill: University of North Carolina Press, 1988.

Wason, Peter. "Reasoning." In Foss, B. M., ed. *New Horizons in Psychology*. London: Penguin, 1966.

Watson, J. B., and R. R. Watson. "Studies in Infant Psychology." *Scientific Monthly* 13 (1921): 493–515.

Weinberger, David. "A Melding of Sci-Fi, Philosophy: Review of *His Master's Voice*." *Philadelphia Inquirer*, May 7 (1983): D04.

Weiss, Eric A. "John Updike's Version of Computing." *Abacus* 4 (1987): 45–48.

Weissmann, Gerald. "Ecosentimentalism: The Summer Dream beneath the Tamarind Tree." In Gross, Paul R., Norman Levitt, and Martin W. Lewis, eds. *The Flight from Science and Reason*. New York: The New York Academy of Sciences, 1996: 483–90.

Wiggins, David. *Identity and Spatio-Temporal Continuity*. Oxford: Blackwell, 1967.

———. "Locke, Butler and the Stream of Consciousness: And Men as a Natural Kind." In Amelie O. Rorty, ed. *The Identities of Persons*. Berkeley: University of California Press, 1976.

———. *Sameness and Substance*. Oxford: Blackwell, 1980.

Wilkes, Kathleen. *Real People: Personal Identity without Thought Experiments*. Oxford: Clarendon, 1988.

Will, Clifford M. *Was Einstein Right? Putting General Relativity to the Test*. 2nd edn. New York: Basic Books, 1993.

Williams, John D. *The Compleat Strategyst*. New York: McGraw, 1966.

Wilson, Edward O. *Consilience: The Unity of Knowledge*. New York: Knopf, 1998.

Winograd, Terry, and Fernando Flores. *Understanding Computers and Cognition*. Norwood, NJ: Ablex, 1986.

Wright, Robert. *The Moral Animal*. New York: Pantheon, 1994.

Wyer, Robert S., Jr., and Thomas S. Srull. *The Content, Structure, and Operation of Thought Systems*. Hillsdale, NJ: Lawrence Erlbaum, 1991.

Wynn, Thomas. "Symmetry and the Evolution of the Modular Linguistic Mind." In Carruthers, Peter, and Andrew Chamberlain, eds. *Evolution and the Human Mind: Modularity, Language and Meta-cognition*. Cambridge: Cambridge University Press, 2000: 113–39.

Index